PRAISE
FOR
RECONCILING THE BIBLE AND SCIENCE

"*Reconciling the Bible and Science* is a valuable new contribution to the growing body of literature in theology and science focused specifically on a constructive theological appropriation of biological evolution. The authors describe and assess the current debates on all sides, concluding that 'nothing in creation ... conflicts with biological evolution.'"

> —Dr. Robert John Russell, The Ian G. Barbour Professor of Theology and Science in Residence, The Graduate Theological Union, and Founder and Director, The Center for Theology and the Natural Sciences, Berkeley

"Reading *Reconciling the Bible and Science: A Primer on the Two Books of God* will be invaluable to those who wish to clarify their thinking on the continuing Bible and science controversy. The authors provide a compelling examination of the history and state of current ideas."

> —Dr. Randy Isaac, Executive Director, American Scientific Affiliation

"*Reconciling the Bible and Science: A Primer on the Two Books of God* will clear up much of the confusion about the actors and issues in the public debates involving the Bible and science. It should be required reading in all Evangelical colleges. The book is faith affirming. It provides the believer with a perspective that allows him/her to assimilate the best of modern science AND honor the Bible as the revelation of God's love."

> —Dr. Ron Highfield, Blanche E. Seaver Professor of Religion, Pepperdine University and author of *Great is the Lord: Theology for the Praise of God*

"*Reconciling the Bible and Science: A Primer on the Two Books of God* should be of great interest to the millions of people of faith who are mystified by the perceived conflict between the Christian faith in which they believe and the science they respect. The book's almost conversational style is very engaging."

—Dr. Francisco J. Ayala, Professor of Biological Sciences and of Philosophy, University of California, Irvine, and author of *Genetics and the Origin of Species*

"Lynn Mitchell and Kirk Blackard have provided a valuable new discussion of the relationship of science and Christian faith in *Reconciling the Bible and Science: A Primer on the Two Books of God*. Religious, philosophical and scientific history provide a helpful context for their arguments. Although brief, the historical context is vital for understanding the contemporary debates. Also, there is a strong emphasis on the importance of reading the Bible in a way appropriate for the types of literature it contains. The authors are not scientists, but recognize that the issue is much more than a scientific one. They take a humble approach to knowledge, both scientific and theological."

—Dr. Keith B. Miller, PhD, Department of Geology, Kansas State University, and Editor of *Perspectives on an Evolving Creation*

Reconciling the Bible and Science: A Primer on the Two Books of God is a timely piece especially while separation of church and state persists as a modern political and social issue. This forthright work provides a convenient historical backdrop and introduces contemporary religious jargon that will stimulate dialog, aid in a detailed study, or help to consider personal positions. These concepts will be particularly helpful to parents attempting to navigate today's education systems.

—Dr. Melinda Jezierski, MD, PhD, Family Physician and Adjunct Assistant Professor of Neuroscience and Experimental Therapeutics, Texas A&M University System Health Science Center

Reconciling the Bible and Science

A Primer on the Two Books of God

Lynn Mitchell
and
Kirk Blackard

To our parents, who encouraged us to seek truth.

CONTENTS

ACKNOWLEDGMENTS

We owe a debt of gratitude to the many people who made this book possible.

While we have attempted to present a fresh and unique look at the Bible and science debate, few if any original theological or scientific concepts are presented. Consequently, we are indebted to a long line of individuals, such as Plato and Newton in historic times, Henry Morris and Phillip Johnson, who did so much to shape the current controversy, Michael Behe and Francis Collins, who continue to think deeply and write eloquently on the subject, and numerous others. We are thankful to have been able to take advantage of the work that many before us have done.

Lynn Mitchell thanks all the professors and students whom he has encountered in his many years of teaching about this controversy at the university level. Their questions, comments, and encouragement have led him to a richer appreciation of this complex topic and have been an important impetus for this book.

We especially appreciate all those members of the Bering Drive Church of Christ in Houston who encouraged—perhaps pushed—the writing of this book and contributed financially in the early stages. We won't try to list all the names, but you know who you are. We thank you.

Several individuals were willing to read the manuscript and provide invaluable input during its development. All their work significantly improved the product and enhanced our belief in its credibility. Our special thanks go to: Dr. Randy Isaac, Executive Director, American Scientific Affiliation; Dr. Ron Highfield, Blanche E. Seaver professor of Religion, Pepperdine University and author of *Great is the Lord: Theology for the Praise of God;* Dr. Francisco J. Ayala, professor of Biological Sciences and of Philosophy, University of California, Irvine, and author of *Genetics and the Origin of Species*; Dr. Keith B. Miller, PhD,

Department of Geology, Kansas State University, and editor of *Perspectives on an Evolving Creation*; Dr. Robert John Russell, The Ian G. Barbour professor of Theology and Science in Residence, The Graduate Theological Union, Berkeley and author of *Cosmology from Alpha to Omega: Towards the Creative Mutual Interaction between Theology and Science;* Dr. Melinda Jezierski, PhD and MD; Dr. Randy Millican, MD; Dr. Dale Richey, MD; and Dr. Brent Isbell, Doctor of Ministry.

Margaret Jordan transcribed tapes of Lynn Mitchell's lectures, which provided a starting point for the book. Paula Yost performed the yeoman's job of editing the entire manuscript and Carol Mitchell did a final review that was extremely helpful. We deeply appreciate your work.

And finally, we thank our families—our parents for all the sacrifices they made for us and for teaching us without brainwashing us, and our spouses and children for their continuing support.

INTRODUCTION

"You are young, my son, and, as the years go by, time will change and even reverse many of your present opinions. Refrain therefore awhile from setting yourself up as a judge of the highest matters."
Plato (427-347 BC)

The story of the two books of God is one of controversy, often involving more assumptions than knowledge, emotion than logic, heat than light. The debate takes various forms, but evidence of an apparent conflict between the book of scripture and the book of nature seems to be everywhere: *Time Magazine* features a debate between a nationally known atheist author and an imminent Christian scientist, a newspaper article condemns those who advocate intelligent design, legislatures fight over what can and cannot be taught in public schools, courts are asked to decide issues of faith and science, three candidates in a presidential debate say they do not believe in evolution and the other seven say they do. The controversy affects national and local policy, influences education, and, some argue, could potentially degrade our way of life if either scientific advancement or religious belief and practice are stifled.

The conflict is being waged on two levels. The public level is a continuing war among relatively few activists: politicians who are looking for votes, civil libertarians who fear the mingling of church and state, scientists who are concerned that religious beliefs foster bad public policy, religious leaders who believe science destroys the very core of faith. We see warring books and articles, contentious town meetings, law suits, legislative agendas, and other efforts by each side to win and make sure the other loses.

The second level of the conflict is largely silent, below the water line. But like the submerged portion of an iceberg, it is larger and more important than the public conflict. It involves those of us who sense an "either/or" conflict between what we have come to believe about religion and what we see, hear, and experience about science; those who check out of religious faith and become "de-facto agnostics;" and those who allow their faith to prevent a robust consideration of all that science offers. The conflict is within our hearts and minds. It has no strategy, no clear battle lines, no obvious winner or loser.

If you are in either camp, you may face a quandary that arises from many unanswered questions about scripture, science, and the alleged conflict between the two. Finding intellectually satisfying answers can be frustrating and even frightening. The search often involves learning new words that sound like so much gobbledygook, reading an array of books and articles that present only one side of a multi-faceted issue and seem to be intended to obfuscate rather than enlighten, considering different and scary biblical interpretations and scientific conclusions, and making judgments without all the facts.

This book tells a story that will clear the fog from the controversy and help you reach better informed conclusions on this important subject. And it is a story. A discussion of religion and science may be part history, part bill of indictment, part brief for the defense, part PhD dissertation. But more than anything, it's a story—with heroes and villains, plots and subplots, passion, humor, mystery, surprise. And it's a true story, that cuts to the very heart of our being and has helped shape the world in which we live.

We have tried to tell the story in a way that will be easily understood by anyone who has an interest in Christianity, wants to understand its relationship to science, or is befuddled by all the fuss. We have avoided theological and scientific jargon where possible. Where such words just have to be used, we have tried to explain their meaning as we go along, and have included an index at the end in case you need to refresh your memory. Telling a story that covers approximately 4,000 years of controversial events and widely varying opinions in one small book is difficult, to say the least. We will have omitted events that some will say are critical, used too much ink on people some will say are unimportant, condensed discussion of ideas when others will think we should have expanded it. But we believe we have painted a brief picture that truthfully reveals the main themes of the conflict and outlines a valid approach for dealing with it.

THE ISSUE

Conflicts involving religion and science have been addressed in different ways by different interests. Perhaps the most common recent approach pits "God vs. science," the subject of a number of recent contemporary books and articles. This is a legitimate approach—one which raises the question of God's existence. But God's existence is not the controversy we are addressing. We are writing principally to believers, and, like the Bible, will take it that God is real.

A second view of the conflict is "science vs. religion," as suggested by Ian Barbour's book, *Issues in Science and Religion,* and other contemporary writings. This also is a valid framing of the controversy, but its implicit inclusion of all of the world's religions goes beyond the Christian perspective that we have elected to address.

Our concern, instead, relates to Christianity and science. And since the Bible is the basis of the Christian faith, we will address the apparent conflict between the Bible and science—a much narrower, and for Christians, more relevant issue than the question of God and science, or religion and science. More specifically, the conflict we will address boils down to different beliefs among Christian people about evolution and how the Bible should be interpreted.

THE BOOK

While we respect those who disagree, we don't believe there is a conflict between the Bible and modern science. Faith in God and a belief in the Bible as we think it should be interpreted do not preclude acceptance of science as it is understood today, and as we believe it will be understood in the future. Showing how these two persuasions are compatible is the primary burden of *Reconciling the Bible and Science: A Primer on the Two Books of God.* We will demonstrate that Christianity and modern science can co-exist—even complement one another—rather than pit one against the other or try to convince you of the validity of evolution or of a particular approach to religious practice. Our case will be made in two parts.

Part I presents a factual summary of how the debate arose and its current status. Chapters 1 through 5 present a short historical context. To understand what is taking place today, we need to look first to the past, as there are clear paths connecting the current conflict with the broad sweep of Christian history. Briefly exploring these paths will help you understand that the current controversy is deeply rooted in the stories of Christians through many centuries. Chapters 6 through 10 paint a picture of the current debate. They briefly summarize the modern scientific method and the present state of scientific understanding in three areas that many feel have religious implications: astronomy, geology, and biology. They then explore the current status of several religious responses to science—primarily to evolution—ranging from creationists who believe in an absolutely literal interpretation of scripture to non-believers who see the Bible as nothing more than a fairy tale. These chapters will help you understand the parameters of the current conflict.

Part II presents our views on the debate, looking closely at the Bible and exploring what it is and how we believe it should be read to discern its fundamental truths. Chapters 11 through 14 argue that the Bible is not a book of science, and that to discover its fundamental truths, we need to read it as a book of theology in the context of the times and purpose for which it was written. We also need to understand the language and style in which it was written, and eschew a too literal interpretation that detracts from its truth. Chapter 15 outlines the authors' personal conclusions on the debate after considering the matters presented in earlier chapters.

We encourage you to consider the story in this book as an important episode in your own personal journey of learning and exploration. Your journey will be unique to you, and one you alone must be comfortable with. We hope you arrive where we have—concluding that there is room for both faith and science in your life. But, what does this suggest if you now believe there is a conflict and either religion or science wins? Is a compromise your only option? Doesn't compromise involve giving in, and shouldn't we abhor giving in on matters of faith or conviction?

We are not suggesting a compromise of beliefs or values, even though we recognize that accepting our views would require a change of mind and heart by those who support a literal interpretation of the creation texts of the Bible. We may, however, be suggesting a different interpretation of scripture or a reassessment of certain philosophies or traditions. Re-evaluation of such important, deep seated, often long held beliefs is never easy, so the change process itself merits some thought.

We change our minds in various ways when we get new information that is contrary to our previous beliefs. Sometimes our belief system remains the same but allows for a few anomalies. Sometimes we change bit by bit without being aware of it. Sometimes we abandon one belief and adopt another. A fourth way is to harmonize old and new ideas into a powerful synthesis—a new perspective or insight that allows information to come together in a new form or structure. This kind of change, often called paradigm change, says, "I was partially right before, and now I'm somewhat more partially right." It recognizes that in the past we only saw part of the picture, and what we see now is only part of what we will see in the future. It acknowledges the deep mystery that is inherent in revealed religion, and is enlightening rather than threatening, enlarging rather than constraining. Paradigm change allows a never ending journey of learning and intellectual and spiritual growth that uses the faculties that set us apart from other living things.

We ask you to consider this dimension of change as you read this book and the Bible, and remember that God can cause new light to emerge that has been there all the time. Consider what you read. Think about it. Think about new views of science and scripture that are perhaps more partially right, and that allow you to continually grow under the guidance of the Holy Spirit and the authority of scripture.

THE AUTHORS

Any story as controversial as ours can be affected by the experiences, beliefs, and worldview of those doing the telling. While your authors have attempted to tell the story for what it is, without personal bias, we believe it's important for you to know where we have been and where we are coming from. In this regard, and in the interest of full disclosure, biological evolution is a concept your authors feel compelled to accept. We also believe the scientific view of evolution is itself still evolving and all will know more about it in the future than we do now. We are led to this conclusion by our understanding of the view of the vast majority of the scientific community, which includes many Christians, and our personal observations. For those who want a full discussion of this issue, libraries are well stocked with books that address it better than we could.

We also believe that there is a God who created the universe and who works in our lives. We perceive this God through a Christian perspective. We do not intend to dismiss or minimize any of the other great religions of the world. It's just that we are Christians and that is the view we bring.

We make no claim to being scientists or to having any special first-hand scientific knowledge. We claim only to be reasonably well informed laymen in the arena of scientific practice. Lynn is a theologian and student of the history and philosophy of science, especially as it pertains to the relation between science and religion. Kirk is an attorney, conflict management practitioner, and author of four books.

Each of us has traveled a journey that positions us to think objectively about these issues and to continue to respect those with whom we disagree. We have traveled from a strong religious, fundamentalist childhood, through a period of uncertainty, to a view that reflects both a faith in God and acceptance of science. In our early religious lives each of us attended a tiny, very conservative Church of Christ in small rural Texas towns where we were immersed, both in water and in what would now be called strong creationist beliefs. In church, and to a considerable extent in school, we were taught that the universe is more or less 6,000 years old and was created pretty much as is in six twenty-four hour days, that evolution is the devil's theory with no basis in fact, and that there is no basis for reconciling the Bible and science. We now have a different view—one that sees no conflict between the two books of God. The following chapters will explain that view.

PART I

CONTEXT

[handwritten: Middle East + England mid 1800s]

How can the origin of the Hebrew Bible thousands of years ago in a tiny area of the Middle East and scientific conclusions developed in England in the mid-1800s, be so profoundly connected to our lives and to today's Bible and science debate? What is that debate all about, anyway? And how can we possibly resolve the argument to our personal satisfaction? *[handwritten: → Can there be pc?]*

We need to know where we've been and where we are to understand where we are going. Accordingly, Chapters 1 through 5 trace a path (admittedly, a sometimes vague, confusing, and controversial path) that starts at a time of important pre-biblical writings, winds through what we know of the Bible's origin, and ends with a discussion of the scientific controversies that arose many years ago in Western Europe and are relevant today. Chapter 6 provides an overview of the modern scientific method and the current consensus of scientists in the areas of astronomy, geology, and biology that are uniquely relevant to the debate. Chapters 7 through 10 describe four different groups in a range of responses to the scientific consensus, from those asserting a very literal interpretation of the Bible to those holding that the Bible is only a fairy tale. *[handwritten: overview]*

A word of warning is in order. Providing an abbreviated summary of such a long and complex development is an almost impossible task. We're writing one book, however, not a huge library. Even if time, space, ability, and attention span permitted, there is not and never has been a single biblical religion or unanimity of opinion on many historical events. Scientific knowledge is continually changing and growing, and Christians have disparate, often changing, views of their religion. We live in a free country where anyone can speak to the issue, and frequently does. Views and positions change and evolve over time,

Conflict
Change

as though Darwin himself were in charge of them. The conflict is wrought with conflicting opinions, charges and countercharges, and claims of intellectual dishonesty—modern day Hatfields and McCoys using words rather than guns.

But we will give it a try in Part I. We will provide factual information about a few pivotal people, ideas, and beliefs that offer a sense of the connection to antiquity, the ebb and flow, the continuing change, and the mixture of biblical and secular beliefs that provide the context for today's controversy. We will present nothing new to theologians or knowledgeable lay persons, but hopefully will help readers focus on those people, events, and ideas most relevant to the issues at hand.

That said, let's start at the beginning. Or at least at what most theologians believe is the beginning.

1

RELIGIOUS ANTIQUITY

"Verily, he is highly exalted in the assembly of the Gods."
Tablet VII, Enuma Elish, *Babylonian epic from 1894-1595 B.C.*

[handwritten margin note: Start of debate]

Incredibly, the seeds of the debate between Christianity and science were planted thousands of years ago in a small area of what we now know as the Middle East, where the Bible and Christianity originated. This world was very, very small indeed compared to the world we experience today. "The principal setting of the biblical narratives is Egypt and the Fertile Crescent, the band of arable land that extends northward from the Nile Valley along the eastern coast of the Mediterranean, curves around the great Syrian desert, and continues southward through Mesopotamia to the Persian Gulf."[1] The area encompassed modern Syria, Lebanon, Israel, Palestine, Jordan, and Iraq, including the land between the Tigris and Euphrates rivers. It also included the "holy city" of Babylon in Mesopotamia (in present-day Iraq), the seat of the Neo-Babylonian Empire from around 2300 BC.

Hundreds of religions, beliefs, and diverse doctrines pervaded the known world at the time of the origin of the biblical story around 4,000 years ago. The Bible, or parts of it, eventually became the foundation not only of Christianity, but also of Judaism and Islam. Notwithstanding the antiquity and diversity of that world, it is the starting point of our story. To understand it, we need to trace a line, however brief and vague, from then to now.

PRE-BIBLICAL LITERATURE

All cultures in the ancient world had origin myths. "Myth" can be defined in different ways. Here, it means a story about the gods in which they are personifications of natural processes. These myths covered a form of creation in great detail. The Middle Eastern stories popular during the time of Abraham—often called the Babylonian genesis—were important background for the biblical book of Genesis.

Babylonian Myths

An early example of Babylonian literature is the epic story of *Gilgamesh*, which was repeated orally for hundreds of years and then, probably around 2000 BC, divided into twelve books and written on stone tablets that still survive. The story, a more fully developed form of earlier Sumerian traditions, describes the adventures of Gilgamesh, the legendary king of Uruk around the end of the fourth millennium BC, with his friend Enkidu. When Enkidu died, Gilgamesh crossed the waters of death to find a plant of life that would revive his friend. Gilgamesh received a warning from a powerful water deity that the gods were plotting to send a devastating flood. An ark was built, and a terrible storm occurred. After the storm, a dove and a swallow were sent out, but they returned when they couldn't find a resting place. Then a raven was dispatched, and it did not return. The parallels between this flood account and the Genesis flood narrative are obvious.

Babylonian literature also included the great epic *Enuma Elish,* believed to have originated during the first Babylonian Dynasty (1894 BC to 1595 BC). While apparently intended principally as a literary monument to honor Marduk, "the wisest of the gods," and to praise Babylon, the tale nevertheless presents an account of the origin and ordering of the universe. It describes a world that began with the mythical merging of the waters of the rivers (the god Apsu) with those of the sea (the goddess Tiamat), with the horizon and the sky emerging. The epic also describes a series of births that culminated with the birth of the storm god Marduk, who became king of the gods and creator of human beings.

Enuma Elish contains a number of similarities to events contained in Genesis 1 and 2. The world begins from the merging of waters in the Babylonian story, and the ordered world is built out of the watery chaos in the biblical story. In the second tablet there is primeval chaos, and Tiamut is enveloped in darkness, while in Genesis the earth is desolate in waste, and darkness covers the deep. In the third tablet, light emanates from the gods. In Genesis, light is created. In the fourth tablet, dry land is created. In Genesis, the firmament is created. In the fifth tablet, the sun and moon are created, as they are in Genesis. Man is created in the sixth tablet, as in the Genesis account. The gods rest and celebrate in the seventh tablet. In Genesis, God rests and sanctifies the seventh day. Thus, the seven-day format in Genesis 1 is very similar to the Babylonian format.

Relationship to the Bible

In addition to *Gilgamesh* and *Enuma Elish*, other Babylonian literature contains stories with somewhat different accounts of the way in which all things came into being. Although it is rarely possible to establish a direct link between a specific story and a particular biblical account, similarities abound. A Babylonian account of the earth's origin is told in seven tablets, and the Genesis creation account is told in seven days. The tablets of the Babylonian accounts and the days of Genesis clearly correspond. Each presents a picture of God bringing the heavens and the earth into existence, followed by statements to the effect that the earth was without form and void, and darkness was upon the face of the deep.

A significant difference exists, however. Although the Babylonians could conceive of a time when there was neither heaven nor earth, they apparently could not conceive of a time when there was nothing at all except an all-powerful deity. The Babylonian account identifies the great deep that is and always has been, with the universe arising out of the great deep. Thus, it is a model of pro-creation—or the growth and generation of the gods and the begetting of the universe from existing and eternal spirit and cosmic matter—rather than of creation, or origin from nothingness. There is only one real story of creation in the ancient world, and that is Genesis 1. Its reference to "In the beginning God created the heavens and the earth..." involves creation and distinguishes it from the pro-creation stories of the Babylonians.

Procreation through generation, or birth, sometimes called emanation, is very different than creation. The difference is the Creator. In the Babylonian myths the watery chaos is the source of the generation of everything. In the Genesis account, the watery chaos itself is a creation, and there is something beyond the watery chaos. This represents a great leap in understanding the nature of God and man, and their relationship to one another.

The extent to which biblical accounts do or do not depend on earlier stories is a controversial issue. Some believe Genesis shows Babylonian influence, while others are just as convinced that it does not. It doesn't seem to matter. If anything, the Babylonian accounts seem to define the polytheistic culture in which the biblical story took place. For our purpose, the important point is that Genesis seems to intentionally critique, or de-mythologize, the Babylonian stories.

The Babylonian stories of many gods and goddesses and the orderly, purposeful human-like arrangement of pre-existing matter are a far cry from the biblical story of one God who creates matter out of nothing and remains one God to the end. If certain parts of the biblical account did derive from the Babylonian epics, they are no less the will of God who is revealing Himself.

The Bible is the story—not a philosophy—about the relationship between God and man, told in the language of the time and against the backdrop of those cultures. Which brings us to a brief look at the Hebrew Bible, commonly referred to by most Christians as the Old Testament.

THE HEBREW BIBLE

The traditional view is that Moses wrote or compiled the first five books of the Old Testament, also known as the Pentateuch, probably between1450 BC and 1400 BC. The consensus of theologians, however, suggests a more complicated authorship.

The Times

The most broadly held view is that this part of the Hebrew Bible, which includes the biblical accounts of creation and accounts of the rise of Israel, had a substantial prehistory as oral tradition— stories handed down orally for some time before being committed to writing—and is a composite fashioned and edited over centuries to attain a historical and theological integrity. For example, some people were part of what was to become the Israelite faith before any part of the Old Testament was written.

direct connection
w/ God

When a covenant was made between God and His people, according to the Hebrew Bible, the only written part was the Ten Commandments, believed to have been written by the finger of God. This suggests that the books of Genesis and Exodus in their present form were written subsequent to the people of Israel becoming God's covenant people, contradictory to the idea of a simple writing in a short period of time. Most biblical scholars also believe that the second creation account (Genesis 2-3) emerged before the first account (Genesis 1). The Genesis 2 account is commonly assigned to the time of Solomon's empire around the tenth century BC. The Genesis 1 account is considered to have originated from priestly hands around the sixth century BC, a period following the Babylonian conquest of Jerusalem and the Israelites' exile from Judah to Babylonia, which God had allowed because of their continuing rampant idolatry.

When the deportees returned to their homeland approximately seventy years later, in the middle of the fifth century BC, they adopted the newly written history and a commitment to study the text. With this, the Israelites became a people of the Law, using the laws and customs to maintain themselves as a people under God. Thus, Judaism was born.

Scholars also believe the remaining books of the Old Testament were written over a period of hundreds of years and involved a succession of prophets. Priests and sages collected and codified religious laws, Israel lore and national history, which led to the acceptance of selected "scriptures" as sacred texts for the Jews. The Torah—a reference to the first five books of the Old Testament—became a central feature in Jewish life during this period.

Malachi, the last book in the Old Testament, is believed to have been written around 430 BC to rebuke the people for their false and profane worship. Approximately 400 years passed from the time of Malachi to the birth of Christ, an era known as the intertestamental period and sometimes called the "silent" years. While Malachi had followed a succession of prophets going back hundreds of years, there were none during this period. The time between the Testaments, however, was one of ferment and change. The Jews came under the influence of the Greek Empire (a group of Jewish scholars even translated the Hebrew Bible into Greek), became independent for a time, and then became unwilling subjects of the Roman Empire. By the time of the New Testament, people were guided by priests and teachers. They worshiped in the Temple of Jerusalem as well as in dozens of synagogues scattered throughout the known world. Priests provided leadership, but people began looking to new religious authorities such as Pharisees, Sadducees, and scribes, who were teachers of religious law.

The Culture

Thus, the Hebrew Bible did not just appear one day on the shelves of some pre-history bookstore. Before being written in manuscript form, stories probably spent many hundreds of years being told time and again from memory. One can imagine a group of Semitic nomads sitting around a campfire listening to tribal elders relating stories, including those that ultimately would become part of the Bible as we know it. They didn't read or hear the stories read because they couldn't read and the manuscripts hadn't been written yet. But they listened and got the essential message.

The Mediterranean area of the world where these stories originated was home to hundreds of religions claiming the existence of super-human beings, practicing sacrifice of all sorts (including humans), maintaining special holy places where divine beings dwelt on earth, and engaging in other such rites. The religions almost uniformly endorsed polytheism—a belief in many gods, with each god often claiming his own territorial jurisdiction. Every nation surrounding Israel was polytheistic, and many Israelites were inclined that way as well. As Conrad Hyers has noted,

> For most peoples in the ancient world, all the various regions of nature were divine. Sun, moon, and stars were *gods*. There were sky gods and earth gods and water gods, gods of light and darkness, rivers and vegetation, animals and fertility. Everywhere the ancients turned there were divinities to be taken into account, petitioned, appeased, pacified, solicited, or avoided.

> In addition, pharaohs, kings, and heroes were often seen as sons of gods, or at least as special mediators between the divine and human spheres ... There was also a considerable

(margin notes:) Hebrew stated before the bible

picking up the cultural background

use of animals throughout the ancient world as vehicles, representatives, or forms of various divine beings ....[2]

While idolatry and worship of many gods was a continuing problem for the Israelite faith, science and natural history as we know them did not exist. The basic question being considered in the campfire stories that became the Hebrew Bible could not have been the scientific question of how or through what processes things attained their current form, nor the historical question about time periods and chronological order. The crucial issue was idolatry—polytheism versus monotheism—not science.

This historical and cultural context indicates that Genesis, and much of the Hebrew Bible, was intended to oppose polytheism, not to present any kind of scientific perspective. This idea will be developed more fully in Part II, where we will argue that Genesis is an affirmation of one God and a refutation of polytheism, syncretism, and idolatry rather than a story of how the cosmos was created. Genesis is not tied to any partic- ular conception of the universe. If it were, its message would have died centuries ago because each time our conception of the universe changed, Genesis would have become less relevant. (This, of course, is what certain modern-day naturalists believe has happened, or is happening.)

Thus, the Hebrew Bible had as a central theme an unquestioning loyalty and devotion to one God who had shown His superiority over heathen deities. It provided a new revelation of the divine nature and purpose that formed the basis of the monotheistic beliefs that followed. It described a divine nature of compassion and forgiveness, but also of stark hatred of injustice, immorality, and oppression. And it laid down concepts of moral law as stipulations of the covenant for future generations. In summary, the cultural setting supports the idea that the Hebrew Bible is an affirmation of faith in one transcendent God, not empirical or speculative theories of origin.

SCRIPTURE AS A SOURCE OF CONFLICT

Notwithstanding its non-scientific theme and purpose, the Hebrew Bible contains language that centuries later emerged as a basis of disputes that continue today. Since these scriptures are at the very core of the Bible and science debate, we will introduce them here as a context for the discussion that follows.

Early Controversies

Several passages were at one time part of the controversy, but years ago gave way to compelling evidence from common observations and scientific investigations. Prime examples are:

- 1 Chronicles 16:30 states, "The world is firmly established; it cannot be moved." Joshua 10 relates the story of an army under Joshua coming to the defense of Gibeon, and in verses 12-13, Joshua said to the Lord, "O sun, stand still over Gibeon, O moon, over the valley of Aijalon. So the sun stood still, and the moon stopped, till the nation avenged itself on its enemies." It was argued in earlier times that the language "world is firmly established" and the commandment for the sun to stand still mean that the sun moves rather than the earth, suggesting a geocentric universe. Today, however, most see the language as an example of biblical poetry, and not even the most conservative literalists argue that the sun rotates around a fixed earth. Some believe God actually extended the hours of daylight, while others suggest that the effect of the sun's heat was diminished in some way so fighting could continue.

- Job 28:24 states, "for he views the ends of the earth" and Daniel 4:11 refers to a large tree being "visible to the ends of the earth," suggesting to some that the earth is flat rather than round. Further, Genesis 1 arguably paints a picture of the earth as a flat surface, resting on the primeval waters beneath and separated from waters above by a blue firmament. While the possibility of a flat earth is not a relevant part of the current dialogue, considering these passages does help paint a historical perspective and illustrate the awkwardness of literalism.

Current Controversies

Other passages from scripture continue to be at the center of the Bible and science debate today. Some of the most important examples, to which we will return in detail, are:

- Genesis 1:1 states, "In the beginning God created the heavens and the earth." It asserts the existence of one God but provides no explanation or defense of the assertion. This is, as far as is known, the first time in history that the idea of one God as the creator of everything was clearly and consistently put forward. The idea was a change from the preceding myths and world view, which seem to have held that natural things had within themselves the power of change, to the more biblical view that nothing has the power to change unless it receives that power directly from God. The language of Genesis 1:1 is the foundation of the Christian theological doctrine of creation, but also the source of conflict about the creation of the universe. Some believe these words introduce a scientific, historical account that explains how the world was created. Others believe Genesis does not present a scientific explanation but instead allows for God's "creation" according to modern theories such as evolution. Some endorse Pantheism, a form of theism that suggests God is not the creator of the universe because He does not exist independent of it. And atheists have no sympathy with Genesis 1:1 regardless of what it says about God or science.

- Genesis 1, when read literally, lists God's creative activities over seven days. People have disagreed as to whether God actually created the universe in six literal days and rested on the seventh. The scientific community almost uniformly holds that the universe came into being over billions of years. Some people believe it was created in 144 hours. Others describe the days as geological periods, or periods of history, concluding that when Genesis 1 talks about a day it actually means an age—the so-called "day-age" theory. Still others endorse a "gap theory," suggesting that in Genesis 1:1, between "God created the heavens and the earth" and "the earth was formless and empty," a gap exists which could have covered millions or billions of years. They observe that the Hebrew version of "the earth was formless and empty," can be translated, "The earth became without form and void," allowing for a passage of time.

- Genesis 1 frequently refers to living things being created "according to their kinds." Some have interpreted the term "kinds" to mean biological species and speciation, suggesting that new species cannot evolve. It's fair to say that essentially no one quarrels with the view that living things change over time and that change within species occurs. However, almost all biologists go much further, believing that all species and diversity of life on earth have evolved over millions of years from common ancestry.

- Genesis 2:7 states that "the Lord God formed the man from the dust of the ground and breathed into his nostrils the breath of life…" Verses 21-22 state that He "made a woman from his rib." Some argue that this language means Adam and Eve were formed as fully developed adults and all creation was mature from the beginning. Others believe this is a prime case of the awkwardness of literalism. They argue that "Adam" means a human being rather than a specific male person, and it is incorrect to say that Eve was created after the man because Eve was created in the "Adam." So adam (humanity) was created both male and female, and Genesis 2 simply underlines the need of male and female for each other, emphasizing that the only suitable mate for a human being is another human being.

- Genesis 3 describes an incident during which a serpent converses with Eve and convinces her to eat fruit from the tree that is in the middle of the garden. She also gave some to her husband, and he ate it. God had ordered Adam and Eve not to eat from this tree. Because of what they did, God caused them to see their nakedness, cursed the serpent and condemned him to crawl on his belly, increased the pain of child birth on women, and required men in the future to work in the fields for their food. Most agree that this scripture addresses the fall of man, but people disagree as to its specific meaning. Some interpret the verses literally, suggesting a talking snake, an actual conversation, a naked couple, and other happenings as literally described. Others see the language as a narrative reflection about life and death and the knowledge of good and evil, which gives us a way to organize, through our imagination, our problems and the fallen world in relation to God.

- Genesis 5 and 11 contain genealogies that have been used by various people to calculate the age of the earth by, generally speaking, adding the chronological ages of all generations back to Adam, assuming he was created as a mature man. Various estimates using this procedure place Adam as living sometime between 12,000 and 4000 BC, much more recently than suggested by modern geology and archeology. Some older King James versions of the Bible note at the top of the first page of Genesis the date 4004 BC, a date calculated around 1650 by Archbishop Ussher of Armagh in Ireland. When certain people came to believe that geologic evidence for a much older age of the earth was irrefutable, they developed the "restitution hypothesis" or "gap theory," referred to above, which allows the earth to be as old as one wants. In a variation of this belief, others allow for a long period of a lifeless earth followed by six literal days of the creation of life. They acknowledge that God may have created the heavens and the earth eons ago, but argue that geological evidence of a biblical flood and biblical chronologies mean that homo sapiens appeared just a few thousand years ago. This view holds that there has not been time for any kind of evolution to work, so human beings must have been created by "special creation."

- Genesis 6-9, read literally, describes a flood of global proportion that destroyed all the earth's land-dwelling animal life except for those on the ark, and arguably could have formed all the major geological features of the earth. Most early Christian and Jewish writers assumed that the events actually occurred as recounted, and some today continue to hold those views and to suggest that proof of the flood would cause the collapse of the Darwinian system of biological evolution. In the face of overwhelming geological evidence contrary to a global flood, others have come to suspect that a very large local flood occurred. Still others see the story as having no scientific or historical basis at all. In this opinion, it was included in the Bible to illustrate and explain important theological ideas.

- Genesis 11:1-9 is the story of the Tower of Babel. It tells of a united humanity that spoke a single language and constructed the tower to reach the heavens in order to make a name for its people. God saw that a united people speaking one language would be able to do whatever they set their minds to, so He confused their unified language and scattered them. Some believe this scripture is to be taken literally, explaining the diversity of languages in the world and accounting for the physical differences among people and distinct races. Others see the world's different languages, races, and physical characteristics as another consequence of physiological or cultural evolution.

While these biblical passages are often part of the Bible and science debate, they are not the entire source of the conflict. Classical Greek philosophers had ideas about God, the origin of the universe, and other issues of the cosmos—ideas that even now are often confused with biblical concepts and therefore are part of the continuing debate. Reconciling the Bible and science requires one to clear up the confusion and acknowledge ideas that are philosophical rather than biblical for what they are. Accordingly, the following section briefly summarizes some philosophical ideas that are often involved in the debate.

THE ROLE OF PHILOSOPHY

Philosophy is a field of study in which people question and create theories about the nature of reality. Philosophers concern themselves with such fundamental issues as whether or not God exists, the nature of being and the universe, truth, consciousness, and right or wrong. Although methods vary according to the philosophical and cultural traditions of the people involved, the basic method of western philosophy is the use of reasoning to evaluate arguments.

As we shall see, over the years philosophy worked itself into the fabric of Christian belief. People adopted philosophical ideas to fill in where revealed scripture didn't answer their questions or give them what they wanted. For example, the absence of a biblical "proof" of God's existence has opened the door for philosophical speculation. Plato and Aristotle, two Greek philosophers who lived and wrote during pre-Christian times, led the way in developing philosophies about God. Their ideas on this and other subjects have had a huge affect on the religion and science controversy, as quite often it is their ideas, rather than scripture, that conflict with modern science.

Plato

Plato was born into an aristocratic family of Athens around 427 BC, during the period the latter books of the Old Testament were believed to have been written. He is considered to be one of the greatest philosophers of all time. A deeply religious man, he was strongly opposed to atheism. His writings addressed several subjects about which the Bible is basically silent—subjects that are at the core of today's controversies.

Plato believed that knowledge is derived from contemplating the perfect forms of truth instead of observing their imperfect embodiment in the changing world. His beliefs planted the seeds for the development by later philosophers of an ontological proof, or a proof from being, that God exists. Ontological arguments are based on reason alone. They start with an idea of God, and, without relying on the external senses or observation of the world, use that assumption as a basis for proving there is a God. Most Christian and Jewish theologians—not just modern atheists and scientists—believe that although the ontological approach might have some value, it was a failure as proof or demonstration that God exists. However, the value of the argument on grounds other than as a proof has produced a significant resurgence of the philosophy with philosophical theologians such as Hartshorne, Tillich, and Plantinga.

Centuries later, Anselm, who became Archbishop of Canterbury in 1093 and was considered the outstanding Christian philosopher and theologian of the eleventh century, became known for his celebrated ontological argument for the existence of God. His argument was basically Platonic or Neoplatonic (as opposed to the cosmological argument which is Aristotelian). So Anselm was not starting from scratch. Like Plato, his ontological argument was an argument from "ontos," or from the being of God. It is a very difficult logic to comprehend, especially for moderns, who usually are not adept at ontological thinking. The logic actually arises out of the general definition of theology as "faith seeking understanding" and the Christian view of God, which comes from revelation and tradition. Under these circumstances, one might seek to explain the existence of God, or at least show it to be reasonable, by reasoning from being (ontos).

The argument received much criticism at the time and was rejected by many Christian theologians. It continues to be rejected by Christian and Jewish theologians as well as non-Christians. Criticism varies, but often is centered on the idea that ontological arguments are invalid because they rely upon the implicit assumption that the existence of

differences of faith

God is a predicate, or starting point, of the entire logic. Some maintain, however, that Anselm actually was not trying to prove God's existence, as evidenced by the fact that his argument was stated in the middle of a prayer. Others argue that although the ontological logic fails as an argument, it still has the great value of reminding us, as Tillich says, "If one does not start with Him, one cannot reach Him."

In his *Timaeus*, Plato raised an issue that people are still arguing about two and a half centuries later—the question of intelligent design. Plato's creator lacked the supernatural ability to create *ex nihilo* (out of nothing) and was able only to organize what was already there. However, Plato proposed that the formation of the universe was the rational, purposive handiwork of a Divine Craftsman who, imitating an unchanging and eternal model, imposed mathematical order on a preexistent chaos. The Divine Craftsman, creator of the cosmos, is a supreme wisdom and intelligence who is beyond personality.

Plato believed God is not the author of everything because some things are evil. He saw the gods as good and pious because it is the nature of divinity to be good. God, the ultimate reality, is also unchangeable since any change would be for the worse. The universe as a whole as well as its various parts are intentionally arranged to produce a vast array of good effects and a world that is as excellent as its nature permits it to be. Many see a conflict between Plato's "good," with its divine intent, and Darwin's "good," which is counted in terms of survival and reproduction.

Like other Greeks of the time, Plato supposed that the heavenly bodies were divine beings that moved in perfect circles, because circles were the only perfect figures. He believed in a geocentric universe in which the earth stood still and everything moved around it. Such reverence for circles obstructed astronomy for about 2,000 years, until Johannes Kepler, working from advances made by Copernicus and Tycho Brahe, formulated the laws of planetary motion, including the law that every planet (including the earth) revolves around the sun.

Platonism had impressive parallels with Christianity as it could be construed as monotheistic. It also taught the immortality of the soul and the formation of the world at a point in time. Therefore, Platonism, as well as other consistent non-Christian philosophies, was welcomed by later Christian theologians. They believed the philosophies were true. Many believed the same philosophies had been largely plagiarized from the Hebrew Bible. And they often saw their adoption as a way of fighting charges that Christianity was intellectually void or backward.

Aristotle

When Plato was sixty, a seventeen-year-old presented himself to the Academy. The young man's remarkable intellectual powers led Plato to call him "The Mind of the School." That student's name was Aristotle. Born in 384 BC in northern Greece, he was the son of the court physician to the Macedonian royal family. After early training in medicine, he studied philosophy with Plato in Athens, where he remained for the next twenty years, until Plato's death. He was a brilliant pupil who opposed some of Plato's teachings.

Like Plato, Aristotle believed the earth was round and stood still at the center of the universe, and that all the heavenly bodies moved in perfect circles around it. He could see everything in the heavens move when he went out at night and looked up. They moved in perfect circles for a theological reason. Planets are divine, and divine things only do things in perfect ways.

Aristotle believed there were only seven planets as we know them. Seven was considered the divine number, and he believed that God only made perfect numbers. Further, he had never seen more than seven planets. From his perspective, therefore, the number of planets he saw corresponded to the number of planets that he knew God would have made.

Aristotle developed a theory of motion based on the idea that everything has within itself the inherent power of change and development, and since there is eternal motion in our world, there must be an eternal cause of the motion. His theory was compatible with his belief that planets moved because they were being pushed. Accordingly, each planet had a "daemon," a spirit, which was part of the divine essence located in the planet, and that's what pushed it. His view was developmental, or teleological—a term derived from the Greek word telos, meaning end or purpose.

Teleology is the supposition that there is purpose or directive principle in the works and processes of nature, and the most important reason for a thing is the purpose or end for which that thing was made or done. A teleological argument (or a design argument) is a case for the existence of God or Creator based on perceived evidence of order, purpose, design and/or direction in nature. Aristotle believed that all nature reflects inherent purpose and direction. His theory envisioned a sense of an "unmoved mover" or "prime mover" that could initiate motion without being set in motion. This logical precursor to today's intelligent design theory will be discussed in some detail later.

He also maintained that individual biological organisms—persons or plants—are "substantial" and their form is eternal, their essence unchanging. While some of his reasoning in this regard seems confusing and convoluted, its legacy has contributed to a belief in the "immutability" of biological forms and species in contrast to Darwin's later conclusions on the evolution of species.

The teachings of Aristotle had a major impact on thought a millennium and a half later, in the late Middle Ages, and his secular learning and reasoned arguments came to be considered a threat to theology and its traditions. When his teachings were embraced by the prestigious theology faculty at the University of Paris, traditional theologians became uneasy. A ban on many of Aristotle's books was issued in 1210 and 1215, but his works were officially sanctioned and comprised the core of the arts curriculum at the university by 1255. In fact, universities of Western Europe emphasized a natural philosophy based on Aristotle's teachings in physics, metaphysics, logic, cosmology, and other topics for approximately 450 years.

The great golden age of Athenian philosophy, which encompassed Plato and Aristotle, only lasted about a hundred years. But these ancient Greek philosophers passed on a spirit of rational inquiry into knowledge that has served as the foundation for all subsequent inquiries. Many of their beliefs continue to play out in today's controversies. As you read later chapters, reflect on the source of various issues. Do they have their origin in scripture or in philosophy? What are the implications of one, and the other?

That unbroken path from antiquity to today continues with the birth and death of Jesus Christ and the development of New Testament Christianity, to which we shall now turn.

2

NEW TESTAMENT CHRISTIANITY

"And I tell you that you are Peter, and on this rock I will build my church, and the gates of Hades will not overcome it." Matthew 16:18

Christianity as we know it, of course, emerged with the birth and death of Jesus of Nazareth. The earliest followers of Jesus were Jews. They lived by the Law of Moses and worshipped in the Jerusalem temple, in local synagogues, and in some homes as they offered traditional prayers and sacrifices. Soon after Jesus' crucifixion in about AD 30, Jews were proclaiming his resurrection and elevation to the right hand of God.

Christianity moved into Palestine and nearby areas, as well as into the Gentile world, largely through the efforts of early Christian evangelists such as Paul of Tarsus. Information is scarce as to when the books that would become the New Testament were written. Perhaps the death of a number of witnesses, often at the hands of enemies, prompted early Christian leaders to start writing down their stories of Jesus. In any case, the books of the New Testament are believed to have been written by various individuals from as early as the 50s or the early 60s to as late as 95 AD.

The Christian church appears to have been established throughout the eastern Mediterranean world, with a significant foothold in Rome, the capital of the Roman Empire, by the end of the first century. The cities of Alexandria in Egypt and Ephesus in Turkey (Asia Minor), as well as the area of modern-day Algeria also became significant centers of theological debate. The people of Alexandria and Ephesus were Greek-speaking, whereas those in the area that became Algeria spoke Latin.

Historically Christianity has involved a diversity of beliefs and practices. Differing views on important questions were an original feature. As suggested by Paul's report to the Galatians in the book of Acts, the early church was a product of a long process of debate and refinement. Catholic, Orthodox, and Protestant traditions ultimately emerged.

THE ROMAN CATHOLIC CHURCH

Early in the second century AD, the Christian church faced many problems, including persecution of its members, heresy, and challenges to the authority of the bishops. The challenges to authority held the seeds of the Roman Catholic Church. With all the conflicting versions of their religion, Christians wanted someone who could tell them which approach was correct. This seemed to be the local bishop. If the bishops disagreed, however, someone with final authority had to decide. This authority was considered to have been the bishop of the church in Rome, which was believed to have been established by the apostle Peter.

After an initial period of sporadic but intense persecution, Christianity was legalized when Constantine 1, the first Christian Roman emperor, issued the Edict of Milan in 313. In 380, Emperor Theodosius enacted a law establishing state patronage of the Catholic form of Christianity. By the end of the fourth century Christianity had become the state religion. Thus was established the Catholic Church, which dominated western Christendom until the Reformation in the 1500s.

Neoplatonism

Christianity became infused with philosophy early in its existence, even before the New Testament was established. The first great philosophical influence was Neoplatonism—the last of the great schools of "pagan" philosophy. Generally, Neoplatonism was regarded to have been founded in the third century AD by Plotinus, considered by many to be one of the most influential philosophers in antiquity after Plato and Aristotle. Neoplatonism was a synthesis of Platonism and Aristotlism with elements from mysticism, some Judaic and Christian concepts, and other philosophies of the time. It came to dominate the Greek philosophical schools and remained predominant until the teaching of philosophy by pagans ended late in the sixth century.

In later years, Neoplatonism sought to replace its earlier mysticism and magic with a more intellectual approach often called "scholasticism"—a medieval movement that flourished from 1200-1500. This approach was a particular way of organizing and practicing theology that emphasized a rational justification of religious belief and attempted to reconcile the philosophy of the ancient classical philosophers with medieval Christian theology. Scholasticism also fostered scientific methods based on the view that a combination of logic, metaphysics, and semantics reveal the fundamental truths of the universe. Such views were contrary to modern science's later emphasis on experiment and observation and therefore tended to impede the growth of modern science.

Neoplatonism exerted a great influence for at least a thousand years and formed one of the bridges by which medieval thinkers rediscovered Plato and Aristotle. Many Christian intellectuals assumed this school of thought was needed to make Christianity respectable and philosophically sound, as it tended to refute the beliefs of other philosophers that Christianity was just a superstition. Neoplatonism appealed to them because of its intellectual and moral structure, which lingered long after its philosophical structure was judged to be inadequate for Christianity.

St. Augustine

Neoplatonism was firmly joined with Christianity by St. Augustine, who was born in 354 AD. Early in life, Augustine seemed to have relished paganism, but he later adopted Manichaeism—a religious movement that for a time was a serious rival of Christianity. Manichaeism was a radically dualistic belief, seeing the world as a struggle between totally independent good and evil. Its proponents, for instance, believed that sex was totally, absolutely unholy.

Manichaeism had a significant impact on Augustine until he finally realized how extreme this philosophy was in terms of human life. At the age of thirty-three he converted to Christianity, although he probably retained a form of Neo-Platonic view initially that sex was the original sin. He changed his mind, however, when he realized that one could not believe the doctrine of creation in the Old Testament while also believing that sex is sin. The Hebrew Bible teaches that sex is the original commandment rather than the original sin. So he modified his view, although he continued to leave the impression that it is holier not to have sex. Thus, the emphasis on virginity that existed in Manichaeism and Neoplatonism was brought into Christianity by Augustine and other philosophers with similar views.

Augustine considered himself a biblical interpreter, particularly of the apostle Paul, and a theologian rather than a philosopher. Biblical interpretation, the foundation of Christian theology, is different from philosophy. Philosophy uses reason and logic to evaluate premises or arguments. Interpretation involves analyzing the historical setting and text of scripture (considering the scripture in a literal-fleshly-historical sense or in an allegorical-mystical-spiritual sense, or both) in an effort to determine the true revelation and meaning intended by the writers. When the Bible says, "God did this," for example, it doesn't try to prove through reason that there is a God, as philosophy might try to do. Or consider the New Testament teaching that God was in Jesus Christ in a way in which He was not in any other human being. This is not a view that comes from reason. Each proposition might be reasonable, and each might be discussed in a reasonable way, but they don't come from reason and they are not philosophy.

Thus, Augustine's aim was to determine what scripture revealed, not to reach an independent conclusion through reason. Interestingly, although he did not consider himself to be primarily a philosopher, Augustine came to be respected as one of the most important philosophers in the history of the West.

Augustine rejected the integration of natural science with the Christian faith, and he was not willing to say that in order to be a Christian one had to accept a particular scientific view. He had no problem with objectively listening to scientific theories. He also didn't quote scripture as a defense against whatever was discovered or thought to be discovered about the world by the scientists of his era because he did not believe that the Bible dealt with such theories. Augustine wrote five commentaries on the Genesis creation narratives. The following from his work, *The Literal Meaning of Genesis*, is instructive:

Usually, even a non-Christian knows something about the earth, the heavens, and the other elements of this world, about the motion and orbit of the stars and even their size and relative positions, about the predictable eclipses of the sun and moon, the cycles of the years and the seasons, about the kinds of animals, shrubs, stones, and so forth, and this knowledge he holds to as being certain from reason and experience. Now, it is a disgraceful and dangerous thing for an infidel to hear a Christian, presumably giving the meaning of Holy Scripture, talking nonsense on these topics; and we should take all means to prevent such an embarrassing situation, in which people show up vast ignorance in a Christian and laugh it to scorn. The shame is not so much that an ignorant individual is derided, but that people outside the household of faith think our sacred writers held such opinions, and, to the great loss of those for whose salvation we toil, the writers of our Scripture are criticized and rejected as unlearned men. If they find a Christian mistaken in a field which they themselves know well and hear him maintaining his foolish opinions about our books, how are they going to believe those books in matters concerning the resurrection of the dead, the hope of eternal life, and the kingdom of heaven, when they think their pages are full of falsehoods and on facts which they themselves have learnt from experience and the light of reason? Reckless and incompetent expounders of Holy Scripture bring untold trouble and sorrow on their wiser brethren when they are caught in one of their mischievous false opinions and are taken to task by those who are not bound by the authority of our sacred books. For then, to defend their utterly foolish and obviously untrue statements, they will try to call upon Holy Scripture for proof and even recite from memory many passages which they think support their position, although they understand neither what they say nor the things about which they make assertion.[1]

The life of St. Augustine seems to have bridged the gap between ancient pagan Rome and the Christian Middle Ages. No human being between Paul and Thomas Aquinas in the thirteenth century was more influential on intellectual thought in the West than this man.

Growth and Controversy

The Church grew larger and became more hierarchical. Confusion over what its message really was drove its leaders in the direction of recognized authorities. Bishops had to deal with a number of movements and groups they saw as distorting Christianity, including Docetism, which endorsed the idea that Jesus was not real flesh and blood; Gnosticism, which held that matter is inherently evil; the Marcionites, who produced a rival Bible edited to suit their needs; and the Ebionites, or Jewish Christians, who continued to observe the Jewish way of life.

To deal with all the controversy, the bishops and theologians drew a line between those writings that reflected the teachings of Christ and the apostles and those that did not. Development of the biblical canon—the list of books considered to be authoritative scripture— was a controversial and gradual process covering centuries. It is generally considered that Marcion began the process in 140 AD, but most issues were not ironed out until a list developed by St. Athanasius, Bishop of Alexandria, was accepted at the Third Council of Carthage in 397. Almost immediately disagreement began regarding the meaning of those books that were included.

The period from the fall of Rome, nominally considered around AD 476, to about the year 1000 has been referred to as the Dark Ages (even if the term has been largely abandoned by scholars). This was a period of instability and insecurity, during which there was a survival mentality and relatively little interest in theological debates. European culture developed very slowly, with anti-intellectual sentiment among philosophers and clergy causing them to focus primarily on defenses of traditional doctrine and practice. Concern with the necessities of life discouraged philosophical speculation. Although many nameless individuals worked to preserve the tradition of what had gone before, few genuine high points in philosophical history were attained for several hundred years.

By the eleventh century, Christianity had become a minority religion in the Eastern Mediterranean region. The center of Christian theological reflection had shifted to Western Europe. One power center focused on the city of Constantinople and comprised a form of Christianity based on the Greek language and deeply rooted in the writings of certain scholars of the Eastern Mediterranean region. Most important for our study, another power grouping focused mainly on regions such as France, Germany, the Low Countries, and northern Italy. Christianity there became centered in the city of Rome with its bishop and was influenced by the writings of Augustine and others.

Following the decline of the Roman Empire, the Church underwent a time of missionary activity and expanded across Western Europe. The eleventh century saw the formal split of the Roman Catholic Church and Eastern Orthodoxy over a number of administrative, liturgical, and doctrinal issues. While Eastern Orthodoxy is today the second largest Christian communion in the world after the Roman Catholic Church, it will not be discussed in the following chapters because of its negligible role in the Bible and science conflict in the United States.

Beginning around 1184 and continuing through the end of the Reformation in the 1600s, a number of historical movements involving the Catholic Church were aimed at securing religious and doctrinal unity within Christianity through conversion, and sometimes persecution, of alleged heretics. A conviction of heresy could involve penalties ranging from a fine to various forms of capital punishment, including burning at the stake.

Thomas Aquinas

The High Middle Ages, generally considered the eleventh through the thirteenth centuries, was an intense and productive period of intellectual ferment in Europe when compared to prior eras. Thomas Aquinas, a Catholic priest who lived in the mid 1200s, was a key thinker of the time. He was bothered by the fact that some Christian theologians were advancing "double truth" theories, arguing that something can be true in Christian theology while the exact opposite is true in philosophy, primarily Aristotelian philosophy. If Aristotle said that the world was eternal, for example, and the Bible seemed to indicate that the world was not eternal, theologians had to develop a form of double truth theory: "According to the Bible, which we believe, the earth was created, but according to Aristotle, whom we also believe, the world was not created."

Aquinas thought such an approach was insufferable, as one cannot have double truth. Yet he liked Aristotle and wanted to make sure people understood the philosopher's beliefs were compatible with Christianity, even though some had to be ignored. Aquinas also believed that most Aristotelian positions could be combined with Christian theological doctrine, and he used Aristotle as a starting point to produce a cosmological argument for the existence of God.

The Bible contains no philosophical or rational argument for God's existence, and biblical people did not believe in God because of logical conclusions or reasoning. They believed in God because they believed He had revealed Himself to them in a historical and personal way.

Although Aquinas held very little hope that philosophy could reveal who the God of the Bible is, he believed philosophy could establish that God exists and that He is One. He explained why God is real in his "five ways," based on reasons he believed one can get from the existence of the cosmos to belief in the existence of God. But proof is a very specific process, and one doesn't establish the existence of the biblical God through philosophy. Each of Acquinas' five ways could be attributed to a different God, and his proofs were not philosophical or scientific establishments of the existence, character, or personality of the God of the Bible. He simply concluded, based on faith, that there is a unique and true God of Christianity. Understanding that Aquinas was more interested in revelation than philosophy helps put his arguments in perspective. Perhaps he was not trying to prove God's existence, but just explaining the reasonableness of God's existence.

Before Aquinas, many of Aristotle's beliefs were fiercely opposed by the Catholic Church. With great courage, however, Aquinas continued to teach Aristotelian ideas and fight for his views to be accepted. He was out of step with other teachers and with the hierarchy of the Church at the time. Not surprisingly, his teachings initially caused quite a furor. But church officials eventually accepted Aristotle when Aquinas got rid of the double truth theory and presented a synthesis that allowed the rationality of Christian faith to be demonstrated on the basis of Aristotelian ideas. This synthesis became a bulwark of rational thought in the High Middle Ages.

It should be remembered that Thomas Aquinas was a dedicated Roman Catholic, so his fights with Roman Catholic priests or bishops were not conflicts between the science of Aristotle and Christianity.

They were conflicts among Christians over how much they should use Aristotle in their theology.

Aquinas' teachings were not fully accepted during his lifetime. He died in 1274 while traveling to participate in a Church Council. Three years later a number of his views were condemned by church authorities. Yet he was canonized in 1323, and in 1879 the Pope issued an encyclical commending Aquinas' works to Catholic scholars. His work became the primary theological underpinning of the Roman Catholic Church in its struggles against Protestant theology and its dealing with the advances of modern science, a subject we will cover in the next chapter.

THE PROTESTANT REFORMATION

The Protestant Reformation began in Germany in the sixteenth century. It was second only to the split of Roman Catholicism and Eastern Orthodoxy in the eleventh century as the greatest rift in the history of Christianity. Various groups, led principally by Martin Luther and often supported by local rulers, sought reform of the Catholic Church by repudiating numerous doctrines, practices, and abuses common at the time. The most significant of these was the selling of indulgences, or pardons, to confessed sinners as a means for them to escape punishment in purgatory for their sins.

In the end, however, the reformers split from the Catholic Church altogether, resulting in four major church traditions— Lutheran, Reformed/Calvinist/Presbyterian, Anabaptist, and Anglican. Reformers within the Catholic Church later launched the Counter Reformation, a period of doctrinal clarification, reform of the clergy and liturgy, and re-evangelization.

Subsequent Protestant traditions generally trace their roots to one of the initial four schools of the reformation. From 1600 onward, increasingly significant immigration to North America transported both Protestant and Catholic traditions to the United States. Protestant Christianity became the prevailing influence in Northern Europe, England and the United States for most of the next 500 years.

During the early decades after the Reformation, many German and Dutch theologians began to focus on dogmatic fine points of church doctrine. Other church leaders felt this approach was imposing a cold rationalism and formalism that was smothering the inner life of faith. These dissenters called for a return to individual piety. By the end of the seventeenth century, they had formed the pietist movement, which spread across the European Continent and into England. Its emphasis on personal repentance, spiritual regeneration, regular study of the scripture, and heartfelt love for believers and non-believers alike was a precursor to what we have come to know as modern day evangelicalism. Pietism profoundly influenced the important figures in the rise of evangelical Christianity in America.

Leaders of the movement traveled extensively in England and the American colonies, preaching the good news of salvation by faith. By the early 1740s the egalitarian message of their revivals was sweeping the colonies. Their efforts led to the Great Awakening, which has had a lasting impact on evangelism and Christianity in general in the United States. A second wave of revivals around the turn of the century broadened the evangelical movement to include more Christian traditions and to move it into the South. American Protestantism emerged from these two awakenings as a powerful force, and its character was largely evangelical.

Recent surveys suggest that about 25 percent of the adult population of the United States, approximately sixty million people, consider themselves to be evangelicals. They come from a wide variety of Protestant traditions, and their worship styles and theological doctrines vary broadly. What loosely holds them together and distinguishes them from other Christian traditions is largely their emphasis on the redemptive death and resurrection of Jesus Christ, on being born again, on the authority of the Bible as opposed to pronouncements of church officials, and on the need to share the gospel and convert others to the Christian faith. Importantly, they are the womb from which modern fundamentalism was born, and fundamentalists are the group with the greatest concerns about Charles Darwin's theory of evolution.

This brings us to the subject of modern science—a movement that developed on a path parallel to, though sometimes considered in conflict with, New Testament religion.

3
MODERN SCIENCE

"Finally we shall place the Sun himself at the center of the Universe."
Copernicus (1473 – 1543)

"*Scientia*" is the Latin word for knowledge. The search for knowledge preceded modern science, and several "scientific" disciplines (including medicine, mathematics, and astronomy) existed during the period of religious antiquity discussed in the previous chapters. Nothing corresponded to modern science, however, and no scientific branches such as physics, chemistry, geology, or zoology existed. What we now call science was called "natural philosophy" until the 1840s. Even Isaac Newton's great book on motion and gravity, published in 1687, was titled *The Mathematical Principles of Natural Philosophy*.

Most of today's controversy involving the Bible and science focuses on developments from the nineteenth century and later, such as the new geology, the theory of evolution, and the big bang theory. But the basic beliefs and general scientific attitudes that underlie the controversy arose much earlier, during the scientific movement begun by Copernicus and Galileo and carried on by Newton and others. This movement, which saw a major change in scientific method, resulted in one of the most important transformations in recorded history.

Medieval natural philosophy—what we would call science today—was primarily deductive, starting from general principles and using reason and logic to explain those principles. Modern science, on the other hand, is an entirely different method that tries to document the factual character of the natural world and then develop theories that coordinate and explain the facts. It is generally inductive, starting from experimental observation and using mathematical reasoning to develop conclusions about the observations. Modern science addresses issues from an empirical point of view (What is the universe made of?) and the theoretical point of view (Why does it work as it does?). It provides specialized technical knowledge, not a philosophy of life.

The forerunners of modern science developed new understandings in five basic areas:

- The earth moving around the sun, rather than the sun moving around the earth
- The modern law of motion—something will continue in its present state of motion until a net force acts upon it
- The law of universal gravitation
- Planets moving in ellipses rather than circles
- Advances in geology

Most early scientists believed their discoveries proved the existence of God. During the "Age of Reason" in the eighteenth century, however, many in intellectual society came to view nature as a self-sufficient deterministic mechanism. According to scholar and author Ian G. Barbour, "God became a debatable hypothesis, defended by some as a reasonable assumption, rejected by others as a dubious dogma of a reactionary church."[1]

Thus, in the eighteenth century much of society transitioned from an age of intense belief to an age of significant disbelief. The change wasn't caused by any particular scientific discoveries, but instead by the spreading influence of the idea of science itself—by the psychological reaction to what was discovered. In a psychological sense, God seemed to be more and more remote, a development that makes it important for us to understand key facts about the major figures of this revolution.

The development of modern science was a complex transformation occurring over many years. A complete survey of this sea-change would include the names Lagrange, d'Alembert, Laplace, Priestley, Lavoisier, Linnaeus, Buffon, and many others. The following brief overview, though, is limited to a discussion of four individuals whose lives and contributions were at the heart of the debate involving Christianity and science, and whose legends live today.

CHRISTOPHER COLUMBUS (1451-1506)

Most people know of Christopher Columbus, the Italian navigator and maritime explorer credited with discovering the Americas, whose voyages to the New World began a European effort to explore and colonize the American continent. Although Columbus was not a scientist in the conventional sense, his beliefs and activities have been a part of scientific discourse for centuries, and his story has a unique relevance in the history of science and Christianity.

A popular story holds that Columbus took a basket of eggs around to monks, priests, and other church people and tried to convince these ignorant folks that the earth was round like an egg. Of course they just laughed at him because they knew the earth was flat. Nothing would change their minds. After many unsuccessful efforts Columbus finally won an audience with Queen Isabella of Spain, who accepted the possibility that the earth could be round and gave him money for his expedition. Sailing to the other side of the world, lo and behold, Columbus proved it was round.

Problem is, the story is not true. Some Europeans still believed in a flat earth, but they generally were pagans, the uneducated, or the very superstitious who believed only what they saw. And they saw what most of us see every day when we go outside—an apparently flat earth.

The fact is, only a few people (virtually no learned monks or priests) believed the earth was flat at the time of Columbus' voyage. Interestingly, Lactanius, who lived in the third century, was perhaps the only important theologian in history who believed the earth was flat. Regarding the idea of a round earth, he observed, "Can anyone be so foolish as to believe that there are men whose feet are higher than their heads, or places where things may be hanging downwards, trees growing backwards, or rain falling upwards?"[2] Galileo made fun of him, and Thomas Aquinas called him an ignoramus.

Long before Columbus, church leaders and Christian theologians knew the earth was round. This is not surprising because Aristotle, Ptolemy, and other philosopher/scientists had the same beliefs. And people believed their scientists. They saw no conflict between their own knowledge and the words of the Bible, from which one could infer a flat earth.

Thus, while we presumably can thank Columbus for his discovery of the Americas, we should be more restrained in crediting him with changing the way people viewed the world. We must turn to others for that.

NICOLAS COPERNICUS (1473-1543)

Copernicus, said to be the founder of modern astronomy, was born in Poland and spent a sheltered academic life as a cleric in the bishopric of Lukas Watzenrode, located in what is now northern Poland. He studied mathematics, optics, and church law. Over time, astronomy became his primary interest. He carried on investigations quietly and alone, making his celestial observations with a "naked eye" from a turret situated on the protective wall around the cathedral. A hundred years would pass before the invention of the telescope.

In 1543, Copernicus published his great work, *De Revolutionibus*, which asserted that the earth rotated on its axis once daily and traveled around the sun once yearly—a fantastic concept for the time. His ideas were contrary to the prevailing theory in the western world, based on the work of Aristotle and Ptolemy, that the universe was a closed space bounded by a spherical envelope beyond which there was nothing, and the earth was a stationary center of the universe.

What did Copernicus do? He lived many years before the seventeenth century scientific revolution, yet his work paved the way for that revolution. Legend holds that he believed theology was a kind of "bunk," and that he produced a view of the world that was contrary to existing theological beliefs. In fact, Copernicus produced a simpler way of understanding the solar system. The prevailing view of the time—that the sun and planets revolved around the earth—required continuing cumbersome and arbitrary amendments and revisions to reconcile the astronomical data that was becoming available. Copernicus, in direct opposition to Ptolemy and Aristotle, proposed a model involving a small number of concentric circles, in which the planets and the earth revolved around the sun. His model agreed with the astronomical data with comparable accuracy, and was much simpler mathematically.

Since Copernicus didn't have a telescope, he saw only what Ptolemy and Aristotle had seen. He didn't discover any particular fact in the universe or make any observations on the nature of the movements of the heavenly bodies that had not been made before. But he did arrange the known facts in a new and simpler way, following a fourteenth century principle called "Occam's razor," which holds that the explanation of any phenomenon should make as few assumptions as possible, eliminating those that make no difference in the observable predictions.

Copernicus' new beliefs were widely considered to be contrary to prevailing philosophical and religious beliefs of medieval times, in particular the idea that man was made by God in His image, was the next thing to God, and therefore was superior to all creatures. Copernicus' work challenged this perceived place of man in the cosmos, as most church leaders believed that man's place in the universe was being demoted to one on a spinning, peripheral planet. As a result, man could no longer legitimately think that his significance was greater than his fellow creatures. Instead, he came to be just a part of nature.

Copernicus was a theologian. His famous work was published by Andreas Osiander, a theologian and ardent follower of Luther. Not surprisingly, however, Copernicus' theories ran counter to the beliefs of many politically powerful churchmen over time. By the beginning of the seventeenth century scientific revolution, many had begun to see the Bible as a source of infallible information about science that had been dictated by God. Those holding this view opposed the Copernican theory as contrary to biblical passages that implied a geocentric universe, such as the reference in Psalm 93:1 that "The world is firmly established, it cannot be moved;" in Ecclesiastes 1:4 that "Generations come and generations go, but the earth remains forever;" and other passages with similar import.

Further, it could be inferred from Copernicus' ideas that there was no need for a God who granted a soul, power, and life to the world and to human beings, as science could explain everything that had been attributed to Him.

Copernicus died in 1543 and was never to know what a stir his work would cause. It was the beginning of a new worldview that was to clash with existing theological beliefs, which were largely a synthesis of scripture and Aristotelianism. The conflict was bound to come to a head, as it did in the Galileo affair roughly a century later.

GALILEO GALILEI (1564-1642)

Born in Italy, Galileo was the son of a mathematician and musician. He attended the University of Pisa and served on the faculty at several universities, teaching geometry, mechanics, and astronomy. He concentrated on science, made many significant discoveries, and is often called the "father of modern physics." He was a devout Roman Catholic who found no conflict between his religious and scientific beliefs.

Galileo is noted for his careful investigations that involved combining theory with extensive use of experiments. A strong supporter of Copernicus' views on astronomy, he used the newly available telescope to seek to conclusively establish the Copernican system, which placed the sun rather than the earth at the center of our universe. In 1610, he moved to Florence to accept a position with the Grand Duke of Tuscany. After a warm reception, he encountered significant hostility against his views.

In 1612, Galileo visited Rome, where he continued to face opposition to his Copernican theories. This was a reactionary period of intrigue and extremely complex social and intellectual circumstances. For religious, sociological, and psychological reasons, people were less free to disagree with the hierarchy of the church than they had been in earlier times.

From the pulpit of Santa Maria Novella in 1614, a church official denounced Galileo's opinions about the motion of the earth, judging them dangerous and close to heresy. Galileo defended himself against these accusations. In 1615 he composed his famous letter to the Grand Duchess Christina of Tuscany, addressing issues of science and faith. Long excerpts of the letter, not published until 1635, are quoted below because they so effectively and eloquently capture the context and spirit of the conflict involving the Bible and science at the time, and also because they seem to so accurately describe much of today's controversy.

> They know that as to the arrangement of the parts of the universe, I hold the sun to be situated motionless in the center of the revolution of the celestial orbs while the earth revolves about the sun.

> Possibly because they are disturbed by the known truth of other propositions of mine which differ from those

commonly held, and therefore mistrusting their defense so long as they confine themselves to the field of philosophy, these men have resolved to fabricate a shield for their fallacies out of the mantle of pretended religion and the authority of the Bible. These they apply with little judgment to the refutation of arguments that they do not understand and have not even listened to.

They pretend not to know that its author, or rather its restorer and confirmer, was Nicholas Copernicus; and that he was not only a Catholic, but a priest and a canon. He was in fact so esteemed by the church that when the Lateran Council under Leo X took up the correction of the church calendar, Copernicus was called to Rome from the most remote parts of Germany to undertake its reform.

They go about invoking the Bible, which they would have minister to their deceitful purposes. Contrary to the sense of the Bible and the intention of the holy Fathers, if I am not mistaken, they would extend such authorities until even in purely physical matters— where faith is not involved— they would have us altogether abandon reason and the evidence of our senses in favor of some biblical passage, though under the surface meaning of its words this passage may contain a different sense.

I hope to show that I proceed with much greater piety than they do, when I argue not against condemning this book, but against condemning it in the way they suggest—that is, without understanding it, weighing it, or so much as reading it.

With regard to this argument, I think in the first place that it is very pious to say and prudent to affirm that the holy Bible can never speak untruth—whenever its true meaning is understood. But I believe nobody will deny that it is often very abstruse, and may say things which are quite different from what its bare words signify. Hence in expounding the Bible if one were always to confine oneself to the unadorned grammatical meaning, one might fall into error. Not only contradictions and propositions far from true

might thus be made to appear in the Bible, but even grave
heresies and follies. Thus it would be necessary to assign to
God feet, hands and eyes, as well as corporeal and human
affections, such as anger, repentance, hatred, and sometimes
even the forgetting of things past and ignorance of those
to come. These propositions uttered by the Holy Ghost
were set down in that manner by the sacred scribes in order
to accommodate them to the capacities, of the common
people, who are rude and unlearned. For the sake of those
who deserve to be separated from the herd, it is necessary
that wise expositors should produce the true senses of such
passages, together with the special reasons for which they
were set down in these words. This doctrine is so wide-
spread and so definite with all theologians that it would be
superfluous to adduce evidence for it.

From these things it follows as a necessary consequence that,
since the Holy Ghost did not intend to teach us whether
heaven moves or stands still, whether its shape is spherical
or like a discus or extended in a plane, nor whether the earth
is located at its center or off to one side, then so much the
less was it intended to settle for us any other conclusion of
the same kind.

I would say here something that was heard from an eccle-
siastic of the most eminent degree: "That the intention of
the Holy Ghost is to teach us how one goes to heaven, not
how heaven goes."[3]

Notwithstanding Galileo's continuing defense of his beliefs, a
cardinal admonished him in 1616 to neither advocate nor teach Copernican astronomy as religious doctrine. For the next several years Galileo
stayed well away from the controversy. In 1632, however, he published
a book on the subject with papal permission and formal authorization
from the Inquisition. In the process, he offended the Pope, who ultimately called him to Rome to explain himself.

Galileo was ordered to stand trial on suspicion of heresy in 1633.
The sentence of the Inquisition required him to recant heliocentric
ideas, which were condemned as "formally heretical." He was ordered

imprisoned, although the sentence was later commuted to house arrest; his book was banned, and publication of his other works forbidden. Galileo spent the remainder of his life under house arrest. He died in 1642, and was formally "rehabilitated" in 1741, when Pope Benedict XIV authorized the publication of Galileo's complete scientific works. In 1758, the general prohibition against heliocentric views was removed from church doctrine. More recently, in 1992, Pope John Paul II declared that the ruling against Galileo was an error resulting from "tragic mutual incomprehension." In 2008, Pope Benedict XVI paid tribute to the astronomer, and top Vatican officials suggested he should be named the "patron" of the dialogue between faith and reason.

Although Copernicus and Galileo could not empirically prove their theory, they (along with other key figures in the astronomical revolution, such as Tycho Brahe, Johannes Kepler, and Isaac Newton) dealt the death blow to Aristotelian astronomy. Galileo had problems with some members of his church, but he apparently had no ultimate intellectual or theological problems with his faith. He held that scripture did not reveal scientific facts but instead offered spiritual knowledge, or truths that are above reason or observation, and that nature is the sole source of scientific knowledge.

ISAAC NEWTON (1642-1727)

Sir Isaac Newton was born in Woolsthorpe, England, in the year Galileo died. In 1661, he went to Trinity College, Cambridge. Unfortunately, the plague was spreading across Europe and reached Cambridge in the summer of 1665. The university closed, and Newton returned home, where he spent two years concentrating on problems in mathematics and physics. He wrote later that it was during this time that he first understood the theory of gravitation, for which he became so famous. Newton also invented calculus, experimented in mechanics and optics, and brought to fruition the alliance of mathematics and experimentation that Galileo had pioneered.

Legend is that Newton saw an apple fall in his garden in Lincolnshire, thought of it in terms of a gravitational force that attracted things towards the earth, and realized the same force might extend as far as the moon. Regardless of the legend, he did develop the idea that the earth's gravitational pull might extend to the moon and, therefore, the moon might be continually falling toward the earth. Ian Barbour has noted that Newton presented:

> a structure of forces and masses rather than a hierarchy of purposes. This magnificent synthesis was rightly admired, and the perfection of mathematical law made a great impact on Newton's contemporaries. It suggested an image of *the world as an intricate machine* following immutable laws, with every detail precisely predictable. Here was the basis for the philosophies of determinism and materialism which later generations were to develop. Newton himself believed that the world-machine was designed by an intelligent creator and expressed his purpose; to later interpreters, impersonal and blind forces appeared to be entirely self-contained, and all sense of meaning and purpose was lost.[4]

Newton was not a priest or a Roman Catholic, but he considered his work to be theological. All his scientific work was done, as he said, to the greater glory of God. He believed there was a God, and God had created everything. Newton wrote in the *Principia:*

> This most beautiful system of the sun, planets, and comets could only proceed from the counsel and dominion of an intelligent and powerful Being....He is eternal and infinite, omnipotent, and omniscient; that is, his duration reaches from eternity to eternity; his presence from infinity to infinity; he governs all things, and knows all things that are or can be done....We know him only by his most wise and excellent contrivances of things, and final causes; we admire him for his perfections; but we reverence and adore him on account of his dominion: for we adore him as his servants; and a god without dominion, providence, and final causes, is nothing else but Fate and Nature.[5]

Newton's thesis is an example of what has come to be called the argument from design. He believed there were certain irregularities in the observed motion of the planets that he could not explain in terms of the law of gravity. If these irregularities were cumulative, they would in the course of time cause great deviations that would upset the whole balance of the solar system. He suggested there must be only one explanation. From time to time, God intervenes and puts the errant planets back on their proper paths. Thus, Newton seemed to be suggesting that he could explain everything except a few irregularities involving the planets and their spheres, and he had to bring God into the equation to correct those situations. Some have inferred from these ideas a "God of the gaps"—a God who seems to work only in areas that man cannot explain through natural causes. However, Newton probably did not envision a God of the gaps in the sense now described by some, which will be discussed in more detail in later chapters.

Newton was not the great intellectual giant who finally got rid of God, as the myth generally assumes. He was a devout believer, who seemed to take his theology even more seriously than his science. Newton did not believe that nature was God, or that nature or fate was all there is. He believed the dominion over nature was the dominion of God. Further, God was not a retired author or a retired creator, and even the law of gravity could be explained only in terms of the power of God.

For example, Newton said, "Gravity explains the motions of the planets, but it cannot explain who set the planets in motion. God governs all things and knows all that is or can be done."[6] He even supposed that his system of celestial mechanics provided a proof for the existence of God, and no doubt would have been horrified to think that his life's work would result in a general undermining of religious faith. He believed that it should have exactly the opposite effect.

Ironically, Newton's work is often seen as one of the primary factors leading to a worldview holding that only science—not the supernatural—matters. He lived at the beginning of the age of machines. The model he had available to him was that of the machine, and his work set the stage for viewing the universe as a mechanical system. It allowed one to think of the world as a machine that was created at the very beginning and is still running under its own steam according to the laws of nature, with God only intervening once in a while to tap something back into place. Such beliefs are not far from a belief that one doesn't need God, as the laws of nature keep the world operating.

So, even though Newton believed that God had created the world and is necessary for the universe to exist, his work probably helped lay the groundwork for various views that question the existence of God, including agnosticism and even atheism.

CONCLUSIONS

We have looked briefly at four individuals whose work, along with that of others, set the stage for much of science as we know it. While their beliefs may seem simple or even outdated now, their fundamental attitudes are relevant to today's debate. It is important to remember that they were Christians, as were essentially all scientists for many years. Most early scientists had no doubt that nature displayed God. As early as Augustine in the fourth century AD, the idea existed that God has two books. One, the book of nature, is read one way, and the other, the book of scripture, is read in a different way. Or as Galileo believed more than a thousand years later, one does not read scripture to find out if the earth revolves around the sun, or if the sun revolves around the earth, because scripture does not discuss that subject. Instead, one uses reason and evidence to determine physical matters and scripture to learn "how one goes to heaven."

Almost all scientists through the nineteenth century held strictly to the idea of the two books of God, and the related conflicts among Christians were essentially conflicts between science and philosophy rather than between science and religion.

This history is important background for today's controversy. There is a bias—perhaps a growing bias—that Christianity has thwarted scientific progress over the years. But the truth is not that clear. There can be no doubt that certain religious beliefs and institutional churches have impeded some scientific advances, as we have seen in the case of the Catholic Church's reaction to Galileo. A credible view is that the institutional church was one of the reasons scientific development was so meager in the Middle Ages. The rest of the story, however, is that in most cases believers like Copernicus, Galileo, and Newton were the ones advocating the advances. So the conflicts were primarily among Christians—often among Christian scientists— and not between secular or atheistic scientists and Christians. Thus, any historical bias against Christians who impeded science needs to be balanced by acknowledging those Christians who fostered scientific progress.

Perhaps more importantly, while the Bible is not a textbook that contains scientific facts, the roots of modern science are deeply embedded in Christianity. The rise of modern science was a complex phenomenon, influenced by many causes. Economic and social conditions were important drivers. Other religions fostered spates of scientific advancement as well. For example, Moslem intelligentsia introduced Aristotle to Europe and produced important scientific thinking before they were expelled, and Jews contributed to the development of modern science, particularly in Spain. However, modern science only developed in the Christian West, where Christianity contained deep truths that made it conceivable for the human mind to explore nature. Speaking very generally, most other religions see matter as impermanent, illusory, or evil and do not acknowledge a Creator God. Christianity, on the other hand, posits a transcendental creator and natural laws that can be understood only by observation, which allowed science to develop on its own terms. Since the world was not an object of worship, it could become an object of study. Christianity also envisioned human beings created in God's image, with the confidence that man's created mind could understand the created realm and the laws of nature. And finally, "The 'Protestant ethic' similarly endorsed *scientific work*; the study of nature was held to be at once intrinsically fascinating, beneficial to mankind, and divinely sanctioned, for it would both reveal God's handiwork and exemplify rational and orderly activity."[7] All considered, such a worldview fostered the experimental method and the investigatory processes of modern science.

The idea of rationality as seen in science permeated human activities in the hundred or so years following the life of Isaac Newton. The eighteenth century came to be called the Age of Reason, during which the Enlightenment movement arose. This movement was a diverse phenomenon that spread across Germany, England, and the American colonies and influenced the climate of thought in the rest of the modern world. Nature was seen as a self-sufficient mechanism that could be explained by natural forces, it was believed that man could achieve the ideal society by applying reason to human affairs, and God became a subject for debate.

However, the last half of the eighteenth and the early part of the nineteenth centuries saw a reaction against the Age of Reason. Conservatism and concern for traditional values revived, new forms of nationalism appeared, literature began to assert the limitations of science and the value of intuition, and new religious movements emerged.

It was into this world that Charles Darwin and his colleagues appeared around the middle of the nineteenth century.

4

CHARLES DARWIN

"I see no good reason why the views given in this volume should shock the religious feelings of any one."
Charles Darwin (1809 – 1882)

Our story of Charles Darwin begins in the early 1800s, on the threshold of the Victorian era in England and in the midst of full-fledged westward expansion in the United States. The industrial revolution had a full head of steam in both countries and around the world, but science as we know it had not yet emerged. Relatively little was understood about science generally or the area of biology. Naturalists knew little about subjects such as fertilization, heredity, or embryonic differentiation— and certainly nothing about DNA, RNA, the human genome, or other topics of today. The study of animal behavior and ecology had barely begun. Few fossils of man or beast had been discovered.

Mainstream western thought going into the nineteenth century had viewed the biological world as orderly and stable, the result of what Greek philosophers, including Plato and Aristotle, had described as an immutable "nature," "form," or "essence" that naturally breeds true for every organism. This concept of static species had been combined with a literal interpretation of the Genesis creation account to foster a theological legacy for the early 1800s.

However, English scientists were coming more and more to accept as "scientific" only those explanations based on natural law and to believe that the formation of new species would be found to be a natural process rather than a direct act of God. Some theologians saw a threat to biblical authority, but most did not. Biblical literalism had long since been questioned, and most theologians did not see a problem with the idea that the earth was very old, or that one couldn't explain geology by Noah's flood, or that living organisms had developed through small changes over long periods of time. Many did not believe that biological life was functionally complete from the beginning, and some believed that human beings had not been created specially as a separate species.

Into this world came Charles Darwin, a rich kid who grew up with the fits and starts, rebellion and uncertainty of so many teenagers today. Ultimately he published the book that would become the focus of the mother of all controversies—one we all continue to live with.

DARWIN'S EARLY LIFE

Charles Darwin was born in Shrewsbury, England, on February 12, 1809, the fifth child of Robert Darwin, a wealthy society doctor and financier, and his wife, Susannah. Although his father was not a believer, Charles was baptized in the Anglican Church and attended the Unitarian Chapel with his mother and siblings. His golden childhood included boarding school, travel, and shooting game, which placed him squarely in the club of the rich and privileged.

After young Darwin spent the summer of 1825 working with his father as an apprentice doctor, his father sent him to the University of Edinburgh to study medicine in the fall. His revulsion at the brutality of surgery led him to neglect his medical studies, however. He developed a keen interest in natural history instead, and became an avid pupil of Robert Grant, an early proponent of evolution by acquired characteristics. This course of study allowed him to participate in Grant's investigations of the life cycle of marine animals, which found evidence supporting the theory that all animals have similar organs, differing only in complexity, and therefore have common descent.

In 1827, Darwin finally came clean with his father about his disdain for medicine. With the army, navy, and the law not being viable considerations, Dr. Darwin pushed his son toward the church. Charles had never given much thought to religion, but after due consideration was able to accommodate himself to the Anglican faith and, for the second time, to a profession his father had selected for him. In January of 1829 he began a course of study to qualify as a clergyman—a sensible decision at a time when most clergymen were provided with high social status and a comfortable income.

Most English clergymen were also naturalists, who saw exploring the wonders of God's creation as part of their duty. Darwin became engrossed in competitive collecting of beetles—a craze of the time— and subsequently matriculated in a natural history course. He became particularly enthused by the writings of one of his teachers, William Paley, including his argument for divine design in nature. Paley argued that if you are walking across a meadow and see a watch lying on the ground, you know it was designed and did not just happen by chance. If it was designed, it had a designer. So it is with the natural world. Something that is so beautiful and works so well must have had a designer, or creator.

After graduation, while waiting on his ordination, Darwin received an invitation to serve as a gentleman companion and unpaid naturalist for Robert FitzRoy, the captain of the *HMS Beagle*, during a two-year expedition to chart the coastline of South America. All English ships had naturalists aboard. Their job was to observe the flora and fauna of the land areas touched during the journey, thereby contributing to the great pile of knowledge being gathered at the time by English naturalists. Darwin accepted the post, over his father's initial objection. Perhaps his objection had to do with the fact that he would be required to financially support his son's personal and professional life while at sea, and that he considered it a frivolous distraction from Charles' chosen profession. In any case, the voyage became a five-year expedition that would lead to dramatic changes in many fields of science.

THE *BEAGLE* JOURNEY

The *Beagle* sailed from England across the Atlantic to South America, around its southern tip, north to the Galapagos Islands, west to Australia, passing the southern tip of Africa, and back to England. Darwin spent two-thirds of the time on land, carefully noting a rich variety of geological features, fossils, and living organisms.

In January, 1832, the *Beagle* landed at Camp Verde Island, off the western coast of Africa. Darwin observed the island's barren landscape with pockets of vegetation and pools of live corals. More importantly, he saw signs of extensive volcanic activity and layers of rock that he believed clearly had been laid down on the seabed and then uplifted and folded over time. He had been reading *The Principles of Geology* by Charles Lyell, which advocated a principle called uniformitarianism—the idea that geologic change was the result of the accumulation of relatively small changes over long periods of time rather than infrequent catastrophic events. Now Darwin was seeing it for himself.

In South America, Darwin covered more than 2000 miles on horseback. He found and excavated rare fossils of very large, extinct mammals, which he took to be something like a rhinoceros, in strata showing no signs of catastrophe or change in climate that might have caused the animals' extinction. Shocked by the people of Tierra del Fuego, he observed, "I would not have believed how entire the difference between savage and civilised man is. It is greater than between a wild and domesticated animal…"[1]

On the Galapagos Islands, which straddle the equator 600 miles off the coast of Ecuador, Darwin most famously observed animal life that he noted was different from that found in similar tropical climates. The animals seemed as strange as creatures from another planet, including great marine iguanas as black as the earth beneath them and massive tortoises whose shells differed from island to island. He saw species of birds he had never seen before, and noted that certain birds, like the tortoises, were different depending on which island they lived on.

Thus, Darwin learned a great deal about many geological and biological subjects, including differences between species. Near the end of the voyage, Captain FitzRoy read Darwin's diary and asked him to rewrite it to provide a volume on natural history. Darwin no doubt gave the matter great thought, and his journals were published to considerable acclaim within a few years. His major work, however, was another matter.

THE ORIGIN OF SPECIES

Darwin didn't publish *The Origin of Species*, the famous book based on his experiences, until 1859, twenty-three years after the completion of his journey. Perhaps his delay was influenced by Captain FitzRoy, a staunch, orthodox Christian who believed human beings were specially created by God. Perhaps it was influenced by his marriage to Emma, a devout Anglican who worried that his lapses of faith would prevent their meeting in the afterlife. Also, Darwin was laid up frequently from various maladies—palpitations of the heart, stomach problems, headaches, boils, and numerous apparently stress-related problems. For the most part, though, he worked on additional editing and publishing projects, continuing research, experimentation, and scientific matters. His focus was on the critical issue of species, as he strived to develop his emerging theory and make it fully credible to his scientific colleagues.

Darwin's Predecessors

We often assume that the theory of evolution emerged suddenly and full blown, like a spring flower, with Darwin's publication of *The Origin of Species*. In fact, elements of the theory had been proposed long before, and his main contribution was to fit the ideas of several forerunners together into a unified theory and to provide evidence to support it.

In the century before Darwin's work, Carl Linnaeus, the most renowned botanist of his time, established conventions for naming and classifying plants that became universally accepted in the scientific world. His conventions, based on the idea that differences among species depend on the presence of separate lineages that do not change, perpetuated the belief that permanent differences exist between species. However, French naturalist Georges Buffon had observed the natural variability of species and suggested that their struggle for survival might cause the extinction of some types. As far back as 1749 he estimated that the earth could be 70,000 years old.

In 1802, Jean-Baptiste Lamarck, another French naturalist, proposed a theory of progressive evolutionary development based on forces from within living things and the inheritance of acquired characteristics. He also suggested that biological species exhibited an ascending hierarchy, from the simplest to the most complex, with each generation progressing to more complexity than its ancestors. Lamarck defended unlimited organic change on the theory that an animal's organs develop through use and that acquired modifications are inherited. For example, a giraffe gets a long neck because it has to stretch it to reach something. If he stretches it enough times, his descendants will inherit a long neck.

Although Lamarckianism was one of the philosophical views some people adopted before Darwin came along, probably more people accepted the creationist concept of stability of species. This view generally prevailed, however, because of ingrained habits and beliefs rather than because of support from the church.

Prior to the early 1830s, the prevailing geologic theory held by scientists was catastrophism, the idea that a sequence of great cataclysms such as Noah's flood had shaped all the world's geologic strata and formations, including the layering and changing of mountains, valleys, and other anomalies, and that God had created new species in the relatively stable times between these events.

In the 1830s, Charles Lyell, an important British geological theorist and a Christian, espoused the doctrine of uniformitarianism, which challenged catastrophism and held that natural processes operating over millions of years in the past are the same as those that can be observed operating in the present. He believed geologic change resulted from the steady accumulation of minute changes over enormously long spans of time. His views were generally not thought to conflict with biblical authority. Most Christian theologians, who long since had seriously questioned biblical literalism, read the Bible in a way that was not contradicted by Lyell's geologic discoveries. Darwin later acknowledged that the views of Lyell, whose book he had read before the voyage, had a significant influence on his own thought.

By the mid-1800s several people, including some clergy, had put forward theories of evolution. For example, Scottish writer Robert Chambers anonymously published *Vestiges of the Natural History of Creation* in 1844, providing a naturalistic explanation of the origin of the earth and the progressive evolution of life toward mankind. Chambers was a generalist, outside the circle of specialist geologists. Although both the scientific and religious communities roundly denounced his book, it became popular with the general public. This success forced geologists to respond, with a concurrent widening of the unspoken boundaries of theories open for discussion. It also helped pave the way for Darwin and reminded him of how vociferous his critics would be.

People also were practicing a form of evolution. Artificial selection of domesticated animals was common among English people, particularly English Puritans and Anglican clergymen, who often bred pigeons, dogs, and other animals to develop different breeds. Thus, it's likely that they understood a form of artificial selection well before Darwin.

Darwin's Work

Although a great deal of scientific work preceded Darwin's publication, few scientists had achieved a perspective as to how it all might fit together in a theory of development. They needed more. One can argue that the theory of evolution was nothing new, and Darwin only found additional empirical data to support it. But data wasn't enough. A scientist needs some kind of hook, or fundamental thesis, upon which to hang scientific facts to develop a scientific theory. Darwin provided that hook.

While continuing his research in London, Darwin read "for amusement" the sixth edition of Malthus' *An Essay on the Principle of Population*. Malthus, an ordained Anglican country pastor, calculated that the human population could double every twenty-five years based on the current birth rate, but he concluded that, in practice, growth is kept in check by death, disease, wars, and famine. A lightening bolt struck, and Darwin had found his hook—the concept of natural selection and its role in preventing the human population from increasing beyond the nourishment available to it. Natural selection provided a possible hypothesis for explaining all the differences he had observed between the species in the Galapagos Islands.

By 1844, Darwin had developed the proposition that species of organisms arise from other species through a process of natural selection. When life conditions change, those organisms better adapted than others because of random variations will leave more offspring in the next generation. And so on for very long periods of time. This, of course, challenged several theories prevalent in the early 1800s, such as catastrophism, the fixity of the species, and the stability of biological form. All were traditional beliefs of the church that originated, not from the Bible, but from the influence of Aristotle and other secular philosophers. Thus, if Darwin had a fight, it was with philosophy rather than the Bible.

Darwin, however, continued to seem hesitant to publish his findings. He wrote a friend that explaining his theory was like "confessing to a murder." And his wife didn't want him to publish. She hoped the theory was not true. But even if it was, she didn't want the book published because she believed it would have a detrimental affect on Victorian morality and the current understanding of the essence of a human being.

Darwin was finally prompted to publish his thesis when an acquaintance, Alfred Russel Wallace, began writing papers on species and evolutionary mechanisms that expressed ideas almost identical to his own. Wallace was very open about what he was working on, shared many of his ideas with Darwin, and presented them publicly to a scientific society. Darwin's friends encouraged him to go ahead and publish his work first. Without informing Wallace, Darwin published *The Origin of Species by Means of Natural Selection of the Preservation of Favored Races in the Struggle for Life*. The book proved more popular than expected, with the entire stock of 1,250 copies oversubscribed by the time it went on sale. So we're now writing about Charles Darwin instead of Alfred Russel Wallace. A sincere naturalist and a devout orthodox Christian who felt a need for a scientific explanation for the origin of species, Wallace is one of those people in intellectual history for whom one might feel pity. But when Darwin published, Wallace became a footnote in history.

The essence of Darwin's proposition in *The Origin of Species* is best described in his own words:

> Can it, then, be thought improbable, seeing that variations useful to man have undoubtedly occurred, that other variations useful in some way to each being in the great and complex battle of life, should occur in the course of many successive generations. If such do occur, can we doubt (remembering that many more individuals are born than can possibly survive) that individuals having any advantage, however slight, over others, would have the best chance of surviving and of procreating their kind? On the other

hand, we may feel sure that any variation in the least degree injurious would be rigidly destroyed. This preservation of favourable individual differences and variations, and the destruction of those which are injurious, I have called Natural Selection, or the Survival of the Fittest.[2]

The first edition of Darwin's book carefully avoided discussion of the application of evolution to the origin of human beings, and later editions barely alluded to it. However, in a subsequent book, *The Descent of Man*, published in 1871, Darwin concluded that Africa was the cradle of humankind and spelled out his views as to how human beings evolved.

The publication of Darwin's ideas was like throwing cold water on hot oil. In his 2006 book, *Why Darwin Matters*, Michael Shermer constructed the following syllogistic reasoning, based on a speech William Jennings Bryan had planned to deliver at the Scopes "Monkey Trial," which illustrates the type of condemnation Darwin's theory received:

Evolution implies that there is no God, therefore...
Belief in the theory of evolution leads to atheism, therefore...
Without a belief in God there can be no morality or meaning, therefore...
Without morality and meaning there is no basis for a civil society, therefore...
Without a civil society we will be reduced to living like brute animals.[3]

Many earlier scientific discoveries, such as those involving modern science's challenge to a geocentric universe or even the geologic age of the earth, went through a period of early controversy. But typically their proof was strong enough, and the inferences from them benign enough, that the issues evaporated after a period of time. Not so—or at least not yet—with the question of evolution. More information seems to confuse rather than clarify. Conflicting beliefs and theories become more strident, but resolve nothing. Unlike other scientific issues, the evolution theory advocated by Darwin's book goes directly to the heart of our very being. It presents difficult questions such as from whence we came and who we are and why we do what we do. It teaches that human beings share a common ancestry with other living organisms. It poses the theory of natural selection, under which nature "selects" the reproductively fit and eliminates others. It suggests a world of chance, apparent randomness, blind experimentation, and impersonality. It has been viewed by some as questioning the need for God, as well as encouraging atheism and moral degeneration. People seem to use Darwin as they will to support their own purpose, as James R. Moore has noted:

> The works of Charles Darwin (1809-1882) have been cited more frequently than read, and read far more often than understood. Religious reactionaries and the sycophants of scientism have alike forced Darwin to serve their dubious ends, while even persons of moderation have represented as Darwinism either more or less than the primary texts allow.[4]

We turn now to this continuing controversy.

5

DARWIN'S AFTERMATH

"The struggle for existence holds as much in the intellectual as in the physical world. A theory is a species of thinking, and its right to exist is coextensive with its power of resisting extinction by its rivals."
Thomas Huxley (1825 – 1895)

Controversies involving earlier scientific discoveries were the opening act. Darwin provided the show. *The Origin of Species* immediately set off the era's key scientific controversy, which he monitored closely, keeping press clippings of thousands of reviews, articles, satires, and other responses. The reactions quickly focused on the unstated implications of "men from monkeys," and people took all sides. Many considered Darwin's work an abomination, but a core circle of friends defended him against his many critics and actively pushed his conclusions to the front of the scientific and public stage. With their help, he was awarded—by a ten to eight vote—the Royal Society's highest award, the Copley Medal, in 1864. But that didn't stop the controversy.

THE SCIENTIFIC DEBATE

The debate that followed *Origin* involved various issues, a great deal of confusion, and intermingled levels of discussion. However, it was almost exclusively among Christians, as there were few non-believers at the time. The real battle was between different scientific perspectives—largely between Darwin's defenders and Baconian scientists.

Bacon's Influence
Francis Bacon was a sixteenth century philosopher and devout Bible believer who advocated the presence of two books—the book

of God's word in scripture and the book of God's work in science. With respect to the book of God's work, Bacon introduced the inductive thinking method. The Baconian method, as it came to be known, aimed to draw knowledge from the natural world through experimentation, observation, and testing of hypotheses.

Prior to Bacon, most philosophies were rooted in deductive logic, emphasizing the process of reasoning, where one starts with general theories and derives verifiable observations from them. Bacon's inductive process, on the other hand, minimized the theoretical, creative, imaginative aspects of science and allowed discovery to be a more routine, automatic, mechanistic process that required patience rather than difficult abstract thought. Baconianism became the dominant philosophy of English science because of the appeal of its empirical and inductive methods, which came to be considered the universal means of acquiring truth.

Bacon's inductive process presented a problem for Charles Darwin, who had worked from an elaborate theory that he admitted could not be empirically proved in its entirety and was not the final answer on the matter. *The Origin of Species* contained mountains of observations and facts. Yet, at the end of the day, natural selection was set forth as a theory or hypothesis without absolute proof. It depended very little on Bacon's inductive spirit, an underpinning of scientific exploration at the time, even though the predominantly Baconian scientific community wanted just the facts rather than theory. Thus, Darwin had a much larger problem convincing many scientists and members of the Royal Academy of Science than he had with the religious community.

The Huxley/Wilberforce Debate

The most famous confrontation took place when Darwin's ideas were presented at an 1860 meeting of the British Association for the Advancement of Science in Oxford. The association was comprised primarily of Christian scientists who generally believed, like Newton and Bacon, that their science was actually the study of God's book of nature. They knew that a vast amount of new scientific information had been gathered recently, but no member had as yet ventured any theory of development of the species. So Darwin's thesis held great interest.

Darwin was not present at the meeting. His health problems continued, he was rather sickly and bashful, and he disliked controversy, which perhaps suggested he was the author of the wrong book. Thomas Huxley, a noted English biologist, defended Darwin's views and established himself as "Darwin's bulldog"—the fiercest defender of evolutionary theory. Samuel Wilberforce, the Bishop of Oxford, argued against Darwin. Wilberforce was an educated man, one of England's most popular public speakers, whose family had been largely responsible for the abolition of the slave trade in England. He also was a very pious Christian. However, he had no training or interest in natural history.

The debate is largely mythologized in modern stories, which typically hold that Huxley was an intellectual giant and Wilberforce an intellectual pygmy. The story is that Wilberforce asked Huxley whether he was descended from monkeys on his grandfather's side or his grandmother's side. Huxley immediately muttered, "The Lord has delivered him into my hands," and then openly replied that he would rather be descended from an ape than from a cultivated man who used his gifts of culture and eloquence in the service of prejudice and falsehood. A simplified form of the story, that may or may not have been true, spread around the country that Huxley had said he would rather be an ape than a bishop. The actual record of the debate reads nothing like the mythology. Wilberforce was a reasonable man, not a nincompoop, and he was representing some of the best scientists of the day, who basically fed him his arguments. But he did object to Darwin's theory—a theory that completely revolutionized the way that almost all scientists of his day looked at species and their origin and development.

The Public Controversy

Darwin's ideas didn't become a major controversy until they spread among the general populace, where there was a tremendous shock— probably much like the shock to Mrs. Darwin, who may never have been convinced that the theory of evolution was correct. Within ten years of the publication of *The Origin of Species* all the diversity of opinion we see today existed or was beginning to emerge.

Darwin admitted problems with his theory and understood it couldn't be the final answer because he still did not have answers to a great number of questions. The scientific community was divided. Some scientists, including William Dawson, a Presbyterian geologist from Canada and Luis Agassiz, a German-educated geologist and zoologist who immigrated to America, resisted Darwin's basic conclusions as strongly as they could. Agassiz, a Harvard professor and liberal Unitarian, was Darwin's most formidable opponent and one of the last prominent zoologists to resist Darwin's theory. His belief in the fixity of species and special creation of man led him to reject the theory of evolution.

American botanist Asa Gray, an orthodox Calvinist Christian theologian and Harvard professor, carried on a continuing series of conversations with Darwin. Like many others, Gray accepted parts of the theory but was not fully converted. Darwin's principal defender in the United States, Gray maintained that one could believe in evolution and still be an orthodox Christian. Darwin never attacked his orthodoxy, perhaps because Gray publicly defended evolution. Thus, there was at Harvard an interesting juxtaposition—a rather liberal Unitarian who was Darwin's foremost opponent, and an orthodox Calvinist theologian who was a proponent.

Another group, including Thomas Huxley, enthusiastically supported Darwin's new scientific model in the continuing debate that followed the book's publication. Huxley was concerned that many religious people interpreted Genesis so literally that they were developing an anti-scientific argument against Darwin's theory, and that they were beginning to believe one could not be a Christian theist and accept the theory of evolution. He wanted evolution to be accepted with open minds by Christians because most of the scientists in Britain at the time were Christians. Since they were not going to change their theology, Huxley understood that in order to get Darwin's theory accepted, he had to convince scientists that one could accept evolution and be a Christian theist. Notwithstanding these ideas, he coined the word "agnostic" to describe his own views and as an alternative to Christian or theist views on one side and atheist views on the other.

In summary, the bombshell of Darwin's theory of evolution caused a complex relationship in American and British thought. The debate was not a clearly aligned standoff, where all the agnostics and naturalists lined up on Darwin's side and all the Christians and creationists lined up against him. Scientific acceptance of evolution might have been deferred for years if that had happened, as most scientists were Christians, and non-Christians could not have created the critical mass necessary to assure acceptance of the theory. In fact the sides were mixed, and the support of Christian scientists was a major factor in evolution becoming generally accepted by the scientific community.

Darwin's Theology

One of the interesting sidelights of this history is that when Darwin was writing *The Origin of Species*, perhaps still influenced by his theology studies at Cambridge University, he had not given up on the idea that God was the creator. He just believed God was not a special creator, responsible for what is called special creation—the idea that human beings were created as species separate from animals at some time in the recent past.

Darwin believed in creation until the latter years of his life, when he started wondering whether there was a God or a creation. He became very pessimistic about human life, no doubt partly because of his theory. In addition, he was devastated by the death of his daughter Annie at age ten after a long, lingering illness. This loss no doubt contributed to his pessimism about human life and his doubts about religion and God's providence.

Darwin was a complex human being. The reasons he wavered in his faith were complex, involving his theory of evolution, the problems of suffering, and the difficulty of understanding God's way with human beings. In a letter in 1879, just three years before his death, he wrote, "In my most extreme fluctuations I have never been an Atheist in the sense of denying the existence of God. I think that generally (and more and more as I grow older), but not always, that an Agnostic would be the more correct description of my state of mind."[1] He refused to endorse antireligious or radical atheistic causes and never made direct arguments against Christianity or theism, while admitting that one reason for his silence may have been deference to his wife, Emma.

EVOLUTION AND RELIGION

Within two decades of the publication of *The Origin of Species*, almost no working American naturalists opposed Darwin's concept of organic evolution and natural selection. But the public controversy continued. In the 1870s, a number of church leaders raised an alarm against the teaching of evolution, particularly within denominational colleges and seminaries. The last third of the century also saw several technical challenges to Darwin's theory. Some evidence available at the time suggested that the universe might not be old enough for slight, random variations to work, and questions were raised as to how inherited differences within organisms would be preserved when individuals bred within their species. Alternative ideas were widely discussed that supported design in nature and illustrated the wisdom and goodness of the creator, even if they didn't fit squarely with traditional Christian doctrine.

Modernism

Around the turn of the century many liberal Christian "modernists" embraced evolution (although a significant number questioned the details of Darwin's selection theories) and began to use rationalistic arguments to challenge the Bible's origin, historical accuracy, and accounts of the supernatural. More orthodox Christians generally kept their mouths shut, as they were less concerned with science than with modernism and such fundamental Christian beliefs as the divinity of Christ, the fact of the virgin birth, and the reality of His resurrection. Evolution was not at the forefront of their attention. Consequently, by early in the twentieth century, historians and essayists rather than theologians and scientists were mainly responsible for the public perception of a conflict between science and religion.

Fundamentalism

In the early part of the twentieth century, however, the tenor began to change due in large measure to the writing of George M. Price. A Seventh-Day Adventist, Price was inspired by Ellen G. White, the Adventist founder whom some saw as a modern-day prophet and others saw as a cult figure and plagiarist. White thought some of the attitudes of her Christian contemporaries toward science were too accommodating. She claimed to have received a direct revelation from God that told her the book of Genesis should be read absolutely literally.

You don't have much wiggle room when your prophet tells you how to interpret the Bible, so the Seventh-Day Adventists set out to develop a creation science that would support their belief. Price and others focused primarily on geology and maintained that various interpretations of the rock and fossil record refuted the idea of evolution, as all fossil life forms had lived at the same time and any order that seemed to exist in rocks and fossils was a result of sorting at the time of the Noah flood. When they were compelled by the evidence to acknowledge fossil ordering, they advanced other theories for reconciling flood geology with biblical literalism. Scientists today hold most of their views to be untenable. However, the efforts of Price and others eventually led the way to modern creationism.

The first two decades of the 1900s saw an outpouring of publications focusing on the seemingly critical role of Darwinism in the conflict between science and religion. In 1909, *The Fundamentals*, a twelve-volume series of booklets, was published by a committee of men from several Protestant denominations to oppose modernist views and set forth the fundamentals of the Christian faith, including, among other important concepts, biblical inerrancy. It was not an assault on evolution. In fact at least three contributors, George Frederick Wright, B. B. Warfield, and James Orr, believed in some form of the theory of evolution. Three million copies of *The Fundamentals* were distributed to influential Protestants between 1910 and 1915. Although the immediate effect was limited, the pamphlets helped give rise to what became known as the fundamentalist movement within a few years.

The 1920s saw Darwin's conclusions begin to influence children's education, as new courses in biology began using textbooks touting evolution through natural selection at a time when high school attendance was increasing greatly, especially in the South. Tolerance for evolution largely disappeared after the First World War, however, as the fundamentalist movement came together, largely comprised of the following Christian groups who were committed to biblical literalism and inerrancy:

- Premillennialism, fostered largely by Adventism and other more orthodox fundamental churches, brought a tradition of rigid biblical interpretation and a belief that the end times were close, after which Christ's second coming would replace the fallen world with a new age of peace and justice. A more elaborate form of premillennialism called dispensationalism traces its roots largely to British Plymouth Brethren theologian John Nelson Darby. Dispensationalism was popularized in America largely through the Scofield Reference Bible.
- Theologians at Princeton's Presbyterian Seminary brought their theory of biblical inerrancy—a belief that the scripture is divinely inspired and absolutely accurate.
- The holiness movement basically emerged out of Methodism and stressed the work of the Holy Spirit in cleansing man if he has had his sins forgiven through faith in Jesus.
- The Pentecostalism movement placed emphasis on speaking in tongues and special focus on the direct personal experience of God through the baptism of the Holy Spirit, as shown in the biblical account of the Day of Pentecost.

The fundamentalist movement's main foe was modernism, described by one of its leaders in 1924 as "the use of scientific, historical, and social methods in understanding and applying evangelical Christianity to the needs of living persons...."[2] The fundamentalists' campaign against modernism stoked the fires of the continuing war between Christianity and science, and no doubt was an underlying cause of one of its first major public battles.

THE SCOPES MONKEY TRIAL

William Jennings Bryan led the campaign that saw the fundamentalist movement give birth to a popular crusade against the teaching of evolution in public schools. A man of deep faith, Bryan was a prominent progressive Christian with a long and distinguished public career. He was elected to Congress in 1890 as a thirty-year-old populist Democrat.

Nicknamed the "Boy Orator of the Platte," he became his party's nominee for president, narrowly lost a bitter election, and subsequently received the nomination twice more. Bryan felt evolution or, perhaps more correctly evolutionism, contradicted his Christian values. He believed it was closely related to atheism, eugenics (a social philosophy that advocates the improvement of human hereditary traits through various forms of often forced intervention), and white supremacy.

Under Bryan's leadership, the anti-evolution movement sought legislation to restrict the teaching of evolution in public schools in a number of states, particularly in the South. In March 1925, the state of Tennessee passed a law making it unlawful for a state school teacher to teach any theory that denied the biblical story of creation and taught that man had descended from a lower order of animals.

Concerned that the new law violated the constitutional separation of church and state, the American Civil Liberties Union offered to defend anyone accused of a violation. Several prominent citizens of Dayton, Tennessee, saw an opportunity to put their small town on the map. They convinced the local high school football coach, John T. Scopes, to admit that while substituting for a biology teacher, he had used a textbook that explicitly described and endorsed the theory of evolution. Based on his admission, he was indicted for violating the Tennessee law and brought to trial. After considerable wrangling as to who the attorneys for each side would be, Bryan was selected to represent the prosecution. Clarence Darrow, a staunch agnostic with a national reputation and a long history of representing controversial causes, was selected to represent the defense.

Bryan's public strategy was to advance the right of the people to control their schools through legislation. Privately, he hoped to discredit evolution, which he contended was morally pernicious. Darrow quickly abandoned the ACLU's original defense strategy—to attack the law on constitutional grounds—and instead attacked Bryan's literal interpretation of the Bible as well as his limited knowledge of other religions and science. On the sixth day of the trial Bryan volunteered to be a defense witness. He was cross-examined by Darrow, and became the focus of his opponent's contempt and ridicule. The judge held the examination to be irrelevant to the case and expunged it from the record, so Bryan was never able to examine the defense lawyers in return.

The case ended with a whimper rather than a bang. The judge did not allow the jury to hear the defense testimony about the Bible, and Darrow encouraged the jury to find Scopes guilty, hoping to argue the case on appeal. Following eight days of trial, the jury found Scopes guilty after nine minutes of deliberation. The judge fined him $100, which Bryan offered to pay. On appeal, the court found the statute constitutional but set aside the conviction on a legal technicality relating to whether the judge or jury should have set the fine.

The press coverage of the so-called "Monkey Trial" was overwhelming across the nation and internationally, with a majority ridiculing Bryan and his anti-evolution defense. H. L. Mencken, one of the reporters at the trial, probably did more than anybody to make Americans think that William Jennings Bryan was some kind of boob or numbskull, even though they had considered him for decades to be very important in providing progressive political thought to American life. Bryan never recovered from the characterization typified by Mencken's reporting.

The single most influential retelling of the event occurred in 1955, with the stage play (and later movie), *Inherit the Wind*. The play, which sought to cast the Scopes trial as foreshadowing the McCarthyism of the 1950s, was very loosely based on the trial, but with significant differences. The least important difference was that, perhaps inevitably, the Scopes character gained a fiancée. More importantly, the play portrayed the teacher as the innocent victim of a mob-enforced anti-evolution law. This could not have been further from the truth. The drama transformed Bryan into a mindless, reactionary creature of the local mob who focused on narrow biblical grounds, rather than an elder statesman with broad social concerns. Darrow was portrayed as a hero who became ever more likable as the play progressed—with even hints that he came to question his own agnosticism. While the introduction indicated that the play was not journalism, its long run in New York and around the country, along with the subsequent movie, created a popular impression that may have had more effect on the creationist movement than the actual trial.

No creationists—those advocating a strictly literal interpretation of the Genesis creation account—were involved in the Scopes monkey trial. All the theologians who were involved believed in evolution. Bryan sought the best scientific minds in the creationist camp to serve as expert witnesses, but was unable to get any to testify. Even he eventually conceded that the world was far more than 6,000 years old and that the days of creation were probably longer than twenty-four hours.

Not surprisingly, the Scopes decision led people in other states to try to move in the same direction as Tennessee. In 1927, thirteen states in both the North and South considered some form of anti-evolution law, and at least forty-one bills were introduced. While Mississippi and Arkansas passed anti-evolution statutes, most efforts failed. The movement was basically rejected by the established political system because of two serious problems. The movement's leaders couldn't agree on a theory of creation, as they held views ranging from recent creation in six twenty-four hour days, to defining the days of Genesis as ages, to a gap theory involving two separate creations, and other variations. In addition, a critical mass of scientifically trained creationists did not exist.

Thus, the movement began to turn its efforts inward in an attempt to build an institutional base of its own. Modern scientific creationism, which will be discussed in detail in Chapter 8, began to emerge in the 1930s.

THEOLOGICAL ISSUES IN EVOLUTION

Many arguments against Darwin's conclusions had their origin and meaning in science and philosophy, but owed their intensity to religion, as the theory of evolution seemed to many to exclude God from the world and reflect negatively on His omnipotence and beneficence. If evolution is true, then God presumably created everything by evolution, but that raises several problems. God created everything, but Darwin addressed only the biological world. God designed what He created, but Darwin suggested natural selection with its many tiny, purposeless variations. God created man in His own image, a rational species, but Darwin said man evolved from lower animals in an uninterrupted line of descent. God created everything in His character, but Darwin claimed a brutal struggle for existence in which only the fittest survive.

Ian Barbour, in *Issues in Science and Religion*,[3] has explored such inferences from Darwin's work and identified four largely theological underlying issues that gave rise to the continuing controversy. The following is a brief discussion of those problems.

Challenge to Scripture

Advances in science from Copernican astronomy to the new geology had much earlier cast doubt on biblical literalism, but evolution was the first threat to central biblical beliefs such as the purposefulness of the world, the dignity of man, and the drama of man's creation and fall. For many Christians, the only defense was to reassert the doctrine of biblical infallibility that had been typical in earlier periods of Protestant orthodoxy. When some leading scientists linked evolution to their atheistic viewpoint, biblical literalists could not compromise. For them, Genesis clearly described the creation events, and if Darwin disagreed, he was simply wrong. They believed God put all those fossils in a plausibly misleading pattern in order to test man's faith. Creation occurred in 4004 BC, and the date could be determined on the basis of biblical genealogies.

Others viewed scripture as not inconsistent with evolution. The majority of Protestant authors interpreted the biblical creation account as a symbolic and poetic affirmation of the world's dependence on God. The modernists went further, contending that the Bible was a purely human doctrine. In general, Catholic thought avoided the extremes of both literalism and modernism, and gradually came to a position that acknowledged man's physical descent from lower animals but preserved his uniqueness as a spiritual being.

Challenge to Design

Darwin believed that change results from chance—a very large number of independent, random, spontaneous variations, where the final result is accidental and unpremeditated. Further, he believed that the laws by which life evolved were a matter of chance. They did not express the wisdom and constancy of God implicit in design, but instead were autonomous, mechanical operations of impersonal forces. All this chance seemed to be the opposite of design as exemplified in Paley's watchmaker analogy.

The Bible contains no argument from design, cosmological argument, or argument for the existence of God, so Darwin's challenge to design is not necessarily a threat to biblical Christianity. However, the challenge to design is where Darwin is most threatening to some forms of traditional Christian theology that incorporate such a philosophy. Proponents of these philosophies assume God's creativity to be mechanical, like that of a workman, and evolution makes this analogy untenable.

Challenge to Human Dignity

In Christian tradition, man was set apart from all other creatures, totally different in kind, having an immortal soul that defined his true being and his relationship to God. Man shared some things in common with other creatures but was "outside" nature. The theory of evolution, which claimed that all creatures derived from the same source, seemed to deny this distinctiveness. Further, Darwin claimed that man's moral sense, which had been considered one of his most distinctive capacities, had also originated by natural selection.

Perhaps Darwin looked for the similarities and minimized the differences between man and beast. Some biologists, including A. R. Wallace, emphasized the distinctive characteristics of man—the human brain, the intellect, and distinctive processes that Darwin's biological framework ignored. Even some of Darwin's friends, like Charles Lyell, the noted geologist and advocate of uniformitarianism, struggled to accept some of the implications of Darwinism. Though Lyell interpreted the Bible to include a world that is hundreds of thousands of years old, it was more difficult for him to compromise the uniqueness of human beings.

At the end of the day, however, belief in evolution was often equated to belief that man is nothing but an animal. This challenge to human dignity is where the fear and anxiety still lies, and it is largely responsible for keeping scientific creationism alive today.

Challenge of Evolutionary Ethics

Darwin himself was aware that when speaking of the "fittest to survive," a biologist is expressing relative physical endurance rather than true progress or moral advancement, and that survival of the fittest may in fact be a retrogression in certain important ways. This is the essence of evolution. However, the belief that competition promotes progress fit well in society at the time, and the theory of natural selection was extended to mankind, morality, and human progress. Thus, biological and political ideas merged in what has been called evolutionism or social Darwinism, which is a part of the evolution myth but not a part of Darwin's theory of biological evolution. Darwin's theory of evolution is concerned with how living organisms change over time. Evolutionism applies the ideas more broadly, suggesting that there is a force within nature, or within matter itself, that will eventually produce progress and change, ultimately resulting in an evolutionary outcome within human society.

Many people in America, most famously William Jennings Bryan, became concerned about the impact of evolutionary thinking on our understanding of the nature of morality, ethics, and the country's political ethic. They were afraid of what might happen to American political thought if the Darwinian theory of evolution led to evolutionism or social Darwinism. They were concerned about a rogues gallery of "isms" that put a great deal of stock in evolution as a theory of politics and society.

Karl Marx, the influential German philosopher who believed in communism rather than capitalism, considered himself to be a Darwinist and dedicated his work to Charles Darwin. Marx saw the theory of evolution as a scientific justification for his particular political philosophy and his philosophy of nature. Further, the philosophers surrounding Adolf Hitler generally based their conception of Nazism on Darwin's theory. Darwin himself was a scientific racist, in the sense that he believed different races were the result of different levels of evolutionary development. While Darwin was a Victorian who wouldn't have justified what the Fascists, the Marxist/Leninists, or the Nazis did, they often used Darwin to justify their actions.

Summary

In summary, while actual science did present some issues for religion, the larger problems were presented by the philosophical implications that many assumed the theory of evolution might forecast. Evolution was thought to substitute a philosophical and a scientific explanation of the origin and continuance of things—one that would not need a specific biblical conception of God—for the traditional theistic and Christian views. After Darwin published his theory, evolutionists took it up and elaborated on it philosophically. Darwin bore little direct responsibility for this expansion of his views. From his perspective, evolutionists were taking a purely scientific theory and making it into a social and philosophical theory. Thus, the relationship between Darwin and evolutionists during his lifetime was very tenuous. Evolutionists liked him and accepted his views because they thought he had provided a scientific justification for their philosophy. But Darwin disagreed vehemently with evolutionism because he didn't like the philosophy it expounded, such as eugenics and the application of his ideas to societies generally.

Ultimately, however, the philosophical implications of Darwinism have no bearing whatsoever on whether biological evolution is in fact a correct understanding of man's origin and development. But people don't give up easily, and the controversy continues—perhaps stronger than ever, with many different views articulated by different groups in different ways. Our next task is to describe this situation as it exists today, within the context of recent patterns of change. We start with Chapter 6, which provides an overview of the basic scientific method as well as the current consensus of scientists in the areas of astronomy, geology, and biology that are uniquely relevant to the debate.

6

SCIENCE

"I do not feel obligated to believe that the same God who has endowed us with sense, reason, and intellect has intended us to forgo their use."
Galileo (1564 – 1642)

When one poses a debate between "the Bible and science," what science is one talking about? The term comprises such breadth and depth as to be almost incomprehensible. In today's world it conjures ideas ranging from physics to psychology, from optoelectronics to wine science. And the state of scientific knowledge continues to expand at warp speed. To understand the debate, however, one must start with a basic understanding of the current state of science in relevant areas.

Fortunately, the crux of the controversy can be boiled down to a small number of misunderstandings or disagreements. They start with a frequent failure to appreciate the scientific method and how that method differs from theology, and they include a relatively few current scientific conclusions—intellectual and emotional lightening rods that appear time and again as the conflict rages. In this chapter we will briefly summarize the current view of the scientific community concerning the scientific method and important issues found in three overlapping areas: astronomy, geology, and biology.

We noted in Chapter 1 that neither of your authors is a scientist by training or experience. On each of these issues, however, the questions are clear enough, and the scientific consensus so strong, that we feel comfortable in summarizing the current scientific understandings. In later chapters we will summarize the responses of several religious (or anti-religious) groups to these understandings.

THE SCIENTIFIC METHOD

It seems that, more often than not, the root of the Bible and science controversy lies in failure to appreciate the modern scientific method rather than in disagreements concerning specific conclusions derived from the use of that method. For example, the key issue in most of the court cases concerning science in public schools (discussed in future chapters) has related more to the scientific method than to specific scientific theories or conclusions. A significant portion of the writing of proponents of intelligent design is aimed at trying to establish the movement's scientific credibility rather than advocating specific conclusions. And opponents of the Intelligent Design Movement at times agree with certain ID beliefs, but strongly disagree that such beliefs are based on science.

While faith has on occasion been seen to conflict with the conclusions of science—after all, that's what we are writing about—more frequently, that has not been the case. Recall from Chapter 3 that most of those responsible for the early development of modern science were Christians. The scientific world today is heavily populated with Christians, and efforts exist on many fronts to reconcile science and Christianity. A number of organizations, including Christians in Science, Affiliation of Christian Geologists, Affiliation of Christian Biologists, and others, have been established for this purpose. A leader in this effort is the American Scientific Affiliation, "a fellowship of men and women in science and disciplines that relate to science who share a common fidelity to the Word of God and a commitment to integrity in the practice of science."[1] A key reason many can reconcile the two is that the methods of science and religion are so different, involving differences of kind, where touch points for conflict scarcely exist.

Theological Method

There is an important difference between the scientific method and Christian theological method. The working definition of "theology" has changed over the years, and considerable disagreement exists as to what the "theological method" is and what role scientific method plays in theology. A broadly held view is that the theological method aims to answer three questions: What does the Bible say? What does the Bible mean? How does the Bible apply to the reader? Within this context, theology draws upon scripture, tradition, and experience as data for theological analysis of the fundamental ideas of the Christian faith. Christian beliefs are not the product of logical reasoning from the data. Instead, they flow from faith—a personal trust and confidence derived from the data provided by scripture, tradition, and experience.

Scientific Method

The scientific method is very, very different. Generally speaking, it is a body of techniques for investigating observed phenomena and acquiring new knowledge. Although procedures vary somewhat from field to field, and have been described differently by different people, it's fair to say that the method essentially always involves some form of the following scheme:

- Ask a question about something that has been observed: how, what, when, who, which, why, or where
- Gather information and resources about the question
- Form a hypothesis, or an educated guess about the answer, perhaps including a prediction
- Perform experiments and collect data to test the hypothesis
- Analyze the data and form a conclusion as to whether the hypothesis is true or false
- Communicate the results

The scientific process is iterative, and often various steps must be repeated in a process of testing, challenging, reformulation, and retesting in an effort to find the truth.

Richard Feynman, a Nobel Prize winning American physicist known for expanding the theory of quantum electrodynamics, has stated, more succinctly, that there are really only two steps in the scientific method: "Make a guess, and see if you're wrong." "Make a guess" requires the scientist to gather information through observation and make a hypothesis or theory based on that information. "See if you're wrong,"—the core of science—requires experimentation to determine if the guess was right or wrong.

Thus, the requirements of a theory and systematic experimentation distinguish the scientific method from other forms of explanation, and certainly from faith and theology. The word "theory," often used in relation to evolution, has a special meaning. In common usage, theory often signifies an opinion or a speculation. In science, however, theory signifies a testable model that can predict future occurrences, be tested through experiment or otherwise verified through empirical observation, and is "falsifiable"—that is, there must be some experiment or possible discovery that could prove the theory untrue. For example, Einstein's theory of relativity made predictions about the results of experiments that could have produced results contradicting his theory. Therefore, the theory was (and still is) falsifiable. In contrast, beliefs about who God is or how God works are not falsifiable. The beliefs may be true, but how does one design an experiment that could possibly prove them to be true or untrue?

In science, a theory is said to be "true" if it agrees with all known experimental evidence. However, even the best of theories have often been incomplete. Although a theory might explain interesting phenomena or predict new and exciting results, eventually new experiments show a discrepancy between the workings of nature and the predictions of the theory. In a strict sense, this means that it was not "true" after all, even though it was the best understanding at the time. For example, when Isaac Newton proposed his theory of gravitation in 1666, it explained observed facts and made predictions that were later found to be correct within the accuracy of the instruments being used. Newton's theory was considered to be true. But later, after more accurate instruments were used to test his theory and note some discrepancies, Einstein proposed his theories of relativity, which explained the new observations and made more predictions.

When an accepted theory cannot explain new data, scientists try to construct a new theory. This task gets increasingly more difficult as our knowledge increases, for the new theory should not only explain the old data but all the new data as well. Thus, our understanding of the "truth" of scientific theories changes over time, which certainly has happened to theories relating to the Bible and science debate. The following sections outline in simple terms the current state of scientific knowledge in three important areas. Although they may change or be better defined in the future, they represent the "scientific position" in the current debate.

ASTRONOMY

How did our universe begin? How old is it? How does the cosmos operate? How did matter come to exist? Such questions have existed for centuries. Astronomical questions were the source of the main conflict involving Copernicus, Galileo, and the Catholic Church. The case for a heliocentric universe was thought by many at the time to conflict with the Christian faith and to reduce the standing of human beings from the center of the universe to a position on the periphery. After a time, however, the science of astronomy was simply too compelling. People accepted the obvious and figured out ways to reconcile their old biblical interpretations and conclusions of faith with the new scientific conclusions. The same happened for other issues, but questions remain. The astronomical issue most relevant to the current debate, and one of the most persistently asked questions is—How was the universe created?

Many philosophers, beginning with Aristotle, believed that the universe had no beginning or end and was truly infinite. However, some people from early times have looked to scripture and found a different answer. Genesis 1:1 notes that "In the beginning God created the heavens and the earth," and Paul states in Acts 17:24, "The God who made the world and everything in it is the Lord of heaven and earth and does not live in temples made by human hands."

Scripture has been thought by many to endorse the idea of creation *ex nihilo*, or creation by a transcendent God from nothing, rather than the universe emanating from God Himself. Thus, during the time of the early church, there was conflict between philosophical beliefs that the universe was eternal—with no beginning or end, and in which God only gave shape to pre-existing things—and the Judeo-Christian belief that the world is a product of God's creative work.

Steady State Theory

In the first part of the twentieth century, a group of individuals found the idea of a sudden beginning to the universe philosophically unsatisfying, so they developed the steady state theory. This idea claimed an expanding universe whose average density remains constant, with matter being continuously created throughout to form new stars and galaxies at the same rate that old ones recede from sight. Thus, a steady

state universe does not change its look over time and has no beginning or end. Problems with this theory began to develop in the 1960s
when scientists observed that the universe was in fact changing, and
the big bang theory began to emerge as the dominant view of most
scientists.

Big Bang Theory

The big bang theory suggests that the universe is not infinite and
instead possesses the properties of a finite phenomenon with a beginning and a history. Most scientists believe that discoveries in astronomy
and physics have shown beyond a reasonable doubt that our universe
did in fact have a beginning. Prior to that moment, a primordial condition of infinite density and temperature existed. During and after that
moment there was something—our universe. The big bang theory is
an effort to explain what happened during and after that moment.

According to this theory, the universe was created sometime between
ten billion and twenty billion years ago from a cosmic explosion that
hurled matter in all directions, and distant galaxies are continuing to
recede from one another. (Some experts say there was no explosion.
They believe, instead, there was and continues to be an expansion.
Rather than imagining a balloon popping and releasing its contents,
imagine an infinitesimally small balloon expanding to the size of our
current universe.) Scientists believe that in a minuscule fraction of the
first second after creation, the primordial condition began to evolve
into what we now know as the universe. However, what is known of
these brief moments in time is largely conjectural.

A combination of evidence from astronomy and high-energy
physics makes the big bang plausible. The theory was initially suggested
because it explains why distant galaxies appear to be traveling away
from us at great speeds, which supports the idea that the universe was
once compacted and is now expanding. Other evidence also supports
the theory. Radiation that scientists predicted would have been left
over from the explosion was discovered in 1965, and the abundance
of hydrogen and helium found in the observable universe is consistent
with the big bang model of origins.

The big bang theory provides a viable solution to one of the most
pressing questions of all time, but it is important to understand that

it is constantly being revised. As more observations are made and more research conducted, the theory becomes more complete and our knowledge of the origins of the universe more substantial. It is fair to say, however, that it is today's dominant scientific theory about the origin of the universe.

Theological reaction to the theory has been mixed. Some say it has nothing to do with religion. Some believe the big bang theory offers nothing and the steady state theory itself was just as compatible with the Christian doctrine of creation as the big bang theory because one can interpret creation to mean that the universe has always existed. Some say the big bang is inconsistent with the six-day creation scenario of Genesis. And some believe that the theory is the greatest thing that's ever happened for Christian theology because it is compatible with the ideas of the universe having a beginning at a distinct time in the finite past and continually expanding, whereas the steady state theory was not. Specific reactions of various groups to the theory will be discussed in the chapters that follow.

GEOLOGY

Over the years, astronomers were concerned with establishing the eternal design of the cosmos, but generally were content to rely on religion to describe how the world developed. While many of their new ideas—such as placing the sun rather than the earth in the center of our solar system—were potentially disturbing, they did not challenge revealed religion in quite the way that geology would.

Geologists, on the other hand, posed ideas that seemed to more directly conflict with literal biblical accounts considered by many to describe the creation of the world and of human beings. Their discoveries about the development of the earth raised two primary issues: whether geological findings contradict or confirm the Genesis account of creation and the flood, and whether the events in Genesis were a result of natural laws or evidence of a divine purpose. Different groups adopted different positions, ranging from extreme naturalists who held that natural laws ruled with no divine design or final cause, to those who believed the development of the earth was all the work of God, as revealed in scripture.

Historical Perspective

Around the end of the Middle Ages, the prevailing view in the West was that earth history should be derived principally from a literal reading of the book of Genesis. During the period of the Renaissance and Reformation, a tradition of scholarly chronology developed, which combined genealogical information from the Bible, astronomical calculations, and other non-biblical information sources and concluded that the earth was created about 4000 BC, give or take a few thousand years either way.

The consensus was disturbed, however, by the discovery of ancient Egyptian and Chinese records and information emerging from European exploration of other countries. Such information led to much speculation that the earth was a great deal older, that humans had existed long before Adam, and that there was no way the earth could have been repopulated after the flood from the descendants of Noah and the animal inmates of the ark.

In the late 1400s, Leonardo da Vinci considered the question of how it was that shells and remains of other living creatures were found in rocks on the tops of mountains. Some believed they had been placed there by the biblical flood, others thought they had grown in the rocks, and some believed they were the work of Satan, intended to deceive human beings about revealed truth. Da Vinci saw no way that living creatures could have grown there. He doubted the existence of a single worldwide flood, noting that there would have been no place for the water to go when it receded. And he believed shells carried by a muddy deluge would have been mixed up and separated from each other rather than deposited in regular layers. His conclusion, remarkably close to the modern one, was that fossils were once living organisms that had been buried at a time before the mountains were raised.

In the mid seventeenth century, Rene Descartes proposed that the creation did not fix the present state of the earth, which was instead the result of natural laws governing the development of the original matter over a long time span. Because of prevailing attitudes of the time, Descartes kept a low profile in relation to Catholic authority. He suggested his ideas were only a hypothetical suggestion and a demonstration of how God might have produced the earth and its life forms very slowly by natural secondary causes, rather than an account of how God really did create the world.

In the latter part of the seventeenth century, various speculative theories about the shape of earth history were advanced. Perhaps the most influential one was advanced by John Woodward, who claimed that the whole sequence of the earth's geologic strata (layers of rock) had settled in order of specific gravity as a consequence of the Genesis flood. While this theory diverged from a literal interpretation of Genesis, it did not directly challenge the basic historical accuracy of the biblical account.

Geologists also developed the concept of catastrophism, with the major catastrophe being the flood of Noah. Georges Cuvier, the most important and influential figure in French science in the early nineteenth century, was a primary proponent of catastrophism. He studied the composition and fossil record of the different strata and became convinced that the breaking to pieces and overturning of the strata, along with the apparently abrupt changes in fossil animals and plants between adjacent strata, had been sudden and violent, caused by a series of huge catastrophes. He believed the effects of present processes were too small, slow, or local to have such a result, and the evidence suggested some extremely unusual and overwhelming force. Cuvier did not suggest a physical cause for repeated catastrophes, and he believed the geological record could not be explained simply by one major flood. Even though he avoided religious speculation in his writing, Cuvier's work became quite popular, perhaps because part of his theory gave strong support to the notion that the last such catastrophic flood could be dated at roughly the same time as many people dated the flood described in Genesis. Others used his work to assert the literal authority of the Bible.

During the eighteenth century, the focus of studies of the earth changed from developing a "theory of the earth" to the much more mundane goal of discovering mineral resources. Nevertheless, new ideas continued to emerge. Naturalists concluded that many of Woodward's ideas on the strata were implausible, but they did generally support his idea that the earth's strata were an indication of a time sequence. They also concluded that the earth's most ancient rocks had no fossils, while more recent, superficial strata contained them. The biblical flood was identified only with relatively recent deposits. The older strata, which contained no human remains, came to be accepted as evidence of pre-human earth history—indicating a separation of the origin of the earth from the origin of mankind, and a long earth history that predated mankind. Such conclusions were often reconciled in one way or another with the biblical account, but remained suspect among some conservative religious groups.

Late in the eighteenth century, William Smith, a canal digger in England, discovered that the rocks he was excavating while building canals were arranged in layers that could always be found in predictable positions, and that fossils in each of the layers were different. Smith saw his discoveries as a way to build better canals, as well as a clue to the earth's history. He used the information to develop the first modern geological map, one that displayed the hidden underside of England. His breakthrough ideas provided the basis for estimating the age of the earth until the advent of radiometric methods many years later.

Uniformitarianism

During the same time period, James Hutton, generally acknowledged as the founder of modern geology, advanced the principle of uniformitarianism. This idea challenged catastrophism and committed scientists to explaining the past events of the earth's history in terms of processes still at work, which excluded miraculously powerful events such as the biblical flood that are not known to occur today. Charles Lyell, the influential scientist who actually popularized uniformitarianism, insisted that, given enough time, present-day forces operating at present rates could have produced all observable geological phenomena. The concept suggests that catastrophic processes were not responsible for the land features that exist on the earth's surface. Instead, it maintains that the earth's landscape developed over long periods of time through a variety of slow geologic processes—an idea obviously in conflict with ideas based on a literal biblical interpretation of the history of the earth.

The conflict between catastrophism and uniformitarianism—the two leading schools of geology in the early 1800s—had important theological overtones. The catastrophists' belief, that the history of the earth could only be understood by intervention of inexplicable events, supported a faith in a living God who is involved in the world on a continuing basis. Uniformitarianists, on the other hand, emphasized permanent laws of nature that were always at work, excluding the idea that God intervenes with inexplicable processes.

Uniformitarianism was the prevailing view by the time of Darwin and in some senses prepared the way for Darwin. For those who accepted it, Lyell's teaching of the uniformitarianism principle had already destroyed a traditional understanding of the age of the earth. This view of nature allowed time for evolution to take place. Including man within it was a logical next step.

The Earth's Age

There can be no question but that the overwhelming view today—perhaps a unanimous view—of credible scientists is that the universe is in the range of 14 billion years old and that the earth is in the range of 4 ½ billion years old. Studies of chemical elements, star clusters, and cosmological models have been used to estimate the age of the universe. The fossil record, rock layers, and ordering of rock strata have for years been used to determine the relative chronology of geological periods and to indicate that the earth is very old. Formation of the strata and deposition of the fossils by natural processes, such as the slow deposition of silts at the bottom of oceans that no longer exist, would have taken a very long time indeed. More importantly, the discovery and investigation of radioactivity and radioisotope systems, after the time of Darwin, have allowed paleontologists to provide an absolute age of the earth and much of life. Based on stratigraphic and fossil data, scientists are convinced that the global flood suggested by the literal language of Genesis 6 – 9 just did not happen.

Scientific views in these areas of geology are so convincing, or perhaps not threatening enough, that most in the Intelligent Design Movement have accepted them, and many in the creationist camp have found ways to accommodate them. Several hypotheses have been developed in an effort to live with the idea of an older earth. Some have reinterpreted the Genesis flood as a local or tranquil one. These ideas will be discussed in the chapters that follow.

BIOLOGY

We now jump from the frying pan into the fire. If astronomy and geology led to conflict, biology led to war. Biology involves the mystery of living beings being made of the same things as non-living substances, yet with that special something called life and the ability to grow and reproduce. It involves the relationship between human beings and lower animals, and the idea that chance or evolution from a common ancestor has any role in the development of mankind seems to destroy our humanity and our special place as God's children.

Biology involves fiddling with our very being. Biology and faith meet frequently on ideas about contraception, abortion, the right to die, assisted suicide, cloning, and other hot-button issues of critical importance to individuals and society. Opinions are abundant and strong.

Evolution

Although the idea of evolution "evolved" over a significant period of years through the work of many people, we have seen that Charles Darwin really started the train rolling in 1859 with publication of *The Origin of Species*. By 1900 the predominant public stance of scientist in the English-speaking world endorsed Darwin's theory. The twentieth century saw additional developments in evolutionary biology, and scientists continued to accumulate evidence supporting the general theory of evolution as well as the idea that variations and natural selection are the main causes of evolutionary change.

Before going further, let's recall that biological evolution can be understood to have at least three different meanings. First, it can mean that life forms change over time. For example, cows can be bred to give more milk or to develop body weight for beef. This type of change over time is often called "microevolution." A second meaning of evolution, often called "macroevolution," is a general concept that assumes a common ancestor for all biologic organisms and allows for radical, naturally occurring change. This concept includes the development of new species. For example, fish become amphibians, which become reptiles, which become mammals or birds. The third meaning, also often considered macroevolution, is a combination of the following three specific concepts melded into one theory.

- Random mutation: The genetic material of an organism is sometimes damaged or changed in such a way as to alter the genetic message carried by that gene. Such damage or change is purely by chance.
- Natural selection: The more fit organisms will produce more surviving offspring than the less fit. If a mutation makes an organism more fit than its competitors, then natural selection works over time and causes that organism to have more off-spring than its competitors.
- Common descent: Different kinds of modern creatures can trace their lineage back to a common ancestor.

As we shall see, the scientific community holds a strong consensus that this third definition—random mutation, natural selection, and common descent—is the most accurate and complete definition of biological evolution. Population genetics research uses mathematical tools to study hereditary variation and the influence of natural selection, chance, mutation, and the transfer of genes from one population to another. The work in this field greatly enhanced scientists' understanding of the natural selection and inheritance of variations. Such understandings became a vital ingredient in the modern evolutionary synthesis, which holds that evolution occurs slowly and gradually by the accumulation of small changes often induced by a changing environment.

Scientists of Darwin's era understood natural selection primarily as the survival of the fittest in a competitive struggle. Twentieth century scientists, however, came to see it as equated with differential reproduction and survival that could result from cooperation as well as competition; i.e., sometimes cooperation between two species allows both to survive. More recent work involving the comparison of the molecular structure of similar proteins in various species allows scientists to estimate the time when lineages diverged. Other studies have suggested that behavior, and even an animal's internal psyche, can be important in evolutionary change.

Microbiological experiments in 1944 showed DNA, rather than protein, capable of transferring inherited characteristics. Within the next ten years, scientists were able to determine the structure of DNA. Investigations of many organisms, from bacteria to humans, revealed a genetic code that is universal to all known organisms. The emerging genetic theory was combined with Darwin's theory into a synthesis on which modern "neo-Darwinism" evolution theory is based.

Francis S. Collins, head of the Genome Project, and author of *The Language of God*, provides the following conclusion and comments:

> What does all this mean? At two different levels, it provides powerful support for Darwin's theory of evolution, that is, descent from a common ancestor with natural selection operating on randomly occurring variations. At the level of the genome as a whole, a computer can construct a tree of life based solely upon the similarities of the DNA sequences of multiple organisms.... Bear in mind that this analysis does not utilize any information from the fossil record, or from anatomic observations of current life forms. Yet its similarity to conclusions drawn from studies of comparative anatomy, both of existent organisms and of fossilized remains, is striking.
>
> The examples reported here from the study of genomes, plus others that could fill hundreds of books of this length, provide the kind of molecular support for the theory of evolution that has convinced virtually all working biologists that Darwin's framework of variation and natural selection is unquestionably correct. In fact, for those like myself working in genetics, it is almost impossible to imagine correlating the vast amounts of data coming forth from the studies of genomes without the foundations of Darwin's theory. As Theodosius Dobzhansky, a leading biologist of the twentieth century (and a devout Eastern Orthodox Christian), has said, "Nothing in biology makes sense except in the light of evolution."[2]

But the debate continues. Noted paleontologist/archaeologist Richard Leakey wrote in his 1994 book, *The Origin of Humankind*, that the origin of people like us is the hottest issue in anthropology, adding, "Very different hypotheses are vigorously debated, and hardly a month passes without a conference being held or a shower of books and scientific papers being published, each of these putting forward views that are often diametrically opposed."[3]

The current scientific debate involves questions of when and how—not whether—human beings have been part of the evolutionary process. Disagreements continue to exist on issues like what comprises a "human being," the exact sequence of evolutionary events, when such events occurred, and other important details of the process. However, scientists have used three methods of analyzing fossil remains—the study of changes in anatomy, the study of changes in technology (primarily tools), and molecular genetics—to conclude that human beings are in fact a part of the evolutionary process. Notwithstanding the disagreements on the details, there is a strong scientific consensus that *homo erectus*, or "upright man," is in the neighborhood of two million years old or older.

Further, scientists have concluded that our world's languages have evolved from one another over time. Darwin recognized the similarity between biological and linguistic evolution, and modern scientists agree. They have concluded that the idea of descent with modification applies to languages in much the same way as it does to the origin of species, and the mechanisms of the two are similar. The available evidence clearly demonstrates that the various languages arose through gradual transformation from earlier, ancestral forms.

Collins put it all in perspective, noting that scientific conclusions lead inexorably to the understanding that humans share a common ancestor with other living things, and that unless one is willing to take the position that God has intentionally misled us, "...the conclusion of a common ancestor for humans and mice is virtually inescapable.... The placement of humans in the evolutionary tree of life is only further strengthened by a comparison with our closest living relative, the chimpanzee. The chimpanzee genome sequence has now been unveiled, and it reveals that humans and chimps are 96 percent identical at the DNA level."[4]

The Conflict

The vast majority of credible scientists, both Christian and non-Christian, support the theory of evolution and its application to the origin of man. For example, The National Academies—a consortium comprised of the National Academy of Sciences, the National Academy of Engineering, the Institute of Medicine, and the National Research

Council—takes the public position that while the details of evolution are still being investigated, scientists universally accept that our universe and life itself evolved and continue to evolve.[5] The website of the National Center for Science Education, an organization whose purpose is to keep the teaching of evolution in public school science education, lists over fifty separate statements from education associations from around the country in support of the teaching of evolution.[6]

Yet the conflict does not end. Disputants still appear from seemingly every direction. We think it is fair to characterize the current state of the scientific debate as follows: At the center is an overwhelming majority of credible scientists who unequivocally endorse macroevolution. They are convinced that, among other things, plants and animals of today are different from those of the distant past, offspring differ from parents in ways that accumulate over time, new species come into being, and human beings and other animals have evolved from a common ancestor, with natural selection operating on randomly occurring variations.

Around this majority is a small gaggle of other scientists and non-scientists—often identified with creationism or the Intelligent Design Movement—who are trying to discredit those who believe in evolution or use science to support their own ideas. While most would agree that some form of microevolution has occurred, some argue that macro-evolution in any form simply did not happen. Some agree it happened and aim to show how it supports their biblical views, or at least how evolution can be accommodated to their views. Others say it happened partially, and pick the part they like.

The general public is much more evenly divided. According to a 2008 Gallup poll, about 44 percent of Americans believe that God created human beings pretty much in their present form at one time within the last 10,000 years, and 50 percent believe in some form of evolution. Of those who believe in evolution, 36 percent believe that God guided the process and 14 percent believe that humans evolved without any supernatural intervention. The remainder is unsure about the entire matter.[7]

Not surprisingly, these disparate views have generally coalesced around a few core positions representing a range of beliefs. The next four chapters will discuss these views, starting with non-believers in Chapter 7.

7

NON-BELIEVERS

"To you I'm an atheist; to God, I'm the Loyal Opposition."
Woody Allen (1935 -)

The language of Genesis 1—"In the beginning God ...."—raises the most fundamental of questions, about which there is broad agreement in some respects and broad disagreement in other respects. The language assumes there is a God but offers no proof.

Almost everyone agrees there is no philosophical or scientific proof, within scripture or elsewhere, of God's existence or non-existence. Even Henry Morris, often considered the father of creationism, has stated, "One must simply *believe*—either in eternal, omnipotent Matter or else in an eternal, omnipotent Creator God. The individual may decide which he considers more reasonable, but he should recognize this is not completely a *scientific* decision either way."[1] Stephen Meyer, a leader in the Intelligent Design Movement has said, "You can't absolutely prove—or disprove—the existence of God."[2] And atheist Richard Dawkins has noted, "the absolute impossibility of proving or disproving God ...."[3]

Since this issue finds no resolution in scriptural understanding or science, people resort to faith, philosophy, and reason for their answers. And they have developed a broad range of views. At one end of this range of beliefs are proponents of "fideism"—the view that all we need is faith, that faith alone justifies a belief in the existence of God, and that reason, philosophy, or other logic outside the Christian faith are not appropriate. The other end of the range holds that only evidence and reason count and that God's existence can, or cannot, be demonstrated by reason.

As we have previously discussed, medieval philosophers relied on various lines of reasoning to support God's existence. Plato and others, including Anselm, believed in an ontological proof, or proof from being, with the universe as the rational, purposive handiwork of a divine craftsman. Aristotle proposed a "teleological" argument based on evidence of order, purpose, design and/or direction. The Prime Mover of Aristotle's universe became identified with the God of Christian theology. Plotinus believed God is an all-sufficient unity at the top of a hierarchy of the universe, from which the natural world emanated. Aquinas used Aristotle as a starting point and produced a cosmological argument—the "five ways" based on reason—for the existence of God.

In more modern times, views have varied significantly and much ink has been spilled defending the existence of God, particularly by those prominent in the religion and science debate. Stephen Meyer and William Dembski, two leaders in the Intelligent Design Movement, have articulated a model of reasoning they call "inference to the best explanation." In this form of reasoning, "if we want to explain a phenomenon or event, we consider a whole range of hypotheses and infer to the one which, if true, would provide the best explanation." They conclude, after assessing the evidence available to them, that "the existence of God explains this broad range of evidence more simply, adequately, and comprehensively than any other worldview ...."[4]

Francis Collins, a proponent of a form of theistic evolution, has noted that "...the Moral Law still stands out for me as the strongest signpost to God. More than that, it points to a God who cares about human beings, and a God who is infinitely good and holy."[5] To Collins, the Moral Law comprises that "something" within human beings that appeals to right and wrong and fosters our strong preference for doing the right thing as we attempt to appeal to an unstated higher authority.

So the Bible announces a God, but science cannot prove the existence or non-existence of God, and human philosophy and reason go in all different directions, like a well-struck rack of billiard balls. Believers accept God because of faith, a worldview, a personal assessment of the evidence, or a combination of all these things, not because of absolute proof or irrefutable reason. Non-believers, on the other hand, think God is either unknown or unknowable, or that there is no God. For them, science wins hands down in its contest with religion, or in fact there is no contest because science has no competition.

An open mind is important for investigating almost all subjects, and certainly questions concerning religion and the existence of God. Accordingly, academic study of religions has been dominated for many years by the idea that scholars should adopt a neutral, value-free position and restrict themselves to describing, classifying, and comparing religious phenomena without allowing any personal ideas to affect their investigation. This approach, often called "methodological naturalism," allows academics to analyze the beliefs of others with a process that is as non-judgmental and scientific as possible, but it says nothing about their actual theological beliefs. Methodological naturalists may have a strong belief in God, or they may have none at all. Our purpose in this chapter, however, is to briefly discuss the views of non-believers—views that, not surprisingly, vary significantly and do not always lend themselves to easy labeling. Two relatively broad labels, agnostic and atheist, have generally been applied to these individuals.

AGNOSTICISM

The term "agnostic" literally means no knowledge. The dictionary defines agnostic as a person who believes that the human mind cannot know whether there is a God or an ultimate cause. But individual beliefs differ. Some simply question whether God exists. Others believe the nature and attributes of God are beyond the grasp of man's finite and limited mind. Still others believe there is likely to be a definitive answer; they hope to know it some day, but don't know it today. This all seems to get us back to "no knowledge."

David Hume, who lived in the 1700s and is generally regarded as the most important philosopher to write in English, provided an early philosophical basis of agnosticism. He believed that we cannot prove the existence of anything and insofar as we have any idea of God, we can conceive of Him either as existing or not existing but one cannot prove the matter either way. In Hume's view, any conclusion not arrived at by abstract reasoning or by observing factual data is meaningless. Since all statements about God are outside these parameters and cannot be proved either by reasoning or by factual data, knowledge of God is impossible.

Hume's writings, widely and deeply influential then and now, were denounced by many of his contemporaries as works of skepticism and even atheism. However, disagreement continues as to whether his skeptical position can be properly characterized as agnostic or as atheistic. Regardless how one views Hume's work as a whole, it is clear that one of his most basic objectives was to discredit orthodox religious belief. He significantly influenced other important thinkers, including noted philosopher Immanuel Kant, Charles Darwin, and Thomas Huxley.

Huxley, a fierce defender of evolution, is credited with originating the term "agnostic" to describe his own belief. His description of how he came to coin the term is a good explanation of its meaning:

> When I reached intellectual maturity, and began to ask myself whether I was an atheist, a theist, or a pantheist; a materialists or an idealist; a Christian or a free thinker, I found that the more I learned and reflected, the less ready was the answer; until at last I came to the conclusion that I had neither art nor part with any of these denominations, except the last. The one thing in which most of these good people were agreed was the one thing in which I differed from them. They were quite sure that they had attained a certain "gnosis"—had more or less successfully solved the problem of existence; while I was quite sure I had not, and had a pretty strong conviction that the problem was insoluble....So I took thought, and invented what I conceived to be the appropriate title of "agnostic." It came into my head as suggestively antithetic to the "gnostic" of church history, who professed to know so much about the very thing of which I was ignorant.[6]

Two basic types of agnosticism are generally acknowledged—the limited or weak form holding simply that we do not know God, and the unlimited or strong form claiming that God is unknowable.

Limited Agnosticism

Nothing is inherently unreasonable about being a weak or limited agnostic because, as Hume suggested, all the empirically verified knowledge available to us leads toward uncertainty about God. In fact, some modern theologians, like Paul Tillich, call themselves agnostics because they cannot know, in a scientific sense, that God exists. That doesn't prevent them from being believers, though, because there is knowledge other than that which is empirically verifiable. Similarly, many scientists are agnostic. As a group they tend to be more agnostic than the public generally, although many are believers and some are relatively conservative in their perspective. Science does not require them to be unbelievers, as it does not logically prove or disprove the existence of God or the meaningfulness of religion. If a person doesn't believe in God, his belief is for reasons other than a career in science. Other self-proclaimed agnostics, in fact, believe there is a world beyond the physical but are disillusioned with organized religion and have no other proper way of articulating their views. Importantly, limited agnosticism of whatever ilk is not a threat to Christianity. It simply acknowledges a finite knowledge of the infinite.

Strong Agnosticism

Inconsistent with Christianity is the claim of unlimited or strong agnostics that the existence or non-existence of God is unknowable. From a philosophical viewpoint, many Christian apologists argue that strong agnosticism is also inconsistent with reason, as it implies knowledge about reality in order to deny the possibility of the reality of God. They note also that there is no way short of omniscient awareness (which human beings don't possess) that one can make a sweeping claim that God cannot be known.

At a more practical level, strong agnostic beliefs often suggest not only the suspension of judgment on all ultimate issues, but a secular attitude toward life where God is irrelevant, or even an emotionally charged, anti-Christian attitude. In fact, the difference between strong agnosticism and atheism is often a very fine line. Many who actually reject God, and perhaps are actually more properly characterized as atheists, prefer to be considered agnostics. The agnostic is spared the social stigma associated with atheism and also appears to avoid the burden of having to prove his belief. To assert or deny anything requires a reason, while professing ignorance requires no reasons.

Finally, some agnostics feel their beliefs are a form of atheism and therefore consider themselves to be both agnostic and atheist.

ATHEISM

Richard Dawkins, perhaps one of today's better known defenders of atheism and of the view that science wins in a death match with religion, has presented the following alternative to a God who deliberately designed and created the universe and everything in it:

> This book will advocate an alternative view: *any creative intelligence, of sufficient complexity to design anything, comes into existence only as the end product of an extended process of gradual evolution.* Creative intelligences, being evolved, necessarily arrive late in the universe, and therefore cannot be responsible for designing it. God, in the sense defined, is a delusion; and, as later chapters will show, a pernicious delusion.[7]

This leads to the question—If one cannot prove the existence or non-existence of God, how does one become an atheist? Perhaps the answer depends on the definition. The term "atheism" is defined differently by different sources. Some describe it as the simple absence of belief in deities, which would include agnostics and people who have never heard of God. It is, however, more commonly defined as the positive denial or the deliberate rejection of the existence of a deity or deities. Some have described the former belief—the absence of belief in the existence of God—as "weak atheism" and the latter— the firm conviction that no deities exist—as "strong atheism."

Atheists tend to accept secular philosophies such as "scientific naturalism," which includes any method of inquiry or study that is limited to natural, physical, or material approaches and does not distinguish the supernatural from nature. All phenomena or hypotheses commonly labeled as supernatural are false, unknowable, or not inherently different from natural ones. Similarly, "metaphysical naturalism" holds that the supernatural does not exist and the Bible is irrelevant to anything, thereby fostering strong atheism. These philosophies are to be distinguished from other forms such as "methodological naturalism" which assume that observable events in nature are explained only by natural causes, without assuming the existence or non-existence of the supernatural.

Humanism is a broad philosophy or worldview that affirms the dignity and worth of all people, believing individuals can determine right and wrong by appealing to human qualities and their best understanding of individual and common interests. Specific beliefs vary among proclaimed humanists. Some consider themselves religious and embrace some form of the supernatural, without necessarily being involved in organized religion or accepting the authority of divinely revealed texts. Others reject theistic religious belief, faith, and the existence of a supernatural; they are, therefore, atheistic in their approach. "Secular humanism" is a term often used pejoratively by some conservative Christians to refer to humanism and even to suggest that humanism is really a religion.

Although ideas that would today be viewed as atheistic existed several centuries before the birth of Christ, atheism did not play a significant role in Western culture until the eighteenth century. Interestingly, the rise of modern science and the work of Copernicus, Galileo, Newton, and their colleagues did not give rise to atheism, as they generally believed in God and, in some cases, strongly supported the validity of the Bible. A more powerful force for atheism was a rebellion against the oppressive authority of the French royal family and church leadership, who were seen as harsh, self-promoting, hypocritical, and insensitive to the needs of the common man.

As discussed in Chapter 5, Darwin described himself as an agnostic rather than an atheist, but one can argue the point. As he was approaching age seventy, he made a series of notes for his children in which he discussed his religion. He wrote in one note, made public years later, that he had worked through the positions that had caused him to slip away from the religion of his youth and, "Disbelief crept over me at a very slow rate, but was at last complete. The rate was so slow that I felt no distress, and have never since doubted even for a second that my conclusion was correct."[8] Those opposing religion often looked to Darwin for support, which he declined to offer in any direct way. Correctly or incorrectly, however, his theory of evolution has been used as a powerful weapon in the atheists' arsenal against spirituality.

A litany of personalities, from "professional atheists" to noted scientists are non-believers who have rejected God and faith. Sigmund Freud argued that belief in God is just wishful thinking. Karl Marx called religion "the opiate of the masses." Woody Allen said, "If it turns out that there is a God, I don't think that he's evil. But the worst that you can say about him is that basically he's an underachiever." Madalyn Murray O'Hair filed and won lawsuits that effectively banned most public prayer and Bible reading in the United States public schools. Carl Sagan, a prominent spokesman for naturalism in science, declared in the PBS series, *Cosmos*, that the "cosmos is all there ever was, all that is, and all that ever will be." Bill Maher's film *Religulous* lampoons religion. And Richard Dawkins, Oxford professor and author of the 2006 book *The God Delusion*, has taken the gloves off:

> The God of the Old Testament is arguably the most unpleasant character in all fiction: jealous and proud of it; a petty, unjust, unforgiving control-freak; a vindictive, bloodthirsty ethnic cleanser; a misogynistic, homophobic, racist, infanticidal, genocidal, filicidal, pestilential, megalomaniacal, sadomasochistic, capriciously malevolent bully. Those of us schooled from infancy in his ways can become desensitized to their horror. A *naif* blessed with the perspective of innocence has a clearer perception.[9]

Christopher Hitchens, a British-American author, journalist, and literary critic followed in 2007 with the equally bombastic *god is not Great: How Religion Poisons Everything*, in which he argues that religion misrepresents the origins of humankind and the cosmos, demands unreasonable suppression of human nature, leads to violence and blind submission to authority, and is hostile to free inquiry.

Atheists tend to defend their beliefs by opposing arguments of those who do believe, as proving there is no God is a difficult proposition. For example, they argue against the philosophical proofs of God, such as those of St. Anselm of Canterbury and Thomas Aquinas. Or they attempt to contradict those who believe they have personally experienced God in the form of a vision, or in hearing Him speak, or in other significant events. Atheists also deny that the Bible contains conceptual proof of God's existence.

Atheists also often attempt to disprove God through arguments from the moral sphere. Some argue that the presence of evil in the world, which indisputably exists, denies the presence of an all-powerful, all-good God—a God who could and would destroy evil if He existed. Similar arguments apply in the case of innocent or unjustifiable suffering. Atheists ask, for example, "If God exists and is good, why does He allow the suffering of even one innocent child?" They see the lack of a good, compelling answer as evidence that there is no God.

A number of arguments seeking to disprove God are derived from the nature of man and freedom. Some contend that if there is a God, He knows and controls everything; if God knows and controls everything, humans are not free; humans are free, though, so there is no God. Others argue that God arises only from man's wish, desire, need, or imagination—none of which suggests in any way that God actually exists and works in our lives.

The atheist or humanist worldview sees a conflict between science and the Bible that science wins. Not surprisingly, atheists believe scientific cosmology is inconsistent with the existence of God and object to the view that because the universe began to exist, it must have had a cause. Quentin Smith has argued in an article, "Big Bang Cosmology and Atheism: Why the Big Bang is No Help to Theists"[10] that the premise for such argument—whatever has a beginning to its existence must have a cause—is simply false, with no evidence whatsoever to support it. He further maintains that a theory called the Wave Function of the Universe, developed by Stephen Hawking and others on the basis of observable evidence, implies that it is 95 percent probable that our universe came into existence without a cause.

Fundamental to the atheistic view, and to the Dawkins school of atheism, is the belief that evolution, particularly natural selection, explains the origin of mankind and biological complexity, so there is no need for God. This argument is presented in Chapter 4 of *The God Delusion*, "Why There Almost Certainly is No God," which clearly seems to confirm our earlier statement that God's existence cannot be proved or disproved. The chapter title makes the point. Dawkins argues against several aspects of the intelligent design argument, particularly the argument of irreducible complexity and the gap theory as it applies both to the evolution of species and the origin of the universe.

While he often acknowledges the appearance of design in the universe, he contends that this cannot be attributed to actual design because "the designer hypothesis immediately raises the larger problem of who designed the designer."[11] But his is a defensive fight that aims to negate the beliefs of others in the existence of God, and he presents no actual evidence to disprove that God had a creative plan that may have included evolution.

Quantifying the extent of atheism is difficult. As we have discussed, the term "atheism" does not have hard boundaries and can cover a range of belief and non-belief. In addition, some atheists may not report themselves to avoid the possibility of social stigma or discrimination in certain cultures, and polls tend to be plagued with non-random samples and low response rates. That said, atheism, or at least what may be called "virtual" or "practical" atheism, is known to be relatively common in many parts of the world, including the United States. Several polls suggest a range of from 3 to 9 percent of Americans do not believe in God, or are atheist or agnostic. Recent polls also suggest that atheism may be as high as 88 percent in East Germany, and that atheists and agnostics comprise up to 40 percent of the population of Great Britain.

There is, of course, another view. Norman L. Geisler has summarized key arguments of believers as to why atheism does not measure up:

> First, its arguments are invalid and often self–defeating. Second, many atheistic arguments are really reversible into reasons for believing in God. Finally, atheism provides no solution to basic metaphysical questions regarding the existence of the universe or the origin of personality and the actualization of the world process. Atheists must believe that something comes from nothing, that potentials actualize themselves, and that matter generated mind. It seems much more reasonable to believe in a God who made something where there was nothing, who actualized the potentials that could not actualize themselves, and whose Mind formed matter.[12]

Those who subscribe to such views, not surprisingly, cover a range of specific beliefs. We turn now to the most "fundamental" of them—creationism.

8

CREATIONISM

"No geological difficulties, real or imagined, can be allowed to take precedence over the clear statements and necessary inferences of Scripture."
Henry Morris (1918 – 2006)

In Chapter 5, "Darwin's Aftermath," we discussed what might now be called the "end of the beginning" of modern creationism—the response of early twentieth century conservative Christians to the theory of evolution, modernism, and the teaching of evolution in schools. That time period saw the influence of Seventh-Day Adventists Ellen G. White and George M. Price, the publication of *The Fundamentals* and the birth of fundamentalism, and the Scopes Monkey Trial with its aftermath.

Creationism continued to simmer over the next several decades. The early 1960s saw a broad release of new public school biology textbooks with major sections on evolution, and a resurgence of concern among fundamentalists about the decline of traditional values and growing secularism in society. The creationist movement became more active, emphasizing a literal interpretation of the Bible and the book of Genesis as the sole source of knowledge about origins. The issue of evolution, religion, and public school textbooks resurfaced in the late 1960s as creationist parents began efforts to shield children from influences contrary to their religious beliefs. In the late 1960s and early 1970s, several organizations were formed to promote the idea that Genesis was supported by scientific data, and the terms "creation science" and "scientific creationism" came into use. Several such organizations still exist, and creationist ideas continue as an important force on the Bible and science landscape.

SCIENTIFIC CREATIONSIM

Henry M. Morris, one of the most influential of modern creation scientists, has described the basic idea of scientific creationism as a "purely scientific" explanation of the origin based on a model that:

> postulates a period of special creation in the beginning, during which all the basic laws and categories of nature, including the major kinds of plants and animals, as well as man, were brought into existence by special creative and integrative processes which are no longer in operation. Once the creation was finished, these processes of *creation* were replaced by processes of *conservation*, which were designed by the Creator to sustain and maintain the basic systems He had created.[1]

Within this broad definition, the creationism mosaic is a confusing picture covering a spectrum of beliefs that defy easy labels.

Morris, an engineering teacher at Rice Institute in Houston at the time, had been raised a Southern Baptist and a believer in creation. He drifted away from his religion, but, after a period of reevaluation, returned with a vengeance as a believer that creation occurred in six literal days "…because the Bible clearly said so and God doesn't lie."[2] Having earned his Ph.D. in hydraulic engineering, Morris teamed with John C. Whitcomb Jr. In 1961, the two brought out *The Genesis Flood*, which proposed a scientific basis for creationism, including flood geology, as explained in Genesis. Their book, seen as one of the most important in the development of creationism, evoked an intense debate among evangelicals and broad condemnation by critics.

The Creation Research Society

With impetus from *The Genesis Flood*, ten like-minded scientists founded the Creation Research Society (CRS) in 1963. Previously, these men had found it difficult to publish information favorable to the creation viewpoint in established scientific journals and they believed other scientists probably were having similar experiences. So they established the CRS in the state of Michigan as a non-profit corporation for educational and scientific purposes. It continues today as one of the country's major creationist organizations.

The organization's website indicates the CRS is independent and unaffiliated with any other organization, religious group, or church body. The site also states that CRS members include research scientists from various fields who are committed to full belief in the biblical record of creation and early history. Memberships and subscriptions total around 1,700 worldwide, with about 600 voting members and 250 foreign members/subscribers.

The Society publishes a quarterly journal, conducts creation-related research, provides speakers to churches or other groups, maintains a directory of creationist organizations, and runs an online bookstore for books and videos on special creation. It advocates special creation (as opposed to evolution) of the universe and of the earth. Membership requires agreement with the following Statement of Belief:

1. The *Bible* is the written Word of God, and because it is inspired throughout, all its assertions are historically and scientifically true in the original autographs. To the student of nature this means that the account of origins in *Genesis* is a factual presentation of simple historical truths.

2. All basic types of living things, including man, were made by direct creative acts of God during the Creation Week described in *Genesis*. Whatever biological changes have occurred since Creation Week have been only changes within the original created kinds.

3. The great flood described in *Genesis*, commonly referred to as the Noachian Flood, was a historic event worldwide in its extent and effect.

4. We are an organization of Christian men and women of science who accept Jesus Christ as our Lord and Savior. The account of the special creation of Adam and Eve as one man and one woman and their subsequent fall into sin is the basis for our belief in the necessity of a Savior for all mankind. Therefore, salvation can come only through accepting Jesus Christ as our Savior.[3]

The Creation Research Society has established a small station in north-central Arizona for the purpose of aiding members and visiting scientists in their efforts. They encourage a spectrum of research to develop and test a creation model, and they administer a grant program under which modest funds are distributed for the conduct of creation-related research.

Creation Moments

Creation Moments, Inc. (formerly the Bible-Science Association) was also established in 1963. Its stated purpose is to promote, teach, and study the divine creation as revealed in the Bible. The organization communicates its message through radio broadcasts, seminars, publications, and a bookstore outreach. CMI's mission is "to glorify God by presenting scientific evidences for the literal truth of the Bible." Creation Moments offers individuals, students, churches, home-school parents, and professionals various products intended to support its purpose.

The current organization has an eight-point Doctrinal Statement, the first five of which apply directly to our subject:

1. God has spoken in scripture and has acted in creation and human history. We believe that the autographs of the 66 canonical books of the Bible are objectively inspired, infallible and the inerrant Word of God in all of their parts and in all matters of which they speak (history, theology, science, etc.).

2. The message of the Bible is communicated in the most basic meaning of the text as understood in its historical and grammatical context.

3. God has acted to create the cosmos *ex nihilo* in six 24-hour periods in the recent past.

4. A divine design and purpose exists in nature and this purpose is to point to and glorify the Creator.

5. A universal Noachian flood occurred, which destroyed all life on earth except those saved in the Ark (Noah, his family, and the animals).[4]

Creationism in Public Schools

The year 1968 saw a significant legal development change the landscape of the creationist movement. In 1928, shortly after the Scopes trial, the state of Arkansas had adopted a law that prohibited the teaching of "the theory or doctrine that mankind ascended or descended from a lower order of animals" and the use of any textbook which taught the same in any public school or university. In the mid 1960s, the Arkansas Education Association sought a declaratory judgment challenging the law. In the case of *Epperson v. Arkansas*, the trial court found the law unconstitutional, but the Arkansas Supreme Court subsequently reversed the trial court. On further appeal, the U.S. Supreme Court concluded:

> Arkansas' law cannot be defended as an act of religious neutrality. Arkansas did not seek to excise from the curricula of its schools and universities all discussion of the origin of man. The law's effort was confined to an attempt to blot out a particular theory because of its supposed conflict with the Biblical account, literally read. Plainly, the law is contrary to the mandate of the First, and in violation of the Fourteenth, Amendment to the Constitution.[5]

Thus, the U.S. Supreme Court concluded that the statute's downfall was the fact that the state was trying to prevent its teachers from discussing the theory of evolution, "because it is contrary to the belief of some that the Book of Genesis must be the exclusive source of doctrine as to the origin of man."[6]

Not surprisingly, this decision by the country's highest court led creationists to change their strategy in the 1970s from trying to outlaw the teaching of evolution to requiring schools to give evidence of creation equal time. They feared attempts to require the teaching of the biblical account of creation without balancing it with the teaching of evolution would meet a fate similar to the Arkansas law. Therefore, the creationists began pushing for teaching practices that acknowledged both the evolutionary theory and arguments against evolution, and presented evidence for a recent worldwide flood, while omitting all references to the Bible. This approach, which came to be referred to as "scientific creationism," or "creation science" was generally considered a repackaging of their earlier views in a way thought to be more palatable to the judicial system.

The Institute for Creation Research

Perhaps today's leading creationist organization, The Institute for Creation Research (ICR) was established in 1970 by Dr. Henry M. Morris, whose book, *The Genesis Flood*, had been an impetus for the establishment of the Creation Research Society in 1963. The ICR's mission focuses on research, media, and education in fields of science particularly relevant to the study of origins. The Institute has a Graduate School that offers on-site Master of Science degrees in Astro/ Geophysics, Biology, and Geology and online degrees in Science Education. The school is committed to creationism and to full biblical inerrancy and authority, and it views evolution, at the most, as an idea about history rather than an observational science. Its purpose is "...to serve as an education, research, and communications media institution specializing in the study and promotion of scientific creationism, Biblical creationism, and related fields."[7]

In 1974, the ICR published two editions of a textbook, *Scientific Creationism,* authored by Dr. Morris. The edition intended for use in public schools did not mention the Bible. The one for use in Christian schools contained a chapter on "Creation According to scripture," which includes the following:

> ...the creation chapters of Genesis are marvelous and accurate accounts of the actual events of the primeval history of the universe. They give data and information far beyond those that science can determine, and at the same time provide an intellectually satisfying framework within which to interpret the facts which science *can* determine.[8]

The Institute has a statement of faith for its faculty and students, incorporating most of the basic Christian doctrines in a creationist framework, organized in terms of two parallel sets of tenets—Biblical Creationism and of Scientific Creationism. Each set of tenets has nine points that correspond to a point in the other set. A side-by-side comparison of the first three of the nine points indicates the extent to which Scientific Creationism is equivalent to Biblical Creationism, but without reference to God or the Bible.

Biblical Creationism

1. The Creator of the universe is a triune God -- Father, Son and Holy Spirit. There is only one eternal and transcendent God, the source of all being and meaning, and He exists in three persons, each of whom participated in the work of creation.

2. The Bible consisting of the thirty-nine canonical books of the Old Testament and the twenty-seven canonical books of the New Testament, is the divinely inspired revelation of the Creator to man. Its unique, plenary, verbal inspiration guarantees that these writings as originally and miraculously given, are infallible and completely authoritative on all matters with which they deal, free from error of any sort, scientific and historical as well as moral and theological.

Scientific Creationism

1. The physical universe of space, time, matter and energy has not always existed, but was supernaturally created by a transcendent personal Creator who alone has existed from eternity.

2. The phenomenon of biological life did not develop by natural processes from inanimate systems but was specially and supernaturally created by the Creator.

3. All things in the universe were created and made by God in the six literal days of the creation week described in Genesis 1:1-2:3, and confirmed in Exodus 20:8-11. The creation record is factual, historical and perspicuous; thus all theories of origins or development which involve evolution in any form are false. All things which now exist are sustained and ordered by God's providential care. However, a part of the spiritual creation, Satan and his angels, rebelled against God after the creation and are attempting to thwart His divine purposes in creation.[9]

3. Each of the major kinds of plants and animals was created functionally complete from the beginning and did not evolve from some other kind of organism. Changes in basic kinds since their first creation are limited to "horizontal" changes (variations) within the kinds, or "downward" changes (e.g., harmful mutations, extinctions).

The creationist movement has continued to publicize its views in speeches, debates, and other venues. It also continues efforts to have school children taught its beliefs. In 2001 they opened Dinosaur Adventure Land, a small creationist theme park and museum that claims to teach children "the truth about dinosaurs"—with Genesis, not science, telling the story of the creation. In addition to this venture and instruction in private schools, they offer a number of summer camps for children with the teaching of creationism as a key objective.

Based on admittedly scanty evidence, there is reason to believe that in 1982 nearly as many people in the United States believed in some form of recent special creation as accepted various theories of evolution. That number has not changed significantly to the present time. As discussed in Chapter 6, a 2008 Gallup poll concluded that about 44 percent of the American public accepts what is basically a creationist account of the origins of life, while a roughly comparable number accepts the idea that humans evolved over time.[10] The adherents of creation science are themselves divided, however, based on their view of several issues, particularly the age of the world.

YOUNG EARTH CREATIONISM

The central thesis of the young earth creationists' belief system, according to Henry Morris, is that the biblical record, accepted in its natural and literal sense, gives the only scientific and satisfying account of the origin. According to Morris, "If the Bible is the Word of God—and it is—and if Jesus Christ is the infallible and omniscient creator—and He is—then it must be firmly believed that the world and all things in it were created in six natural days and that the long geological ages of evolutionary history never really took place at all."[11]

Young earth creationists believe the book of Genesis is literally true in every respect and that God created all things in six consecutive twenty-four-hour days. Further, they believe that radiometric and isochron dating of the earth's age are debatable assumptions, while the Genesis genealogies are essentially complete and accurate. Thus, God created the earth, its life forms, and the rest of the universe fewer than 10,000 years ago, probably about 6,000 years ago, generally as calculated by Archbishop Ussher in 1650 (see Chapter 1). So there was instantaneous creation, and only very minor changes within various species (microevolution) have occurred since creation. No new species have evolved or been created (macroevolution).

The flood of Noah was a global event, according to creationists, and all of today's animal life, including human beings, descended from those on the Ark. The Tower of Babel explains the origin of the various root languages of the world. God created a number of unique languages in order to scatter mankind and retard man's technological advancement.

Thus, many creationists explicitly reject the idea of evolution of languages and believe God specially created different languages as explained by the literal story of the Tower of Babel. This action effectively divided humans into several groups and allowed physical differences to develop. Consequently, the Tower of Babel helps explain why humans exist as multiple distinct races today.

Astronomy

Not surprisingly, scientific creationists don't like the astrophysicists' big bang theory because it doesn't take the Genesis account literally enough. For Henry Morris, a veritable Pandora's box of dire fates awaits those who accept the theory or are said to compromise on a literal interpretation of Genesis and thus permit an accommodation with any potentially contradictory views. Morris has written:

> It is obvious by definition that neither the big bang theory nor the steady-state theory has any observational basis. In fact, they *contradict* both Laws of Thermodynamics. There-fore, they are philosophical speculations, not science, secondary assumptions to avoid the contradictions implicit in the evolution model.
>
> The creation model, on the other hand, in effect *predicts* the two Laws of Thermodynamics, as noted before. A special creation of space, matter and time, by an omnipresent, omnipotent, eternal Creator is the only logical conclusion to be drawn from the two most certain and universal laws in science.[12]

Articles posted on the website of the Institute for Creation Research, introduced earlier, also reflect this view. "The Big Bust," an article by Henry Morris, refers to the "badly flawed big bang model of evolutionary origins. A second article, "Were You There?" by Kenneth Ham states, "Yet there is no scientific proof for the big bang theory. It is just a story, based on the speculations of scientists—fallible human beings who do not know everything and who were not there to see it happen." Emphasizing the last point later in the article, he observes, "Carl Sagan's Big Bang theory is WRONG! How do we know that for sure? Because God was there—Carl Sagan wasn't! God knows every-thing—Carl Sagan doesn't."[13]

Geology

Young earth creationists generally support catastrophism rather than uniformatism, as Henry M. Morris has noted in *Scientific Creationism*:

> The creation model is fundamentally catastrophic because it says that present laws and processes are *not* sufficient to explain the phenomena found in the present world. It

centers its explanation of past history around both a period of special *constructive* processes and one or more periods of special *destructive* processes, both of which operated in ways or at rates which are not commensurate with present processes.[14]

Creationist presses have published reams of data by flood geologists that claim to support the young age of the earth by explaining all the strata and formations in terms of one great catastrophe. From their perspective, the scientific objections to catastrophism don't hold water because a miracle of God is involved. In this context, the flood was a great miracle because it was caused by God, and forces were unleashed that are not now available for scientists to study.

The Institute For Creation Research website also includes an article titled "How Long Does it Take for a Canyon to Form?" by John Morris. It maintains that the geologists' view that the Grand Canyon was formed over millions of years by the action of the Colorado River has been disproved, and that it instead was formed by "a great volume of water rushing through the area at a high velocity not very long ago which carved the canyon" that "bears eloquent testimony to the great flood of Noah's day." A second article, "Radiometric Dating and the Bible: A Historical Review" by Henry Morris, notes, "We need to remind ourselves over and over that there is no hint whatever—anywhere in the Bible—that the earth is significantly older than the few thousand years of recorded history. There are numerous biblical statements, on the other hand, that clearly require a young earth."

On another front, the Creation Research Society website maintains that all basic types of living things, including man, were made by "direct creative acts of God during the Creation Week described in Genesis," and "the great flood described in Genesis, commonly referred to as the Noachian Flood, was an historic event worldwide in its extent and effect."[15]

Biology

Predictably, from a biological standpoint, young earth creationists reject the idea that man has slowly evolved from a non-human ancestor. Instead, they believe, "The creation model requires man to be created directly as man, with a fully human body and brain from the beginning." They further argue, "The Scriptures are very clear in their teaching that God created all things as He wanted them to be, each with its own particular structure, according to His own sovereign purposes."[16]

Creationists maintain that while there no doubt has been some change over time within species, or some microevolution, there has been no development between species, or no macroevolution. They believe that species are divided from each other by an immutable "essence" as God formed animals "according to their kinds" as specified in Genesis 1: 25-26, and various races of human beings can be traced to the scattering of languages at the Tower of Babel.

A primary contention of creationists is that there is a missing link in the fossil record—the common ancestor of man and ape or the transitional link leading up to man—and that this absence in the record is evidence that species did not evolve. This claim, involving an issue of which Darwin himself was aware, continues to come under serious attack with advances in archeology, and scientists believe many transitional fossils do exist. A recent example is the controversy surrounding the "Turkana Boy," a fossil unearthed in Kenya in 1984. This skeleton, probably the most complete of a prehistoric human ever found, is thought by scientists to be 1.6 million years old and has characteristics of modern humans and of apes.[17] While scientists believe it is the clearest record yet of evolution and the origin of man, creationists in Kenya's evangelical Christian movement view the scientific conclusions as silly and aim to boycott exhibits of the skeleton.

On the other hand, some proponents of evolution advance the idea of "punctuated equilibrium" to explain the apparent absences in the fossil record. Punctuated equilibrium has been popularized by a number of individuals, prominently the late Steven Jay Gould, an influential Harvard paleontologist and evolutionary biologist. He acknowledged that after 150 years of intense archeological exploration, scientists still have not shown the fossil record to produce enough evidence to sustain Darwin's theory of evolution. However, fossils indicate that a living thing comes into existence, remains the same for millions of years, and becomes extinct. Another organism seems to appear out of nowhere and continues for millions of years. And so on. Therefore, although the earth is millions of years old, the fossil record indicates that there might have been development of new species in relatively short periods of time. This idea—that periods of equilibrium have existed for millions of years, interspersed with periods of explosive evolutionary creativity—is referred to as the theory of punctuated equilibrium. Proponents believe the theory conforms to the fossil record, explains the gaps, and tends to support Darwin's theory.

The most frequently cited example is the Cambrian explosion, which creationists cite as their best case of a failure of the fossil record to support evolution, and which evolutionists cite as a great example of punctuated equilibrium. The Cambrian explosion refers to the apparently sudden (over a period of around thirty million years) appearance of animal fossils at the beginning of the Cambrian geologic period about 550 million years ago. Creationists argue that the 30 million years, more or less, were not enough time for the evolution of animals to occur. Those supporting evolution argue that the "explosion" occurred over millions of years, more than sufficient time for evolution to work. And in any case, the fact that geologists haven't found a complete fossil record doesn't mean the organisms weren't there to support evolution. The fossils could be unavailable for many reasons.

Nevertheless, some who believe the fossil record is inadequate, and also consider themselves in the creationist camp, can't quite reconcile a literal, seven-day interpretation of Genesis with the geologic evidence. Inventive minds have found a way.

OLD EARTH CREATIONISM

Sometimes the scientific evidence just seems too compelling. Many Christians who cannot live with the basics of biological evolution have nevertheless accepted the scientific community's assessment of the earth's age and interpreted scripture in keeping with the evolutionary timeline. This approach, often called "concordism," is the belief that the biblical account of creation, when properly understood, will be in concord (agreement) with correct scientific conclusions. This view generally characterizes the approach of "old earth creationists," also referred to as "progressive creationists." They believe that God created the universe and the earth, and especially created human beings, but concede that the world is billions of years old, as geologic and radiometric dating have shown. They accommodate scripture by adopting one of two theories of old earth creation science—the gap theory or the day/age theory.

Gap Theory

The gap theory, also called the restitution hypothesis, allows people to have the earth be as old as they want by having all the artifacts and fossils that suggest a very old age fall in a gap of perhaps millions of years that is assumed to exist in the creation story. This theory suggests that a vast period of time elapsed between the events of the first and third verses of Genesis, allowing life to be recently created on a preexisting earth. While there are some variations of the theory, the basics are something like this: Genesis 1:1, "God created the heavens and the earth," is considered a first creation, which included the creation of the heavens, the earth, plants and animals, and even a race of humans preceding Adam. Genesis 1:2 says "Now the earth was formless and empty," but the Hebrew writing of this verse can be translated, "The earth became without form and void." During this time Satan and his angels corrupted the inhabitants of the earth, and God judged and destroyed it and all its inhabitants. Thus, "the earth became void" and remained that way for eons. After this huge gap of Genesis 1:2, perhaps billions of years, God said in Genesis 1:3, "Let there be light," and began the six-day creation sequence. Thus, under this view, the earth was initially created in the distant past, and all geologic events pointing to an old earth took place before some event that returned the earth to a state of formlessness or chaos as described in Genesis 1:2, and before the creation of Genesis 1:3.

This gap theory of creation is not to be confused with the expression "God of the gaps" often heard today. As science has provided more and more convincing explanations for natural phenomena, questions or gaps of knowledge still exist. This argument acknowledges these gaps in scientific knowledge and holds that they are best explained as acts of God. An early, famous example of this explanation involved Sir Isaac Newton, famous for his law of gravity and considered by many to be one of the greatest intellects the world has known. When Newton saw certain irregularities in the motion of planets that his theory of gravity could not explain, he stated that these were the result of direct intervention by God. Later, when astronomers and physicists provided a natural explanation, "God" was no longer necessary. Not surprisingly, most credible scientists and theologians agree that even if some answers are still unknown, God should not be used as a hypothesis to fill the gaps in scientific knowledge. Doing so diminishes the concept of God and merely creates a "God of the gaps"—an idea to be explored more fully in the following chapter.

Day-Age Creation Theory

Day-age creation, or progressive creationism, is another way of harmonizing the language of scripture with current scientific understandings. This idea assumes that the days of creation were actually long lengths of time, meaning that a day in Genesis 1 represents not a 24-hour day, but an eon or a very, very long period of time, usually an indefinite period such as the Jurassic Period or the Cambrian Period. This theory accepts the evolutionary time scale—simple to complex over millions of years—but with more input from God than evolutionists generally believe. It proposes that God specially created various kinds of organisms and later man, but over a long period of time.

In his book, *Creation as Science*, Hugh Ross, who holds a Ph.D. in Astronomy from the University of Toronto, explained the day-age view as follows:

> In light of what the Bible says about His unlimited power, God could have chosen any time scale, however short or long, to perform His creative work. As for the six "days" of creation, Hebrew allows for more than one literal possibility. The word translated "day" in Genesis 1, *yom*, has four different literal definitions: (1) a portion of the daylight hours, (2) all of the daylight portion of a 24-hour day, (3) a 24-hour day, and (4) a long but finite time period. RTB's [Reason To Believe, Ross' organization] model posits that the fourth definition affords the greatest consistency with all the biblical accounts.[18]

Quite a number of today's old earth creationists accept the day-age creation theory, because it allows them to read the Bible literally without having to rebut scientific findings about the age of the planet. Each day could represent eons. This leads to discussion of six geological eons—one for each "day" of creation—which could have been an indeterminate number of years. Advocates typically believe that the universe is 14 or 15 billion years old, and that the earth is millions of years old. Human beings have existed for as long as the earth but did not develop from ape-like creatures; instead they were the result of special creation by God. Noah's flood could have been universal or local, but it is not needed to explain all the geological and fossil evidence.

Interestingly, William Jennings Bryan, a defender of creationism in the Scopes Monkey Trial, was an early fundamentalist who accepted the day-age theory. That was one reason he got into so much trouble during the trial. When Clarence Darrow interrogated Bryan and asked him about geology, Bryan's famous comeback was, "I'm more interested in the Rock of Ages than in the age of rocks." Bryan believed that the earth was very old, and he was an old earth creationist. However, as a true modern politician, he didn't want to admit his beliefs on the stand because most of the people in his audience—who had hired him—were young earth creationists.

Since the 1920s, creationists have maintained efforts to have their views represented on an "equal access" basis in public schools when evolution is taught, but they have consistently come up short because their views have never been considered "science." This leads us to the Intelligent Design Movement.

9

INTELLIGENT DESIGN

". . . the inference we think is inevitable, that the watch must have had a maker --
that there must have existed, at some time and at some place or other, an artificer or
artificers who formed it for the purpose which we find it actually to answer,
who comprehended its construction and designed its use."
William Paley (1743 – 1805)

Intelligent design (ID) holds that the complex characteristics of living things are better explained as having an intelligent origin than as resulting from "mindless" evolution. The fundamental idea originated well before the days of Darwin and has surfaced often over the years. In the fourth century BC, Plato posited a supreme wisdom and intelligence as the creator of the cosmos, and Aristotle developed the idea of a natural creator, or "Prime Mover" of the universe. Years later, in the 1200s, Thomas Aquinas argued that design in nature pointed toward God. In the 1800s, William Paley, whose work Darwin studied while in college, contended that the world is not governed by chance, but rather by design. The idea continues to live, and in its modern incarnation is a controversial issue—perhaps the most controversial issue—in the current debate between religion and science.

Intelligent design has been described as follows in the introduction to *Mere Creation: Science, Faith & Intelligent Design,* a compendium of writings of prominent leaders in the movement:

> What has emerged is a new program for scientific research known as intelligent design. Within biology intelligent design is a theory of biological origins and development. Its fundamental claim is that intelligent causes are necessary to explain the complex, information-rich structures of biology

and that these causes are empirically detectable. To say intelligent causes are empirically detectable is to say there exists
well-defined methods that, on the basis of observational
features of the world, are capable of reliably distinguishing
intelligent causes from undirected natural causes.

The empirical detectability of intelligent causes renders
intelligent design a fully scientific theory and distinguishes
it from the design arguments of philosophers, or what has
traditionally been called natural theology.[1]

Like scientific creationism, intelligent design covers a range of
specific beliefs, and various proponents ascribe different details to
the designer and the design. All go further than scientific creationists, however, in acknowledging the conclusions of modern science. In
fact, many ID proponents feel that critics have unfairly aligned them
with creationism, in the face of their stated differences and the Intelligent Design Movement's efforts to be seen as a scientific endeavor
not based on the Bible or the God of the Bible.

THE MOVEMENT

The modern Intelligent Design Movement has an interesting and
controversial history, which has led some detractors to suggest that it
is simply a form of gussied up creationism. Its proponents, obviously,
disagree.

Important Court Decisions
Two 1980s court cases were watershed events in the religion vs.
science debate and seem to have fostered the Intelligent Design Movement. The first was *McLean v. Arkansas Board of Education*, a 1982 case
in the U.S. District Court in Arkansas.[2] This case considered the validity
of the *Balanced Treatment Act of Arkansas*, a law passed in response to the
U.S. Supreme Court's 1968 decision invalidating an Arkansas law that
had prohibited teaching of evolution in public schools, as discussed
in Chapter 8. The act required public school instruction to balance
the teaching of what, in essence, was young earth creationism and the
teaching of evolution science. The suit was filed, not by proponents of

evolution, but by a coalition that included Christian and Jewish church leaders who were concerned about damage that insistence on the teaching of creationism would do to the credibility of their religions.

The court found that although the *Balanced Treatment Act* did not mention the Bible, the creation science it contemplated was clearly inspired by the book of Genesis and was consistent with a literal interpretation of Genesis, leaving no doubt that a major effect of the act was the advancement of particular religious beliefs. The District Court stated in its opinion that "…Section 4(a) lacks legitimate educational value because 'creation-science' as defined in that section is simply not science."[3] It concluded that since creation science had no scientific merit, the primary purpose of the act was to advance religion, impermissible under the U.S. Constitution. The court supported a permanent injunction preventing the implementation of the law.

Five years later, in June 1987, the US Supreme Court decided the *Edwards v. Aguillard*[4] case concerning Louisiana's *Creationism Act*, a law that prohibited the teaching of the theory of evolution in public schools unless creation science was also taught. No school was required to teach either evolution or creation science, but if either was taught, the other subject was required. The Court of Appeals had held that the act violated the United States Constitution because it was a law furthering a particular religious belief. The U. S. Supreme Court confirmed the lower court, finding that the law impermissibly endorsed religion by advancing the religious belief that a supernatural being created humankind—a belief that the term "creation science," as contemplated by the state legislature, embraced. The court concluded that the act's primary purpose was to provide pervasive advantage to a particular religious doctrine that rejects the factual basis of evolution, and it therefore violated the First Amendment to the Constitution.

The Response

Thus, the U. S. Supreme Court effectively prevented the teaching of creationism—even when balanced with the teaching of evolution—in public school classrooms. What happened next has been the subject of considerable controversy, but many believe that creationists attempted to circumvent the Court's restrictions by simply repackaging creationism and advancing it without reference to the book of Genesis or to Christian tenets. Whatever the motivation, the result came to be called "intelligent design."

There is not now, nor has there ever been, complete uniformity of thought or action among all proponents of intelligent design. The core of the movement was nominally launched in 1991 when Phillip E. Johnson, a law professor at the University of California at Berkeley and a self-described Christian creationist often called the father of the Intelligent Design Movement, wrote *Darwin on Trial*. The book attempted to demonstrate that evolution by natural selection did not occur, but it did not push any scientific argument for design. In 1997 Johnson wrote *Defeating Darwinism by Opening Minds*, a book aimed primarily to an audience of scientific creationists. This work outlined principles to be used in debate with proponents of evolution and discussed the emerging intelligent design theory that Johnson and others were advocating.

The Intelligent Design Movement began to take its present shape and course in 1996 with the formation of the Discovery Institute's Center for the Renewal of Science and Culture, now known as the Center for Science and Culture. The Discovery Institute was founded in 1990 as a non-profit educational foundation and think tank. Its mission is "to make a positive vision of the future practical," but its practices in support of intelligent design and against scientific materialism have made it quite controversial. The organization has lobbied aggressively for wider acceptance of intelligent design and against evolution, which it seeks to portray as a "theory in crisis." Although it often describes itself as a secular organization, critics and others consider the Discovery Institute to be an explicitly conservative Christian organization that sees Christianity and evolution as mutually exclusive and promotes a specific Christian agenda. Its most ardent critics argue that the Institute intentionally misrepresents or omits many important facts in promoting its agenda, and uses rhetoric, intentional ambiguity, and misrepresented evidence to lead an unwary public to reach the conclusions it wants them to reach.

A key controversy surrounding ID is the question of whether it is, in fact, "science." Its proponents argue, as cited earlier, that intelligent design is "a fully scientific theory" and is to be distinguished from "the design arguments of philosophers, or what has traditionally been called natural theology."[5] However, many scientists see intelligent design as a fringe activity with little credibility within their mainstream community, arguing that it fails fundamentally to qualify as a scientific theory. A scientific theory, they argue, provides a framework for making sense of experimental observations and a mechanism for looking forward to suggest other inquiries and predict other findings. They believe ID falls so profoundly short in this regard that it is a scientific dead end. The controversy was tested from a legal perspective in the 2005 case of *Tammy Kitzmiller, et al. v. Dover Area School District, et al.*[6]

Kitzmiller v. Dover

The Dover Board of Education, to the dismay of many leaders of the ID movement, had added the following statement to the school's curriculum: "Students will be made aware of gaps/problems in Darwin's Theory of Evolution and of other theories of evolution, including but not limited to intelligent design. Note: Origins of life is not taught."[7] The Board required a statement to be read to every ninth-grade student that included references to evolution being a theory containing numerous gaps, and to intelligent design as an explanation of the origin of life that differs from Darwin's view. The statement also advised students that the book, *Of Pandas and People*, a decidedly creationist work, was available as a reference if they wanted an understanding of intelligent design. The Board, in effect, required the presentation of intelligent design as an alternative to evolution—not unlike the state of Arkansas had tried to do with creationism in the 1980s.

Several parents, represented by the American Civil Liberties Union and other organizations, sued the school district to stop implementation of the policy. The U. S. District Court ruled that the Board's mandate was unconstitutional and barred intelligent design from being taught in the district's science classrooms. In its decision, the court concluded that overwhelming evidence had established that intelligent design is a religious view and a re-labeling of creationism rather than a scientific theory. It characterized intelligent design as follows:

> After a searching review of the record and applicable case law, we find that while ID arguments may be true, a proposition on which the Court takes no position, ID is not science. We find that ID fails on three different

levels, any one of which is sufficient to preclude a determination that ID is science. They are: (1) ID violates the
centuries-old ground rules of science by invoking and
permitting supernatural causation; (2) the argument of irreducible complexity, central to ID, employs the same flawed
and illogical contrived dualism that doomed creation science
in the 1980's; and (3) ID's negative attacks on evolution have
been refuted by the scientific community. As we will discuss
in more detail below, it is additionally important to note that
ID has failed to gain acceptance in the scientific community,
it has not generated peer-reviewed publications, nor has it
been the subject of testing and research.[8]

The school board members who had voted for the intelligent
design requirement were all defeated in the next election, and the decision was not appealed. Not surprisingly, however, the case has spurred
its share of dissenters. Some argue that the decision was overly broad,
the act of "an activist judge" who intruded into inappropriate territory
or had factually incorrect findings. They maintain that the court made
several significant errors. First, it assumed the actions of the Dover
School Board were the actions of the Intelligent Design Movement,
when in fact they were contrary to the recommendations of some
leading proponents of intelligent design. Second, the court inappropriately equated ID with creationism, when in fact it was formulated as
something distinct from the creationism that had previously been held
unconstitutional. And third, the court ignored or distorted scientific
testimony and inappropriately ruled that ID was not science. From a
broader perspective, many who disagree with the decision believe that
religion was not treated in a neutral way and that the court applied
different standards to advocates of intelligent design than to advocates
of Darwinian evolution.

The key issue, of course, is whether ID is science or religion.
Dr. Kenneth Miller, a professor of biology at Brown University color-
fully summarized the difference between them in his cross-examination
as a plaintiff's expert witness. Responding to a question concerning the
importance of scientific rules, he stated:

A. These rules are important because if you don't have these rules, you don't have science. The entire—human beings are fallible, and I mentioned that science is a human activity. It's a systematic search for natural explanations for natural phenomena. And if you invoke a non-natural cause, a spirit force or something like that in your research and I decide to test it, I have no way to test it. I can't order that from a biological supply house, I can't grow it in my laboratory. And that means that your explanations in that respect, even if they were correct, were not something I could test or replicate, and therefore they really wouldn't be part of science.

Q. So supernatural causation is not considered part of science?

A. Yeah. I hesitate to beg the patience of the Court with this, but being a Boston Red Sox fan, I can't resist it. One might say, for example, that the reason the Boston Red Sox were able to come back from three games down against the New York Yankees was because God was tired of George Steinbrenner and wanted to see the Red Sox win. In my part of the country, you'd be surprised how many people think that's a perfectly reasonable explanation for what happened last year. And you know what, it might be true, but it certainly is not science, it's not scientific, and it's certainly not something we can test. So, yes, those rules certainly apply.[9]

Thus, the court did not hold that intelligent design is incorrect or wrong. It said only that intelligent design is not science and recognized that reasonable people can continue to believe, on the basis of revelation and faith, that there is a Designer who designed our universe.

Many Christians who generally support the basic concepts of intelligent design concede that the Intelligent Design Movement has not always made a convincing case that its theories and conclusions meet the tests of modern science. Hugh Ross, identified with old earth creationism in Chapter 8, for example, in his book, *Creation as Science*, noted situations when evolutionists have asked for a testable design model and have not received a reply. Further, "Without a model, the ID paradigm cannot be tested or falsified, nor can it generate significant predictions of future scientific discoveries. This lack of substantive testability gives rise to the repeated charge that ID is 'not science.'"[10]

On the other hand, Michael Behe, in his recent book, *The Edge of Evolution: The Search for the Limits of Darwinism*, argues that design is a "completely scientific conclusion" because it "relies heavily and exclusively on detailed physical evidence, plus standard logic."[11]

All of which raises the question of whether it really matters for most of us. While whatever category the issue is placed in—science or religion—is very significant in determining whether it is an appropriate public school subject under our Constitution, how the issue is pigeonholed has nothing to do with whether or not the idea is true. A religious conclusion can be no less true than a scientific one. Thus, our real question does not deal with public school curriculum, but instead is concerned with whether intelligent design is a true and valid concept.

THE CONCEPT

The Intelligent Design Movement coalesces around the central theme that intelligent design is a better explanation of the complexity of living organisms than is Darwinian evolution. A common theme among ID proponents is that they accept evolution but doubt that it can do everything that some evolutionists claim. The movement is not, however, based on a single idea about which all proponents agree. The concept encompasses a range of beliefs about creation and evolution that appear to be evolving over time. While the details differ, all should be distinguished from those of other related concepts—from creationism, discussed in the previous chapter, and from theistic evolution, the belief that God has elected to act through natural laws, including evolution in all its aspects, to be discussed in the following chapter. Specific beliefs vary greatly among those who see design in the universe, but the extremes seem to be set by the writings of two individuals: Hugh Ross and Michael Behe.

Hugh Ross

Hugh Ross and the Reason To Believe organization, introduced earlier as "concordists" and arguably not a part of the Intelligent

Design Movement, seem to characterize the creationist end of the range of beliefs. They advocate a specific biblical perspective, which acknowledges "that a considerable portion of the Bible's creation material contains metaphors and figurative language" but nevertheless holds that "the Bible's creation content is predominantly literal in its descriptions of natural phenomena," and the Bible's creation accounts are "reliably factual in their declarations about the origin, history, chronology, and current state of both the physical universe and life within the universe."[12] Accordingly, they advocate a model of humans emerging less than about 100,000 years ago "from one couple living in one region in the relatively recent past."[13] Since concordists mean "homo sapiens species" when they say "human," their time line concords with the generally accepted scientific time line. Thus, the remaining questions are not when the homo sapiens species arose, but how and where.

Unlike creationists, who object to the big bang theory, those on the creationist end of the range of intelligent design beliefs are overjoyed with the theory. From their perspective, it proves the biblical story of creation and enhances the Christian's case for faith in the biblical creator as the Designer. Ross has written:

> As the empirical support for big bang cosmology mounts and as the model becomes increasingly well understood, signs of a personal, transcendent, loving Creator become increasingly evident. Despite the skepticism of our age, we find the Creator revealed in clear and exciting ways. Many new discoveries are continually enlarging and enhancing the list of features that signal design behind the universe, our solar system, the earth and living things.[14]

However, many theologians conclude that while the Bible certainly does not argue against the big bang theory, it also doesn't contain any element that is parallel to the theory. They argue that Genesis doesn't begin with a bang. It begins with a watery chaos, just like the pre-biblical Babylonian story does, and it is out of the watery chaos that the universe is built.

Michael Behe

Michael J. Behe is perhaps the leading spokesman for the other extreme in the range of ID beliefs. Unlike Ross, who attempts to find agreement between the Bible and science, Behe views intelligent design as a purely scientific endeavor. He wrote in his 1996 book, *Darwin's Black Box*:

> There is an elephant in the roomful of scientists who are trying to explain the development of life. The elephant is labeled "intelligent design." To a person who does not feel obliged to restrict his search to unintelligent causes, the straightforward conclusion is that many biochemical systems were designed. They were designed not by the laws of nature, not by chance and necessity; rather, they were *planned*. The designer knew what the systems would look like when they were completed, then took steps to bring the systems about. Life on earth at its most fundamental level, in its most critical components, is the product of intelligent activity.
>
> The conclusion of intelligent design flows naturally from the data itself—not from sacred books or sectarian beliefs.[15]

Behe's views on the details of evolution have changed somewhat over time. In *Darwin's Black Box*, Behe stated that he had "no reason to doubt that the universe is the billions of years old that physicists say it is" and also found "the idea of common descent (that all organisms share a common ancestor) fairly convincing."[16] He concluded that small-scale, microevolution has in fact occurred, but found no persuasive evidence to support the idea that large changes can be broken down into small steps over great periods of time, or that step-by-step Darwinian processes could explain certain irreducibly complex biochemical structures.

However, Behe's 2007 book, *The Edge of Evolution: The Search for the Limits of Darwinism*, takes matters a step further. He now believes "the evidence for common descent seems compelling" and notes:

> The results of modern DNA sequencing experiments, undreamed of by nineteenth-century scientists like Charles

Darwin, show that some distantly related organisms share apparently arbitrary features of their genes that seem to have no explanation other than that they were inherited from a distant common ancestor. Second, there's also great evidence that random mutation paired with natural selection can modify life in important ways. Third, however, there is strong evidence that random mutation is extremely limited.[17]

Thus, Behe's only real argument with Darwinian evolution is the idea of random mutations. His book, in effect, concedes that a significant portion of the changes in living organisms are random, but argues that the effect of random mutations in higher mammals is limited. Instead, many mutations are non-random, dictated by an intelligent designer. His view as to the origin of human beings is:

The bottom line is this. Common descent is true; yet the explanation of common descent—even the common descent of humans and chimps—although fascinating, is in a profound sense *trivial*. It says merely that commonalities were there from the start, present in a common ancestor. It does not even begin to explain where those commonalities came from, or how humans subsequently acquired remarkable differences. *Something that is nonrandom must account for the common descent of life.*[18]

While his views continue to be criticized by most of the scientific community, they clearly are a long way from the views of creationists such as Henry Morris or concordists such as Hugh Ross. They are much closer to the "two books" views of Galileo, Newton, and the proponents of theistic evolution to be discussed in the following chapter.

THE RATIONALE

Intelligent design proponents support their case with several arguments, all of which have been contested by skeptics who often have suggested that ID is basically the same as creationism except that the

Intelligent Design Movement is more coy about the identification of the designer. The following paragraphs discuss several of the most prominent arguments for ID and some common rebuttals.

The Design Inference

The classic historical case for a design inference in nature comes from William Paley, the eighteenth-century British theologian-naturalist referred to in Chapter 4. Using his now-famous metaphor, Paley argued that if one is walking across a meadow and sees a watch on the ground, he knows it wasn't formed by natural processes and instead can infer that it was designed. The same inference applies to living organisms.

Jonathan Wells, another leader of the ID movement, who holds PhDs from Berkeley and Yale, has described a current view of the design inference as follows:

> It is only when a pattern cannot plausibly be attributed either to chance or to natural regularity that we infer design. Dembski wrote in his 1998 book *The Design Inference*: "Whenever explaining an event, we must choose from three competing modes of explanation. These are *regularity, chance*, and *design* … To attribute an event to design is to say that it cannot reasonably be referred to either regularity or chance." Thus, "these two moves—ruling out regularity, and then ruling out chance—constitute the design inference."[19]

Well's logic for a design inference, which relies on work previously done by William Dembski,[20] is generally as follows: First decide if an event is a regularity—one that occurred by necessary and regular existing physical laws, such as the high probability of getting approximately equal numbers of heads and tails when a fair coin is tossed several times. If the event is not a regularity, then decide if it happened by chance, meaning it is highly improbable and not complex enough to warrant a design inference. For example, picking several letters in sequence from a hat and forming "wdlmnlt dtjbkw irzrezlmqco p" would be by chance—highly improbable, but not complex enough to infer design rather than randomness. However, if the letters form "me thinks it is like a weasel," the event is both highly improbable and complex, and one may infer that it is the result of design.[21]

Howard J. Van Till, a Christian scientist whose views will be discussed in more detail in the following chapter, is not a fan of intelligent design and has a different view. He suggests that the intelligent design conclusion is centered on the claim that a particular organism could not have been created by natural means and must, therefore, have been created by "extra natural" means—which we cannot comprehend. This means that ID in effect honors a "God of the gaps:"

> our present failure to comprehend exactly how some particular species or biotic subsystems came first to be formed is taken to be sufficient evidence that its form was imposed by the action of an intelligent designer. Implicit in this thesis is the expectation that there are gaps in the formational economy of the creation that had to be bridged by acts of intelligent design ....[22]

The design inference logic has also been roundly criticized with claims that the underlying work is riddled with inconsistencies, equivocation, flawed mathematics, poor scholarship, and misrepresentation of others' results. Critics argue that a design inference is subjective, largely in the eyes of the beholder. The difference between a clock and a rock is obvious. The clock was designed. But how does one determine the difference between two chipped rocks—one by natural causes and one by a person? Such decisions are largely a result of our personal experiences and the culture in which we have learned. And finally, some critics argue that design is not a real alternative at all because it raises an even bigger problem than it solves—Who designed the designer?

The Anthropic Principle

A second logic for intelligent design is based on the anthropic principle—generally the idea that the seemingly arbitrary and unrelated constants of physics in our universe are precisely the values that are needed for a universe capable of producing life. Advocates of intelligent design believe that this so-called "fine-tuning" supports a supernatural origin of the universe. Specifically, they believe that for life to exist in our universe, many of the constants of physics—such as the strength of gravity, the strength of the electromagnetic force, the ratio of the masses of protons and electrons, and many others— must be within a very small range of their actual values to support life. For example, the advocates argue that if the strength of gravity were slightly weaker, the universe would have expanded so quickly after the big bang that no planets would have formed. Or if gravity were slightly stronger, the universe would have quickly collapsed on itself. They apply similar reasoning to many other constants. In *Creation as Science,* Hugh Ross states that 322 fine-tuned characteristics of the earth and its cosmic environment were present as of 2004 to indicate intelligent design.[23] He contends that since the ranges of these characteristics are very small, and our very existence shows that they allow life to exist, the probability that our universe arose by chance is so small that we must seek a supernatural origin of the universe.

Skeptics have a different view. One argument is that the universe is not in fact so finely tuned for life as the vast majority is empty space, and most of the little matter that exists, including the other planets in our solar system, is inhospitable to life. A second argument is based on the claim that many universes may exist with many different combinations of physical constants. If there are enough of them, a few would be able to support life solely by chance. And we live in one of those few. This argument seeks to overcome the low probability of having a universe with life in it with a multiplicity of universes.

Skeptics also argue that our universe is not finely tuned for us. Instead, we are finely tuned for it. Life could exist in circumstances very different from ours, but our ignorance misleads us into thinking that a universe must be much like our own to sustain life. Indeed, virtually nothing is known about the possibility of life in other universes. Perhaps most could support life, even if it is of a type that is completely unfamiliar to us. To assert that only universes very like our own could support life goes well beyond anything we know today.

Irreducible Complexity

The last case for intelligent design that we will discuss is "irreducible complexity"—a concept introduced in principle by Darwin himself in *The Origin of Species*: "If it could be demonstrated that any complex organ existed, which could not possibly have been formed by numerous, successive, slight modifications, my theory would absolutely break down. But I can find out no such case."[24]

> Michael Behe has defined irreducibly complex as:
>
> a single system composed of several well-matched, interacting parts that contribute to the basic function, wherein the removal of any one of the parts causes the system to effectively cease functioning. An irreducibly complex system cannot be produced directly (that is, by continuously improving the initial function, which continues to work by the same mechanism) by slight, successive modifications of a precursor system, because any precursor to an irreducibly complex system that is missing a part is by definition nonfunctional. [25]

Behe uses a simple household mousetrap to illustrate the meaning of irreducible complexity. He notes that a mousetrap consists of a flat wooden base, a metal hammer to crush the little critter, a spring to provide the power, a sensitive trigger that releases when pressure is applied, and a metal bar that connects to the catch and holds the hammer back when the trap is set. He contends that this system is "irreducibly complex" because if even one part is missing, one cannot catch a mouse. If the wooden base were gone, there would be no platform for attaching the other components. If the hammer were gone, the mouse could not become pinned to the wooden base. If there were no spring, the hammer and platform would jangle loosely, and again the rodent would be free to do its dastardly deeds. Each part must be present, and each must perform its function. There is no way the trap could be developed gradually because it won't work at all until all the parts are present and functioning. One concludes that all the mousetrap parts, arranged correctly as they are, performing their function, couldn't just happen by chance.

Behe reaches the same conclusion as to organisms like the eye, the human blood clotting process, or the bacterial flagellum—which is the long, slender projection from a cell body that may function in a whip-like motion to propel the organism through surrounding liquid. Simply stated, the argument goes, how could organs that are this complicated come about by chance or natural processes? The eyeball, for example, is so complex that no Darwinian mechanism could possibly have caused it to come into existence. There has not been enough time in the history of the universe for it to have happened by chance. The same goes for many other organisms.

Skeptics accuse ID proponents of using "bait and switch" logic. They claim the proponents first propose an irreducibly complex organism, then science shows it isn't irreducibly complex after all, so proponents redefine "irreducible complexity," thereby confusing the unknown with the unknowable. Scientists suggest that the three examples—human blood-clotting mechanisms, the eye, and the bacterial flagellum— which proponents have used to support irreducible complexity now appear likely to have been assembled by a step-by-step evolutionary process. The human eye, for example is not so complex that total blindness would result if any part were removed. Many people are visually impaired by disease or injury and lose much of their vision, yet can detect light and use their restricted visual capacity.

THEOLOGY

The success of the Intelligent Design Movement is predicated on ID being science and not theology, and many in the movement bend over backwards to avoid identification with any particular interpretation of the Bible. Further, intelligent design per se cannot be said to identify any particular deity with characteristics that one would match with the Christian God.

However, theological inference seems ultimately to be necessary. All the ID proponents might be described as theologians of various levels of competence, and concluding that the universe is designed certainly seems to imply that there might be a designer to which the design could be attributed. In fact, opponents often suggest that advocates of ID have been less than straightforward at times about their religious agenda in order to enhance their chance of getting their ideas into public science education, though, in fact, their religious beliefs are central to ID. And certainly the older "intelligent design" advocates, including Paley, Newton, and others, were not hesitant to envelop their beliefs in a natural theology.

Aside from the scientific arguments and the question as to whether the Intelligent Design Movement endorses a theology at all, some have made the case that ID simply has no theological merit. John F. Haught, retired Chair of the Theology Department at Georgetown University testified in the *Kitzmiller v. Dover* case that intelligent design is appalling theology:

> Well, I think most people will instinctively identify the intelligent designer with the God of theism, but all the theologians that I consider great—people like Karl Barth, Paul Tillich, Langdon Gilkey, Karl Rahner—would see that what's going on in the intelligent design proposal, from a theological point of view, is the attempt to bring the ultimate and the infinite down in a belittling way into the continuum of natural causes as one finite cause among others. And any time, from a theological point of view, you try to have the infinite become squeezed into the category of the finite, that's known as idolatry. So it's religiously, as well as theologically, offensive to what I consider the best theologians…of the 20th century.[26]

Thus, intelligent design has been controversial at best. The judicial system has routinely held that creationism or intelligent design are not to be taught as science in public schools because they are religion and not science, and teaching religion as science violates the United States constitution. The scientific community is generally skeptical as an overwhelming majority of credible scientists believe that intelligent design, like creationism, has no scientific merit. Many theologians see no merit in either set of beliefs. So how are issues of the relationship between the Bible and science to be resolved? Some believe there is simply no conflict between the two. We turn now to the view that there is no gap to bridge, or conflict to reconcile, because the Bible is not a scientific book.

10

TWO BOOKS

"The heavens declare the glory of God; the skies proclaim the work of his hands."
Psalm 19:1

In the last three chapters we have reviewed various beliefs about the Christianity/science conflict. At one extreme, atheism and its undecided sibling, agnosticism, maintain that while science may not have all the answers, it has all the answers that are. At the other extreme, creationism in its various forms supports a literal interpretation—more or less—of the Bible and argues that scripture prevails over science, at least in those areas where science doesn't have a clear and obvious answer. Between the two extremes a number of accommodations have been made. Ultimately these beliefs present either/or conflicts, where one must choose between the two. Each side believes it is the winner, and the other is the loser.

However, there is another way—a way that sees no conflict, no winner or loser, and perhaps two winners. This way calls to mind the "Two Books of God," a metaphor articulated by Francis Bacon in 1605: "Let no one think or maintain that a man can search too far or be too well studied in the book of God's Word or in the book of God's Works, divinity or philosophy….[We should] not unwisely mingle or confound these learnings together."[1]

There is no conflict if we avoid unwisely mingling or confounding the Bible and science. We will consider two different, though somewhat similar, approaches that avoid the conflict as we explore another way in this matter. The first approach, a concept of Non-overlapping Magisteria, suggests that science and religion are such different worlds that they cannot conflict. The second, theistic evolution, recognizes a God and creator who works through evolution. We will discuss three views of theistic evolution referred to by their principle proponents as "fully gifted creation," "bio-logos," and a "noninterventionist understanding of special providence." The remainder of this chapter is largely a summary of these concepts along with a few explanatory or critical comments.

A warning is in order as we begin this discussion. Some might see such ways of avoiding conflict as a cop-out, finding a middle ground or compromise simply to foster peace. While the give and take of compromise often works in resolving conflicts that involve division of resources and interests, this approach doesn't work in matters of truth. Matters of truth stand on their own. Any attempt to reconcile Christianity and science needs to do so as well. Attempts at reconciliation should not build up their own cause by tearing down other beliefs, attempt to synthesize or meld positions when the aim is to be politically correct or more broadly acceptable, or compromise the intellectual integrity of those involved. They should, instead, search for the truth and let the chips fall as they will. We have no reason to believe that the proponents of the positions discussed below have any other standard, and we encourage readers to use this standard to assess the positions.

NON-OVERLAPPING MAGISTERIA

The late Stephen Gould, a self-described agnostic who grew up in the Jewish tradition, was the Alexander Agassiz Professor of Zoology and Professor of Geology at Harvard. He also was the author of *Rocks of Ages*, the thesis of which is that science and religion are not in conflict and cannot be synthesized into any common theme because they are entirely different. Science addresses the factual character of the natural world, while religion addresses the totally different realm of human purposes, meanings, and values. Just as a horse and a house are different—they do not conflict and cannot be combined—religion and science are different and should respect, but not interfere with, one another. Reconciling perceived differences between the two is not a matter of "either/or," where one must be selected over the other, or of imposing an unsatisfying compromise. There is, instead, opportunity for a "golden mean" that provides integrity and dignity to each.

Gould captured his thesis of difference and non-interference by enunciating the Principle of NOMA, or Non-Overlapping Magisteria, which he describes as follows:

> A magisterium ... is a domain where one form of teaching
> holds the appropriate tools for meaningful discourse and
> resolution.

> To summarize, ... the net, or magisterium, of science covers
> the empirical realm: what is the universe made of (fact) and
> why does it work this way (theory). The magisterium of religion
> extends over questions of ultimate meaning and moral value.
> These two magisteria do not overlap, nor do they encompass
> all inquiry (consider, for example, the magisterium of art and
> the meaning of beauty). To cite the old clichés, science gets
> the age of rocks, and religion the rock of ages; science studies
> how the heavens go, religion how to go to heaven.[2]

Gould claims equal status for the two magisteria, noting that even with all their power and wonder, science and its offspring, technology, "can hardly cast a flicker of light upon the oldest and simplest ethical questions that have haunted people since the dawn of consciousness."[3] He also concludes that science cannot contradict scripture, and vice versa. Therefore, if a validated scientific conclusion seems to contradict a conventional reading of scripture, we need to re-examine our interpretation of scripture as "The natural world does not lie, but words can convey many meanings, some allegorical or metaphorical."[4]

The concept of Non-Overlapping Magisteria has very practical implications. It challenges many creationist views, such as the young earth creationists' belief that the earth can only be about ten thousand years old because that's the way they interpret the book of Genesis. Such belief violates NOMA because it tries to impose a particular reading of a biblical text upon a factual issue that is within the magisterium of science, and science has concluded beyond reasonable doubt that the earth is several billion years old. Considering the other side of the coin, a scientist who makes an important and socially relevant invention violates NOMA if he thinks his technical expertise allows him to determine the invention's social or moral implications, which fall within the realm of religion. In summary, NOMA respects the significant differences in logic between science and religion, and urges each to mind its own business, do its best in its own realm, and talk to the other in mutual respect.

The NOMA principle has a number of important defenders. Darwin and Huxley, agnostics like Gould, believed in the principles of non-interference, as have a number of scientists throughout history who also were ordained and devoted clergymen. Gould noted that, notwithstanding an apparently contrary practice during the days of Galileo, the Catholic Church has endorsed positions quite consistent with NOMA from the time of Pope Pius XII in 1950, through Pope John Paul II, to the present time.

But NOMA has also been criticized by both believers and non-believers. Gould notes that the creationist movement, in particular young-earth creationists who believe the Bible is literally factual, disagree. Along with many in the Intelligent Design Movement, they do not separate religion and science. They sometimes find conflict, yet at other times find harmony between much of the Bible and science. They see biblical faith as fact-based, with the words of the Bible describing many aspects of nature. Gould believed they make claims on the basis of religion that, in his view, are clearly within the sole realm of science.

The work of Francis Collins, a proponent of a form of theistic evolution, will be discussed in the following section. While using Gould's work to argue that Richard Dawkins' atheism goes beyond the available evidence, Collins also argues that Gould's principle is potentially unsatisfying. He says it fosters internal conflict and "deprives people of the chance to embrace either science or spirit in a fully realized way."[5]

From an atheistic perspective, Dawkins writes in *The God Delusion* that Gould could not have meant much of what he wrote, and that he no doubt was bending over backwards to be nice to his opponents. Dawkins simply denies that theologians have anything worthwhile to say about much of anything. He further argues that religion and science cannot really be separated, as "The presence or absence of a creative super-intelligence is unequivocally a scientific question, even if it is not in practice—or not yet—a decided one. So also is the truth or falsehood of every one of the miracle stories that religions rely upon to impress multitudes of the faithful."[6]

Unfortunately, Gould died in 2002 and is not around to further defend his position. But his ideas remain influential in the continuing debate.

THEISTIC EVOLUTION

While Gould sought to separate religion and science, proponents of theistic evolution see a need to integrate the two. Keith Miller noted in his preface to *Perspectives on an Evolving Creation*:

> Although science and theology clearly occupy different realms of experience and thought, they do touch and impact one another. Both conflict and independence approaches to science and theology are doomed to failure, because in neither case is a real dialogue established. What is needed are efforts to achieve an integrated Christian worldview which takes seriously both scriptural revelation and the testimony of the created universe.[7]

"Theistic evolution" is the term describing those who hold this integrated worldview and who believe that an all-powerful God is both the source of the universe and the creator of biological complexity, providing the world with rich potentials built into nature from the beginning. Theistic evolution accepts the old age of the earth and the theory of evolution as the mechanism for the development of life on earth, including human beings, from a single common ancestor. Proponents of theistic evolution detect purposefulness through revelation, but agree neither purposefulness nor lack thereof can be proved through science.

As might be expected, the details vary. Some theistic evolutionists believe the origin of life is impossible without a direct act of God. Others take the term to mean that God directly guided the process of evolution, while still others assume God created the universe in such a way that life would eventually result without His further intervention. The views of three individuals, representing a range of beliefs, are discussed below.

Howard Van Till

One of the more prominent advocates of a form of theistic evolution is Howard Van Till, a retired physicist with a Calvinist Christian background who taught at Calvin College and wrote *The Fourth Day*. Van Till dislikes the phrase "theistic evolution," which seems to emphasize evolution rather than theism. He prefers "evolutionary creationism," which makes God's status as creator clear while leaving open the secondary issues of the manner and timing of that creation. He refers to his particular views, briefly discussed below, as "the fully gifted creation perspective."

Like Gould, Van Till rejects "either/or" approaches to religion and science matters, and holds that theology and the natural sciences focus on different aspects of reality. He believes we must carefully distinguish two categories of questions about the natural world. The first category concerns "internal affairs." This is a view through the lens of natural science that reveals information about the world's properties, behavior, and history, and is properly the subject of empirical investigation—and science. The second category involves "external relationships" such as the relationship of the Cosmos to God, wherein Christians can look to the Bible for answers. Within this context, God created the universe and endowed it with the miracle of self-organizing capabilities, obviating the need for a God of the gaps view of creationism and intelligent design on a seemingly ad hoc basis.

Van Till draws a clear distinction between the doctrine of creation and the various pictures of how creation was carried out. His view is that God, as the creator, fully gifted his creatures at the beginning with "creaturely capacities" that enable them to play out His will for creation without further miraculous input. Thus, he believes in God and in creation but believes that evolution is how creation came to be. He poses the issue as follows:

> How can we best describe the character of divine creative action? By reference to occasional interventions in which a new form is imposed on raw materials that are incapable of attaining that form with their own capabilities? Or by reference to God's giving being to a creation fully equipped with the creaturely capabilities to organize and/or transform itself into a diversity of physical structures and life-forms?[8]

Van Till goes for his latter reference as the answer. He suggests that the scientific evidence indicates few if any gaps in the creaturely capabilities of the universe, and God does not have to intervene time and again in order to get his creation right. Further, we should not view natural processes, acting under God's sovereign will, as inferior to interventionist miracles. These processes include biological evolution, which he views as highly credible and quite consistent with the Christian doctrine of creation. Van Till rejects all forms of special creationism (including intelligent design), but he concludes that creation's "formational economy" is capable of organizing and transforming itself "from elementary forms of matter into the full array of physical structures and life-forms that have existed in the course of time."[9]

Importantly, Van Till acknowledges that there will continue to be tension between conclusions of science and religious belief. Since we are not omniscient, and our knowledge of both God and science is incomplete and subject to error, there will always be questions with no easy answer. And there is no simple rule to guide us. He maintains that when tension appears, each set of beliefs should be used in the assessment of the other. In all likelihood we will be more confident in one belief—albeit science or religion—than the other. The more confidently held belief should be retained, and the other re-evaluated. If this approach requires a reassessment of old beliefs about the meaning of scripture, we need to demonstrate the intellectual honesty to make such a reassessment.

Francis Collins

Francis Collins presents a slightly different take on theistic evolution. He grew up in an environment where faith was not important, gravitated to agnosticism, and then to atheism. After Collins became a physician, his work with sick and dying patients led him to observe their often unbelievably strong faith, to question his own atheism, and ultimately to believe in God. One of the country's leading geneticists and the longtime head of the Human Genome Project, he is a vocal defender of faith in the presumed conflict with science.

Collins accepts that there is no proof of God, but has concluded that the best evidence available points to a good and holy God who cares about human beings. The presence of a Moral Law is, in his view, the best evidence of God. As additional evidence of an intelligent creator, he cites the fact that the universe had a beginning, that it obeys orderly laws, and that a remarkable series of "coincidences" allow nature to support life.

Collins endorses a form of theistic evolution he refers to as "BioLogos." He describes the concept as follows:

1. The universe came into being out of nothingness, approximately 14 billion years ago.

2. Despite massive improbabilities, the properties of the universe appear to have been precisely tuned for life.

3. While the precise mechanism of the origin of life on earth remains unknown, once life arose, the process of evolution and natural selection permitted the development of biological diversity and complexity over very long periods of time.

4. Once evolution got under way, no special supernatural intervention was required.

5. Humans are part of this process, sharing a common ancestor with the great apes.

6. But humans are also unique in ways that defy evolutionary explanation and point to our spiritual nature. This includes the existence of the Moral law (the knowledge of right and wrong) and the search for God that characterizes all human cultures through history.[10]

In summary, Collins sees God as creating the universe and establishing natural laws that govern it. To accomplish this, God used evolution to create all living things and give rise to humans, who have intelligence, free will, knowledge of right and wrong, and a desire to seek fellowship with God.

Robert John Russell

Dr. Robert John Russell is the Ian G. Barbour Professor of Theology and Science in Residence at the Graduate Theological

Union and the founder and director of The Center for Theology and the Natural Sciences in Berkeley, California. Russell's paper, "Special Providence and Genetic Mutation: A New Defense of Theistic Evolution,"[11] and chapters four through six of his book, *Cosmology from Alpha to Omega: Towards the Creative Mutual Interaction between Theology and Science*[12] discuss his "noninterventionist understanding of special providence." He pushes the case for divine action further than many who advocate theistic evolution, arguing that nature is an open system that is naturally subject to objective acts of God. He expresses his hypothesis in five steps, briefly summarized as follows:

- God is the creator and absolute source and sustainer of the universe—the continuing actor who, together with nature, brings about the biological evolution of life on earth.
- God not only creates but also guides and directs the evolution of life toward the fulfilling of God's overall purposes.
- God provides evolution as a whole with an overall goal and purpose, and he takes special actions with specific consequences—actions that are recognized through faith.
- God's special actions do not violate, but are within, the laws of nature he made.
- The effects of God's actions occur directly at the level of genetic variation and therefore indirectly affect the course of evolution.

In support of his thesis, Russell argues that a central teaching of the Bible, from the call of Abraham through the life of Jesus, is that God makes new things happen. Further, quantum physics—a physical science that deals with the behavior of matter and energy at the atomic and subatomic level and accurately predicts the physical behavior of systems—can be interpreted philosophically to imply that there are some events in nature for which there is no sufficient efficient natural cause. Given this interpretation, quantum physics can be further interpreted theologically as making non-interventionist, objective divine action possible. Thus, we can say theologically that general divine action that creates and sustains the world, as well as special divine action that can indirectly result in special events in the world, can occur within the laws of nature. In this regard, quantum processes created by God contribute significantly to the genetic mutations that are central to the evolutionary process. While these processes may appear to involve random chance, God can know the future consequences of His present actions without violating the laws of nature. Russell summarizes his case for theistic evolution as follows:

> Unlike atheists, who point to "blind chance" in evolution as undercutting Christian theology, and fundamentalists who agree with them and attempt to replace evolution with a pseudoscience, evolution is precisely what Christians can celebrate as the result of God's creating and providential action in the world. The blind chance science uncovers is the hidden action of the living God who creates life.[13]

It is important to distinguish Russell's views from those of the ID Movement, which aims to include an intelligent designer as an explanation of the evolution of life. Many believe this inappropriately introduces God into the scientific method. On the other hand, Russell accepts current views of macroevolution, commonly referred to as "neo-Darwinism," as the best current theory for explaining the evolution of life, and offers a theological interpretation under which God acts in nature without breaking the laws of nature. Thus, it can be said that the Intelligent Design Movement aims to be a scientific movement but in fact introduces God as an explanatory factor, while Russell's approach is a specific theology that is separate from but aims to be consistent with science, including all aspects of evolution.

SUMMARY

While these forms of theistic evolution have something in common with each of the responses to science discussed in previous chapters—from atheism to creationism—they also are significantly different. For example:

- Theistic evolution differs from atheism and agnosticism as it includes a positive belief in God, and they don't.
- Theistic evolution differs from creationism because it includes a positive belief in evolution, and creationism doesn't.

- Theistic evolution also differs from intelligent design. The Intelligent Design Movement claims to be a scientific, not a theological, concept, while theistic evolution seeks to meld or reconcile the two. Intelligent design adopts many evolutionary concepts but says evolution isn't enough and an Intelligent Designer must have provided certain necessary components during the process—components neither random nor subject to chance. Theistic evolution presumes that once evolution got under way, no supernatural intervention was required. Or, in the case of Robert John Russell, that any such intervention is consistent with nature. Further, theistic evolutionists maintain that the intelligent design claim of a scientific basis does not measure up. ID fails to predict other findings or to suggest other experimentations. More specifically, ID doesn't explain how supernatural interventions give rise to irreducible complexity—a critical component in the ID logic. Many of its examples of irreducible complexity are disappearing in the face of scientific advances.
- Theistic evolution differs from Non-Overlapping Magisteria because it is a synthesis of religion and science rather than a separation of the two. Collins, for example, sees evolution and religion attempting to inhabit the same domain, unlike the NOMA position. He says that if the claims of young earth creationists were true, they would lead to a total collapse of physics, chemistry, cosmology, geology, and biology. In defending science against new earth creationists, theistic evolution proponents would attempt to prove creationists wrong, while proponents of NOMA would say they are in a different magisterium so it doesn't matter.

Those who accept theistic evolution do not interpret the biblical creation account literally. Instead, they believe it is a revelatory story that is symbolic rather than historical or scientific. Forms of theistic evolution are accepted, or at least not rejected, by many prominent theologians, mainline Protestant churches, and the Roman Catholic Church. Paul Tillich noted that "There is no conflict between faith in its true nature and reason in its true nature." Karl Barth wrote that the biblical idea of the creation "...is intended for a solemn marking of the distance between the cosmos and the creator, and precisely not for a metaphysical explanation of the World." Dietrich Bonhoeffer stated, "Then God said 'Let us make man in our image, after our likeness'. This has nothing at all to do with Darwinism. We certainly have no wish to deny our connection with the animal world; rather it is just the opposite."[14] And C. S. Lewis wrote:

> For long centuries God perfected the animal form which was to become the vehicle of humanity and the image of Himself. He gave it hands whose thumb could be applied to each of the fingers, and jaws and teeth and throat capable of articulation, and a brain sufficiently complex to execute all the material motions whereby rational thought is incarnated. The creature may have existed for ages in this state before it became man; it may even have been clever enough to make things which a modern archaeologist would accept as proof of its humanity. But it was only an animal because all its physical and psychical processes were directed to purely material and natural ends. Then, in the fullness of time, God caused to descend upon this organism, both on its psychology and physiology, a new kind of consciousness which could say 'I' and 'me', which could look upon itself as an object, which knew God ....[15]

A majority of Protestant denominations in the United States today either explicitly or implicitly allow for acceptance of both faith and evolution. For example, the United Methodist Church takes no position on evolution or intelligent design but asserts "...that science is a legitimate interpretation of God's natural world," and affirms "... the validity of the claims of science in describing the natural world, although we preclude science from making authoritative claims about theological issues."[16] And the Presbyterian Church holds that "...the true relation between the evolutionary theory and the Bible is that of non-contradiction..."[17]

The Catholic Church has taken the position that faith and scientific findings regarding the evolution of man's material body are not in conflict, that the existence of God is required to explain the spiritual component of man's origins, and that evolution is more than a hypothesis. Recent statements by Pope Benedict and others, however, have raised questions in some minds as to whether a retreat from the Church's traditional teaching that evolution and Catholic dogma are not in conflict could be on the horizon.

On the other hand, many conservative Protestants reject all forms of macroevolution, theistic or otherwise, and some see its advocates as doing nothing more than foolishly capitulating to or compromising with atheistic Darwinism. As a general rule, proponents of the Intelligent Design Movement have problems with theistic evolution. Many see a logical disconnect between a scientific view of a random, undirected, and purposeless world, and a God who could direct the process. This view is summarized in the introduction to *Mere Creation: Science, Faith & Intelligent Design*:

> Theistic evolution places theism and evolution in an odd tension. If God purposely created life through Darwinian means, then God's purpose was to make it seem as though life was created without purpose. Within theistic evolution, God is a master of stealth who constantly eludes our best efforts to detect him empirically. The theistic evolutionist believes that the universe is designed. Yet insofar as there is design in the universe, it is design we recognized strictly through the eyes of faith. Accordingly, the natural world in itself provides no evidence that life is designed. For all we can tell through our natural intellect, our appearance on planet Earth is an accident.[18]

After Howard Van Till published *The Fourth Day*, the Calvin College Board of Trustees received many requests that his beliefs be examined for consistency with Calvinist creeds. An investigative committee spent approximately four years probing Van Till's commitment. While he was officially vindicated, a small but vocal group, whose worldview did not include many scientific discoveries, strenuously objected.

Not surprisingly, most atheists criticize theistic evolution because it includes a belief in a supernatural creator without empirical evidence of one's existence. They claim such a belief violates the scientific method and the falsifiability requirements of scientific philosophy. Such criticism seems reasonable if a theistic evolution proponent is trying to portray his view as a scientific theory rather than a personal religious belief. However, if the proponent's argument is based on personal religious belief, a scientific response seems inappropriate. Science doesn't deal with the question of the existence of a creator, and argues neither for nor against it. Others argue that some forms of theistic evolution are simply a belief in a God of the gaps, where anything that cannot currently be explained by science is attributed to God.

As we stated in our Introduction, your authors accept the scientific view of evolution and also believe in God. We see no conflict between the Bible and science. We are, therefore, most comfortable somewhere within the theistic evolution camp of believers, although we prefer to avoid nomenclature with the emotional or theological baggage often attached to "theistic evolution." In Part II of this work, we will discuss our views on how to read the Bible and make judgments about science, and how those views moved us to our belief.

PART II

Reconciling the Books

We have seen a bewildering array of religious responses to the conclusions of science. Most of them seem to pit the two books of God (the Bible and Nature) against one another and to place the Bible in irreconcilable conflict with science. It's now time to make the case that there is no conflict. In doing so, we are reminded of an old story about a beloved country preacher. One Sunday morning, he preached a real stem-winder on the ills of hard drink. At the end of the service, he took his usual place at the door, greeting congregants as they left the church. A large man with a big red nose and potbelly approached him and said, "Reverend, you weren't so good today. You quit preaching and went to meddling."

We now will quit preaching and start meddling. In Part I, we provided a brief historical perspective and a summary of the current controversy with the aim of being factual and objective. Where matters were disputed, we said so and presented the conflicting viewpoints. In Part II we aim to make the case that there is no conflict between science and the Bible when it is properly interpreted.

Chapters 11 and 12 address some important principles of biblical interpretation, considering the cultural context in which the Hebrew Bible was written and the linguistic/literary relationships within the text. Chapters 13 and 14 apply these interpretive concepts to the specific scripture (introduced in Chapter 1) that so often are the root of the Bible and science conflict. We will not attempt to present a comprehensive interpretation of these passages or even to conclusively demonstrate their meaning. Instead, we hope only to convince you that nothing in them addresses questions of science.

It's easy to say that the Bible and science are different books and that the controversy is not an "either/or" proposition. It's more difficult to decide how we as individuals should deal with this in our lives. But we feel compelled to discuss our personal conclusions. Therefore, Chapter 15 shares our personal beliefs in this matter.

11

BIBLICAL CONTEXT

We can almost see it now. The first copies of the Bible arrived at the big Middle Eastern bookstore today by camel caravan, and the signing party is going full steam. Over in one corner, two well-known clerics are arguing heatedly about the meaning of the Bible.

For as long as people have read the Bible—a very long time—they have disagreed as to its meaning. They have considered it from many perspectives, with many preconceived notions, for many different purposes, with varying degrees of sophistication. They have used different processes for determining its meaning, and they have reached different conclusions. Consider the number of religious traditions to which the Bible has given rise.

How one reads and understands the Bible is a key, we believe the key, to the Christianity/science controversy. Our goal is to read the Bible for what it says and to attempt to understand the beliefs of the writers and how those beliefs apply to us today. Reading the Bible for what it is often does not support tradition and may actually be based on a modernistic reading that varies greatly from what we have understood in the past. Certain traditions hold that sex is the original sin, for example, or that work is punishment for sin, or that cherubs are little babies with wings, or that Satan had a war with God in Heaven before the creation of the world. But the Bible does not support such conclusions.

To separate the traditions from the teachings of the Bible—to read the Bible in a way that conserves its original meaning and to understand the beliefs of the writers—one needs to understand what the Bible is and the culture within which it was written. We introduced these issues in Chapter 1, where we briefly discussed the cultural setting of religious antiquity. We now continue that discussion.

REVELATION

The word "scripture" means writing, and the set of writings called the Bible is considered by most Jews and Christians to be holy and inspired by God. Some say the Bible "was written by God"—a theological affirmation that is not inconsistent with the understanding that the Bible was physically written by a number of human beings over a long period of time. In that sense—that the Bible represents the sum of the ideas and convictions of a group over a period of time relating to questions such as the essential nature of man and how one should live—one might say the Bible is a philosophy. However, it is not philosophy in the later Greek sense that philosophy presents a rational structure based on reason, and it does not involve human reason and logic or the weighing of evidence from the material world.

Instead, Christian theology holds the Bible to be based on divine inspiration and revelation. The Bible claims divine inspiration in a number of passages, such as Moses receiving the Ten Commandments, or Old Testament prophets claiming their message was divine by using the words "Thus says the Lord." This reflects a central theme of Christian theology—that we need to be told what God is like because human attempts to fully understand His nature and purposes always fail. Revelation involves a belief that a supernatural, transcendent God has made His word known, and through His word has revealed Himself. This view holds that the Bible is radically theocentric, with God as its focal point and center of reality. While it doesn't provide a physical picture, the Bible does reveal a theological picture of the nature of God through the eyes of its writers.

Revelation is a complex concept about which theologians have developed several views. These include: seeing revelation as a set of doctrinal statements or propositions that, taken together, create the matrix of Christian theology; God's communication of His personal presence within the believer; God revealed through the personal experience of the believer; and historical events that are seen as acts of God. God is seen as revealing Himself in many ways in addition to scripture, such as through His daily control of the world, man's understanding of right and wrong, visions, miracles, prophets, and more. These things are not seen as mutually exclusive, however, and in fact can be taken together to form a rich view of the breadth and importance of revelation and of man's striving to know God.

Most modern Christians believe the Bible is a form of progressive revelation still in process, in which God has been revealing Himself to His people over the generations. Described this way, revelation provides a reliable yet incomplete description of reality. For example, it's obvious that Abraham did not know everything about God that Moses did, and Moses didn't know everything about God that Jesus did. Our knowledge of God is different than that of people in medieval times, and people in the future will have a different knowledge than we do. That's because of the progressive nature of revelation and the progressive nature of its appreciation in history.

Through it all, people have generally characterized revelation in either of two basic ways that are most relevant to the Christianity and science debate. One view is that we know God from above through His revelation in the Bible. The other view is that God does not reveal Himself from above, and we only know about Him in a naturalistic way from below, based on our experiences and observations. For example, the first chapters of Genesis that describe creation, the origin of human beings, and the fall can be read in different ways. A more conservative person would say that Genesis is God's revelation of man's dependence on God and on the orderliness and goodness of the world. A modernist would read Genesis as a poetic expression of religious convictions—a human expression of our dependence on God and on the orderliness and the goodness of the world.

Perhaps each holds truth, as the two concepts of revelation often have been combined, as described below:

> There is a consensus within Christian theology to the effect that nature (or creation) bears a witness to God its creator. This natural knowledge of God is to be supplemented by revelation, which gives access to information

which is not otherwise available. Yet the idea of revelation implies more than imparting knowledge of God; it carries with it the idea of the *self-disclosure* of God. In speaking about other persons, we might draw a distinction between "knowing about someone" and "knowing someone." The former implies cerebral knowledge, or an accumulation of data about an individual (such as her height, weight, and so on). The latter implies a personal relationship.

In its developed sense, "revelation" does not mean merely the transmission of a body of knowledge, but the personal self-disclosure of God within history.[1]

Thus, both divine and human sources seem necessary to really experience God. The content of the Bible provides the authority as only God can speak for Himself. However, the form of the message and the context in which it is revealed is thoroughly human, grounded in authentic human experience. To experience God to the extent that we can, we need to appreciate that much of the experience is in nature. In the words of Psalm 19: 1-3:

The heavens declare the glory of God;
the skies proclaim the work of his hands.
Day after day they pour forth speech;
night after night they display knowledge.
There is no speech or language
where their voice is not heard.

Notwithstanding the many facets of inspiration, our purpose in this chapter is to shed light on only one—the theological concept of God's revelation through scripture that was written a long time ago in a very different land.

CULTURAL SETTING

Some people seem to view the Bible as just a static piece of holy literature that God himself wrote and dropped out of heaven. Not so simple. As we discussed in Chapter 1, the Bible, sometimes called the Word of

God, is a collection of books written over a period of hundreds of years by dozens of people from different cultures, in different languages, and in different genres. The word "bible" comes from the Greek word *biblia*, which means "the books," not "the book." It is an apt description for the extensive collection of writings that comprise the Bible.

The Bible

The Bible's status is often seen in either of two ways. Some people (usually atheists, naturalists, or humanists) see the Bible as purely human literature and on an equal standing with it—perhaps more than a trashy novel, but not much. Others place the Bible entirely outside of human literature, as if each verse had been written directly by God's finger on a divine computer and e-mailed directly to each individual human being. This characterization frequently leads people to divide the Bible into separate parts that are isolated from each other and from their cultural, historical, and literal context. They may also use their favorite part to support whatever worldview they hold for other reasons.

We need, instead, to view the "Word" as divine revelation as well as writing based on human experience. The Hebrew Bible was written primarily, but not exclusively, by Jews who lived hundreds of years before the Jews who wrote the New Testament. Therefore, unless we subscribe to the idea that God just dropped the Bible out of the heavens, we must conclude that even though the Bible is divine revelation, the form of the message is thoroughly human, the product of human authors who were in turn the product of their age. And in this human communication, vast cultural gaps exist between the writing of the two testaments as well as between the time the New Testament was assembled (several hundred years after the life of Christ) and current times.

The Biblical World

To adequately understand the meaning of the Bible, we need to remember that biblical writers described the world around them as they saw it with their own eyes, rather than in terms of some scientific explanation that we now understand. Each writer had a life and way of thinking that was radically different from ours, and each one was addressing people who were very different from us. All the writers lived in a different geographic area, a different time, and under different political, social, and religious circumstances. The Bible was conditioned by and reflects the culture in which its writers and target audience lived—a largely agrarian, nomadic, oral society that spoke the Hebrew language and worshipped many gods and idols. The Egyptians, Babylonians, and Canaanites endorsed polytheistic paganism and worshipped many gods, mostly of the material world. These gods, including the rivers, seas, mountains, storms, earth, moon, sun, and stars, were considered to be personal and powerful, capable of exerting great influence on the life of each individual. People worshipped and adored them to gain their favor. But Israel was called to be different, to be a people of God who did not worship the gods of the material world.

What an understatement to say that we live in a vastly different world. Think of the differences between the Middle East and the United States today, and multiply that by up to 4,000 years. The gap between biblical times and our current world is a historical, linguistic, and cultural gap of massive proportions, but one that we often forget about as we try to impose our contemporary views on the world in which the Bible was written. It seems that some of us think the apostle Paul would feel comfortable if he were miraculously transported from the first century to the twentieth century, rode his donkey to a contemporary church, walked down the carpeted aisle, sat in a comfortable pew, enjoyed a hundred-strong chorus with an accompanying orchestra, and observed a larger-than-life preacher who appeared to be in several places at once. Paul could not possibly be comfortable in that situation. He would experience a tremendous cultural shock and have a hard time understanding what was going on in a modern church of any ilk. Just as most of us have an equally hard time understanding what went on in his day and before.

From another perspective, imagine a group of Semitic nomads sitting around a small, sputtering campfire somewhere in the Middle East listening to stories, including the ones we now know as the book of Genesis. They are men, women, and children engaged in one of their regular migrations among various seasonal camps throughout the region, or perhaps they are members of a trade caravan moving between cities. Their lives and worlds are ruled by earthly kings and an array of gods they believe to be divine. The people are not hearing the stories read because they haven't been written yet. (Even biblical writings were meant to be shared orally; they are still read aloud in Jewish syna-gogues and most Christian worship services.) But they are sitting there in the dry desert air, with bright stars above, listening carefully to a tribal elder tell a story and absorbing its message. The message is that there is one God, the creator of the cosmos, rather than many gods. The story could not be an attempt to describe in scientific detail how the stars work, or whether the universe is geocentric or heliocentric, or how or in what timeframe God went about creating the universe.

Implications

What do we do with Genesis and other Bible passages now that up to four thousand years have passed since they were first told, and modern science has burst on the scene? Too often we read scripture like a scout manual, a set of assembly instructions, or, God forbid, the IRS code—viewing it as a text answering questions only we could have asked. We disregard time, history, and context as if we were the only people ever to have lived. Instead, we need to remember that biblical authors communicated through their own cultural filters to people in their own or similar cultures who would understand the communica-tion as it was intended. We need to get beyond ourselves, try to return to their world, and try to understand that the Bible is answering ques-tions that people of all times and generations have asked—from those nomads around the campfire to each of us today. Questions about the relationship of God to His creation.

Thus, when interpreting the Bible, we need to look both ways. We need to look back into the biblical world, reconstruct the text's life situation and ideological framework, and understand the intended meaning. And we need to look forward, bridge the gap, and determine how those words play out in our world. Some believe that in bridging this culture and knowledge gap, the Bible reveals modern science. For example, Islam—the Muslim religion that, like Christianity, believes in the God of Abraham as revealed in the Old Testament—maintains that scientific accuracy is strong evidence of the inspired nature of the Koran. More relevant to our discussion, prominent creationist Henry Morris wrote, "it is precisely because Biblical revelation is absolutely authoritative and perspicuous that the scientific facts, rightly inter-preted, will give the same testimony as that of Scripture."[2] Others believe this is a tortured attempt at "Monday morning quarterbacking," and that the historic, culture, and linguistic gaps make it important for us not to try to read the Bible as if a modern person had written it. This view holds that by the very nature of reality, the Bible does not contain modern science. We will have more to say about this in the following pages.

INTERPRETATION

In discussions of conflicts between science and religion, protagonists on both extremes of the range of views seem to assume that the Bible is a book of science and take comfort in a literal interpretation—one that takes all words in their primary, matter-of-fact sense; one that reads "It's raining cats and dogs," and immediately calls the humane shelter to round the critters up. Atheists generally accept the Bible's literal intent but dismiss it as a fairy tale or worse. When noted atheist Madalyn Murray O'Hair (who was murdered in 1995) participated in a series of debates and appeared on several rather sleazy television talk shows, one of her primary tactics was to mock biblical literalism. And in *The God Delusion*, Richard Dawkins, while acknowledging that many Christians do not read much of the Bible literally, nevertheless heaps his greatest disdain on those who do.

Young earth creationists generally understand science in light of a literal reading of the Bible and declare scientific conclusions that are not in conformity with a literal interpretation to be unscientific and wrong. They say, in effect, "Stay away from those scientists who are trying to put forth theories that are only theories and cannot be true because the Bible says differently." Or, as Henry Morris has written, "...the creation chapters of Genesis are marvelous and accurate accounts of the actual events of the primeval history of the universe. They give data and information far beyond those that science can determine, and at the same time provide an intellectually satisfying framework within which to interpret the facts which science can determine."[3]

A third way, often aligned with concordists or the Intelligent Design Movement, attempts to reconcile biblical language with science by agreeing with science where it seems to support the literal language (as with the big bang theory), acknowledging a non-literal interpretation where the scientific evidence is too overwhelming to resist (as in the day-age view of the age of the universe), or advocating a minority— some would say wrong-headed—scientific view where the other options fail, as many believe is the case with irreducible complexity.

Bible Literalists

Many Christians seem to believe that the interpretive coin has only one side, and that biblical language, particularly that concerning creation, must be read literally in order to capture its true and intended meaning. These literalists have some esteemed progenitors as this interpretive approach came largely out of Yale and Princeton, and particularly Princeton during the nineteenth century.

Following a philosophy espoused by Francis Bacon many years earlier, which emphasized inductive thinking and observing just the facts, Princeton theologians saw the purpose of theology as the systemization of the facts of the Bible and the determination of the principles and truths they reveal. They generally taught that "the Scriptures not only contain, but are THE WORD OF GOD, and hence that all their elements and all their affirmations are absolutely errorless, and binding the faith and obedience of men." Further, since truth is apparent primarily in objective facts and is the same for all ages, "the written word was the surest means permanently and precisely to display this truth."[4] Since they believed truth came largely from the written word, reading scripture provided these theologians a general view of science. Their primary focus was defending the "inerrancy" of scripture—the idea that the Bible is totally without error, which does not address the question of interpretation—against the skeptical arguments of modernists. While some Princeton theologians actually interpreted Genesis to allow for some aspects of evolution, they did represent the conservative position that still reflects the thinking of many evangelicals and literalists today.

Bacon's inductive method was eventually overwhelmed by modern science, with its emphasis on a deductive approach that involved hypothesis, testing of observable data, and empirical proof. With this change, the Baconian approach to biblical interpretation used by the Yale and Princeton theologians, which draws science from the literal language of the Bible, has come under more and more challenge. Today, the key issue

170   Reconciling the Bible and Science

is not as much a battle between Christian faith and science as it is a debate among Christians who hold different beliefs about biblical interpretation.

Modern Americans are generally not very good at non-literal interpretation. Think about how few people enjoy the study of Shakespeare in high school. While this was a popular course of study in previous generations, few people enjoy or get much out of Shakespeare now because we've lost so much of our sense of symbolic, metaphorical, and mythological imagination. We are basically literalists who tend to feel that everything not intended to be read literally is not worth spending much time on because it doesn't really tell us much.

The Awkwardness of Literalism

Human communication often has two types of meaning. The literal type involves a speaker using words intended to be understood in their primary, matter-of-fact sense. The non-literal type involves words that are often more interesting, sound better, and perhaps make the speaker's point more clearly. Non-literal language may be false in its standard meaning, but true as it is meant to be understood.

For example, you probably never would say, "I was in New Mexico this summer, and I saw the most beautiful turn of the earth on its axis that I've ever seen." You probably would say, "I saw the most beautiful sunset." Even though you know the sun doesn't set, you've made your point.

Or think of a grandmother who picks up her new grandbaby and says, "What a beautiful gift God has given us." Even a sophomore science major wouldn't say to her, "Grandmother, you're so ignorant. What happened was that Aunt Martha and Uncle John had sex. And he deposited the sperm, and this sperm got connected with an egg, then it produced a zygote, then an embryo, and pretty soon this thing flopped out." All such a statement would prove is that the sophomore is not very profound in his understanding of language. Both statements may be true, and they are not necessarily inconsistent. And neither explanation may be true. It depends on the level of science at the time. One can have an accurate scientific understanding of how babies come into being, yet still believe that the statement, "God has given us a great gift," is true. People in the Middle Ages could think on two levels—perhaps better than we can today—and the Bible contains a great deal of language that requires both levels of understanding.

Not surprisingly, literalists are perhaps over represented in the conflict between science and religion. For example, one of the principles of the Creation Research Society is: "The *Bible* is the written Word of God, and because it is inspired throughout, all its assertions are historically and scientifically true in the original autographs. To the student of nature this means that the account of origins in *Genesis* is a factual presentation of simple historical truths."[5]

While many in the Intelligent Design Movement have, for legal and political reasons, been quite coy about discussing the Bible and its interpretation, Hugh Ross, seen by many as a concordist but often identified with intelligent design, has written:

> RTB's [Ross' organization, Reason To Believe] specific biblical perspective, while acknowledging that a considerable portion of the Bible's creation material contains metaphors and figurative language, nevertheless holds that the Bible's creation content is predominantly literal in its descriptions of natural phenomena. Its accounts are viewed as reliably factual in their declarations about the origin, history, chronology, and current state of both the physical universe and life within the universe.[6]

Even these groups, however, have compromised their literal views in the face of compelling science. Consider the reference in Ezekiel 7:2 to "the four corners of the land," or in Isaiah 11:12 to "the four quarters of the earth," or in Job 37:3 to "the ends of the earth." In these instances, the literal text clearly says the land has four corners, four quarters, and ends—without question, an earth as flat as one can imagine and not at all round. At times the church taught that the world was flat, and perhaps a few people continue to see it that way. In fact, the Flat Earth Society currently claims to have been "deprogramming the masses since 1547." But most of us, including creationists and intelligent design proponents, have moved beyond the literal language and recognized what we know to be true.

Consider the language of Psalm 93:1 that "the world is firmly established; it cannot be moved," and Ecclesiastes 1:5 that "The sun rises and the sun sets," and Joshua 10: 12 where Joshua commands the sun to stand still. Read literally, all these references place the earth at the center of the universe with the sun and stars moving around it—a geocentric universe. It was easy for Ptolemy, Aristotle, and churchmen at the time of Galileo and Copernicus to believe in a geocentric universe, because when they went out in the morning or evening, that is what they saw. People believed that the earth was the center of the universe, both physically and metaphysically, because of their own observations and the scientific authority of Aristotle, rather than because of the words of the Bible. This view was accepted by the church for many years. So what happened? Simple observation and scientific evidence accumulated until someone—perhaps prodded by people like Copernicus or Galileo—decided they ought to reconsider how they had been interpreting those passages and that they weren't to be read quite so literally after all.

An irony of biblical literalism is that, in its consuming passion to be faithful to the scriptures, it turns attention away from the central religious concerns of the Bible's authors. Much religious language was not intended to be read literally, which often leads to our downfall in biblical interpretation. Reading a symbolic or metaphorical passage literally is as big a mistake as reading one intended to be literal in a symbolic sense. To understand the true meaning of symbolic language, we need to remember that imagination is an organ of meaning. And to get the intended meaning, we need to acknowledge and appreciate the fundamental symbolic character of the words.

All this, of course, raises the questions of how one knows whether certain language is to be interpreted literally or symbolically, and if it is to be interpreted symbolically, what it means. A key factor in answering such questions has to do with the language itself. In the following chapter, we will discuss the language of the Bible, how it was written, and how symbolic writing is used to convey the writer's intent. We will maintain that the writers never intended for the Bible to contain any science at all, whether viewed scientifically, historically, psychologically, theologically, or exegetically. It is meant to tell us that there is only one God and that we and everything else He has created are all absolutely dependent on Him, without exception. If we get that lesson from the Bible, we have learned its purpose.

12

SCRIPTURE

I am afraid that the schools will prove the very gates of hell, unless they diligently labor in explaining the Holy Scriptures and engraving them in the heart of the youth.

Martin Luther (1483 – 1546)

We introduced Chapter 11 with the supposition of two clerics arguing about the meaning of the first Bible. If this encounter had happened, we're willing to bet that one read language literally and the other symbolically because that difference is so often the basis of conflict. Language, including the language of the Bible, is used in many forms, and to correctly interpret scripture, we need to acknowledge the forms for what they are. We need to read myths, fables, or other symbolic language as they were intended rather than refuse to acknowledge their symbolic nature. This chapter will acquaint you with the most relevant of these forms. We will discuss the language of scripture, "genres" that indicate a specific type of literary composition, and "literary forms," sometimes called sub-genres, often embedded within the genres.

LANGUAGE

In the last chapter, we discussed the importance of the cultural setting from which the Bible arose. The languages of the time were an important element of that culture, and the culture—date, place, circumstances, audience, authorship of the texts, and other factors—helps establish the intent of the words. Therefore, language that might seem to relate to natural matters often carries subtleties in meaning, and its intent is not always obvious. We often see this in the Bible's use of common language and language that can have two levels of meaning.

Use of Common Language

Biblical language dealing with natural matters, which we would now call science, was the language common people of the day used to carry on their daily communication, rather than the modern scientific language used by today's scientists in their profession. This use of popular language made the Bible a book for all people of all ages. Think about how out-of-date it would be today if its writers had used their best scientific language—whatever that may have been at a time before science existed as we know it—to communicate their message. It would be incomprehensible in today's environment. Instead, the common language lives.

You may be questioning the validity of common people using common language to address divine subjects. Fortunately, you're not the first to worry about this issue and theologians have articulated the "Accommodation Principle" to address it. This principle affirms that God has chosen to reveal aspects of Himself to mankind in ways that mankind is able to understand. The principle allows human authors, acting as God's means for communicating to mankind, to communicate objective spiritual truths about the nature of God. Although the authors themselves were limited and prone to mistakes, the perfect and truthful God works in and through His human agents to reveal information about Himself that is sufficient and complete. Accommodation also holds that in spite of the difficulty of accurately translating the original texts into language we can understand today, God still has the power to use such translations to reveal His nature to people.

The Bible describes what was apparent to the people of the time, rather than the principles and laws relating to nature or theories about how things work. Think of all the Bible's references to natural things—the earth, moon, sun, stars, fish, fowl, cattle, birds, grass, fruit trees, and on and on. But you will find no such references to asteroids, comets, germs, cells, DNA, or flagellum as people didn't know about them because they couldn't see them. Biblical writers described a beautiful sunrise because that's what they saw. Not because of any view, one way or another, relating to whether the sun or the earth is the center of the universe. These descriptions of what people actually saw are timeless because the people saw what we see today, even if they didn't know what we know today.

Two Levels of Explanation

An excerpt from the testimony of John F. Haught, former chair of the Theology Department at Georgetown University, at the *Kitzmiller v. Dover* trial discussed in Chapter 9, illustrates the difference between a scientific explanation and an everyday explanation. Haught says that most disagreements relating to religion and science result from the fact that biblical writers often used a different level of explanation than many readers assume. He explains:

> Suppose a teapot is boiling on your stove, and someone comes into the room and says, "Explain to me why that's boiling." Well, one explanation would be it's boiling because the water molecules are moving around excitedly and the liquid state is being transformed into gas.
>
> But at the same time you could just as easily have answered that question by saying, "It's boiling because my wife turned the gas on."
>
> Or you could also answer that same question by saying, "It's boiling because I want tea."
>
> All three answers are right, but they don't conflict with each other because they're working at different levels.[1]

This example illustrates both a scientific and a common explanation. Biblical explanations fall into the second category. While the language of the Bible is not anti-scientific, it is pre-scientific or non-scientific. If the Bible had been written in scientific language, it would not have been understood by the millions of people who read it before modern science came to be, or by those who read it today without any scientific understanding. Instead, the use of common language that describes what can actually be seen and experienced makes possible a meaningful, timeless revelation that is understandable to all. Thus, as C. W. Shields has stated in *The Scientific Evidences of Revealed Religion*, "In a word, it is because the Bible, though non-scientific, is not anti-scientific, that it is as true for our time as it was true for its own time, and is likely to remain true for all time to come."[2]

Let's turn now to the various forms the Bible's language has taken.

GENRE

A literary genre is a group of written texts marked by distinctive recurring characteristics that constitute a recognizable and coherent type of writing. Identifying the genre of a piece of writing raises certain expectations about how its contents are to be understood. In our day-to-day life we are exposed to many different literary genres—a newspaper column, short story, biography, legend, fairy tale, poem, novel, letter, recipe, or any of many others. Each is written differently, following different conventions, different rules of grammar, and different syntax. Each has a different context for understanding, communicates differently, and needs to be read differently to understand the meaning of the words. We all know, for example, that a love poem is written not at all like a recipe for our favorite chocolate cake, and that we need to read them differently. We read the words with different expectations and interpret them differently, largely because of the genre that each embodies. We expect each genre to fulfill its purpose.

The Bible is composed of a number of different genres, and one should read each for what it is, expecting what one would normally see in that type literature. While different writers would describe them differently, the Old Testament is generally considered to contain narrative and poetry, and the New Testament is generally considered to contain narrative, epistle, and apocalypse. We will focus our attention on narratives (which we will call stories) and poetry because they are most relevant to our topic.

Stories

The Bible is, more than anything, a compilation of stories relating happenings of the past rather than a book of propositions about God. Recall that both the Old and New Testaments were written well after the lives of their principle characters. They were not written from any current or denominational perspective, nor to present historical facts. Instead, they were written for religious purposes with the aim of making God relevant to the writers' and readers' circumstances. They contain books of stories about God in which God reveals Himself.

There are so many examples of the narrative genre, including the stories of Adam and Eve, the fall, Abraham, the people of Israel,

Jesus, and numerous others. In each case, the story is the lesson. For instance, Jesus' lesson is drawn primarily from the story of his life, death, burial, and resurrection rather than from his words. Most of his words were not new, except as they interpreted the old in light of a revelation of the story of Jesus Christ. His story said, "If you've seen the way I relate to you, you've seen how God relates to you." The lessons of Jesus do not give propositions about what God is like. They tell stories that reveal what He is like.

The Ten Commandments are not abstract moral dictums that can be understood or interpreted outside of their story. They begin, "I am the Lord your God who brought you out of Egypt, out of the land of slavery. You shall have no other gods before me." (Exodus 20:2-3) So the First Commandment is the end of a passage that begins with God delivering the people from Egypt and slavery—suggesting that because of this deliverance, they are His people, and if they are to be in a relationship with Him, they need to act a certain way.

Stories often relate a version of events over time, something people normally think of as history. However, a story may or may not be true history as there is a difference between a historical narrative and what has been called a "mimetic" or "imitative" narrative.

A historical narrative aims to present a factual story of real historical events, persons, and places in their correct chronological order. It is history for history's sake and is expected to follow well understood canons or processes of research and documentation—much like modern science—that makes the narrative as objective as possible. For example, Volume 1 of *The Story of Civilization* by Will Durant contains fifty-five pages of "Bibliography" and "Notes" to document its accuracy according to commonly accepted standards. A recent popular history of President John Adams by David McCullough has sixty-nine pages of supporting documentation. Both are excellent examples of the rigor required of modern narrative history.

The Bible, on the other hand, is a mimetic narrative. It contains a form of history and refers to historical times, events, and people, but it does not contain stories that meet the scrutiny of modern historical narrative. For example, the book of Exodus relates the story of how God parted the Red Sea and the people of Israel crossed over on dry land. Eventually, after wandering forty years in the wilderness, they entered Canaan—known today as Palestine or Israel. The story does not follow the scientific methodology required of a modern historian. Just saying, "God opened the Red Sea and the people of Israel walked across," is not an event susceptible to historical methodology. A writer could say, "According to the scriptures, the Hebrews believed that their escape from Egypt was a divinely orchestrated event and that God divided the Red Sea and the Jordan River to bring the people of Israel out of Egypt into their promised land." Although that is what the people of Israel believed, a scientific historian cannot substantiate whether the actual event occurred. Thus, a scientific historian may believe every word of Exodus literally and still refuse to consider it a historical narrative because he understands that it is not susceptible to confirmation in the modern sense of scientific history.

The same thing is true in the New Testament. Some people are bothered because some historians will not affirm the life and resurrection of Jesus as an actual physical event, and because they argue that He was just a compilation of myths from the surrounding culture. Such historians are not necessarily nonbelievers; they just don't have as much evidence as they feel they need. Few if any scholars today, religious or non-religious, will argue that Jesus was just a compilation of myths because it seems evident that there was a man named Jesus and that he did die in Jerusalem around the year 30 A.D. Yet you won't find a history book saying Jesus died in 30 A.D. and rose from the dead because that's not data historians can deal with. What they *will* say is that the early disciples of Jesus believed strenuously that Jesus was raised from the dead after his crucifixion and burial and that he then appeared to his disciples. And that the disciples believed this so strongly that many of them gave their lives testifying to that belief.

Thus, the Bible is not a historical record like the account of Julius Caesar crossing the Rubicon. Instead, the stories of Exodus and of Jesus are examples of the other form of historical story—mimetic narrative. W. Randolf Tate has described this type of story as follows:

> It may be historical without being history in the modern sense. I call it "storicized" history. Mimetic narrative transcends history, for what is found in narrative is a redescrip-

tion of reality, the creation of a literary world or a textual world that reaches beyond itself and beyond its historical milieu. Through a definable and well-structured artistry, it offers to guide the reader into the discovery of some universal truth.[3]

In this kind of narrative—the kind that is in the Bible—the author takes independent, autonomous stories and weaves them together to communicate a truth through the whole. The emphasis is on the truth of the whole, not the literal facts of all the details of each independent part.

The stories people tell, even when they give eyewitness accounts of the same event, frequently differ. Those telling the stories may have seen things differently, have different memories, have different ways of expressing themselves, or have different worldviews. That certainly has been true throughout history. However, one can usually find a logical consistency within each story that helps in understanding what the author is trying to say. In such a case, focusing on details may obscure the truth of the broader story, so one needs to read the narrative from beginning to end to understand its meaning as a single, coherent story.

The story of Jesus has exasperated people for centuries, for example, because it is skimpy on the details. Instead, it communicates truth through the whole. We want to know about this person's ancestors, early life, daily activities, persona, and everything else one can imagine. We don't want to jump from the day He's born to age thirty, which is basically what the gospels do. Thus, the gospels, even those that mention the birth of Jesus, are not biographies. They initially were handed down orally and weren't written until several years after Jesus' death, so each is based on different traditions and tells a different story. Different details are included, and the stories are told to communicate something not necessarily a historical fact. That's not to deny that Jesus was born, but communicating a historical biography was not the reason for recording the life, teachings, and death of Jesus.

The Bible contains four gospels because each is a different way of talking about the same subject. Each comes from a different cultural origin, uses different language and vocabulary, and is directed toward a readership of a different culture. For example, the vocabulary in Mark is vastly different from that in John because each writer is talking to a different group of people within a different culture. This again demonstrates that the Bible is a bunch of books rather than a single one. If they were all the same, only one would have been needed.

The purpose of the gospels, however, was to tell all people of all cultures and times who Jesus was and what He means to the world. From the writers' perspectives, the death and resurrection of Jesus were the most important events in history—world-affirming and world-critical events that give meaning not only to all prior history, but to all future eras. So the writers didn't worry about what Jesus did when He was five or six years old. They tell instead of a year and a half to three years of His life, presenting theological lessons for all time by doing so. Thus, the gospel is a form of story used by biblical writers to convey a certain message or lesson, not to provide a biography. In fact, while biography is a legitimate literary genre, it is not one found in the Bible.

Poetry

Poetry is the second most common literary genre in the Bible. Medieval people seem to have been more poetic than people today. One theory holds that all language was originally pure poetry and only recently was divided into poetry and non-poetry. Poetry generally involves highly structured, figurative, metaphorical language. It is the language of imagery, in which the poet examines concepts by drawing verbal pictures and asking the reader to form mental pictures.

The Bible contains various types of poetry—prayers, songs, liturgies, and wisdom psalms. The unique context, features, language, and intended purpose of each need to be considered for a full understanding of biblical meaning. A good example is the poetry of Joshua 10: 12-13:

> On the day the Lord gave the Amorites over to Israel,
> Joshua said to the Lord in the presence of Israel:
> O sun, stand still over Gibeon,
> O moon, over the Valley of Aijalon."
> So the sun stood still,
> And the moon stopped,
> Till the nation avenged itself on its enemies,
> as it is written in the Book of Jashar.

The ancient "Book of Jashar" is thought to be an Israelite collection of poems and chronicles, which most scholars see as a collection of oral traditions that was probably compiled around the tenth century B.C., though the origin of this work seems uncertain. In any case, these words of Joshua, which literally suggest a scientific conclusion that "...the sun stood still, And the moon stopped," are simply the lines of a poem.

Speaking of the moon, do we really expect it to literally turn to blood? Joel 2:31 states:

> The sun will be turned to darkness
> and the moon to blood
> before the coming of the great and dreadful day of the Lord.

And in Acts 2:20 Peter addresses the crowd with essentially identical words:

> The sun will be turned to darkness
> and the moon to blood
> before the coming of the great and
> glorious day of the Lord.

Both renditions are poems with strong messages, but there is no reason to believe the intent of either is to communicate a scientific fact that the moon will ever drip with blood.

> Or consider the following from the poetry of Isaiah 40: 1-4:

> Comfort, comfort my people, says your God.
> Speak tenderly to Jerusalem, and proclaim to her
> that her hard service has been completed,
> that her sin has been paid for,
> that she has received from the Lord's hand
> double for all her sins.

> A voice of one calling:
> In the desert prepare the way for the Lord;
> make straight in the wilderness a highway for our God.
> Every valley shall be raised up,

> every mountain and hill made low;
> the rough ground shall become level,
> the rugged places a plane.

In reading this passage, there is no reason to believe that hills will actually be leveled and valleys filled in. The meaning is conveyed as much through emotional appeal as through the bare words. Cotterell and Turner, in their book on biblical interpretation, have noted that the communication achieved is quite different than would be achieved by the literal language in the following approximate equivalent: "Tell Judah that they have now been sufficiently punished and so their sins are forgiven. But they must end the wrongs they are committing, and they must begin to do what the law requires, so that Yahweh may again act on their behalf."[4]

One reads poetry very differently than one reads narrative or other genres. W. Randolf Tate has summarized the needed approach as follows:

> The metaphorical nature of most Hebrew poetry requires the reader to experience an effect on one level (the literal level of the metaphor) and then to transfer that experience to another level. The reader must first pause long enough to allow the metaphor or simile to construct the literal picture before too quickly rushing on to the second level of meaning where logical associations are made between the bifocaled levels of the metaphor or simile. Simply put, two thing must occur when reading poetry—a seeing and a thinking.
>
> The seeing occurs on the literal level of the image, while the thinking takes place when we trace the associations and meanings between the literal and interpretive levels.[5]

We have seen that stories and, especially, poetry, require the reader to recognize and understand various literary forms. We now turn to this subject.

LITERARY FORMS

Some people are so afraid of taking anything in the Bible non-literally that they contend that everything that Jesus said was literally true. This approach can run into a brick wall. For example, Jesus says in John 10:1, "I am the gate; whoever enters through me will be saved," but even literalists don't expect to open a latch when they enter through the gate or door that is Jesus. And when Jesus says in John 15, "I am the vine," few people expect to pick grapes. The fact is that many biblical writings were not intended to be read literally and make no sense if they are. Embedded within each genre are non-literal forms of language that help provide a context and meaning for the writing. We will focus on several that are especially relevant to our consideration of the Bible and science.

Symbolic literature is hard for many people, especially Americans, to read. We believe that the Bible is the revelation of God, and we assume God would want everything to be literally historical in His revelation. A major portion of the Bible is symbolic literature, however, and one needs to acknowledge the fundamental symbolic character of religious language in order to understand its meaning.

Myth

Myth is one form of symbolic language used in the Bible. Many assume that "myth" means something that is not true or real—in popular usage, a fictional tale. Religious scholars, however, usually consider a myth to be a legendary narrative that presents part of the beliefs of a people or that explains a particular phenomenon. In myths, natural phenomenon are usually personified—thus, the origin of the "gods." The term does not imply any judgment as to validity or truthfulness, and the presence of a mythological creature does not mean there is no truth to a story. It just means that the writer used symbolic imagination to convey his meaning.

We discussed in Chapter 1 the view that the creation accounts of Genesis are derived from earlier pagan myths, and we suggested that this does not make those accounts any less true when their purpose is considered. Famed Christian apologist C. S. Lewis also concluded that the mythical origin of these accounts does not mean they are not inspired writings, and does not detract from their truth and value. He has stated:

> When a series of such re-telling turns a creation story which
> at first had almost no religious or metaphysical significance

into a story which achieves the idea of true Creation and a transcendent Creator (as Genesis does), then nothing will make me believe that some of the retellers, or some one of them, has not been guided by God.[6]

Genesis 3:24 is a good example of myth: "After he drove the man out, he placed on the east side of the Garden of Eden cherubim and a flaming sword flashing back and forth to guard the way to the tree of life." This literal language says that when Adam and Eve were cast out of the Garden, God put cherubim with flaming swords at the gate of the Garden to block the way to the Tree of Life and keep Adam and Eve from returning. To understand the language, however, we have to understand what a cherub was and how it had mythological meaning.

When we think of a cherub, we normally think of a little baby because we have seen cherubs depicted that way in art and on various Renaissance buildings. But the biblical description is very different. While descriptions vary somewhat among various books of the Bible, cherubim typically are depicted as winged creatures that combine human and animal features, and they often have four faces—human, horse, lion, and eagle. If one reads Genesis 3 literally, she reaches the interesting conclusion that somewhere in Iraq there is this big thing that looks like an animal with four heads that is guarding the Garden of Eden. She, of course, is missing the point. In the Bible, cherubs are mythological creatures that guard the presence of God.

Neither God, the throne of God, nor the guardians of God can be depicted literally. How would you describe God's guardians? But they can be represented in some fashion, and that fashion happens to be as a cherub. The symbolism suggests that we all, as human beings, have eaten of the tree of the knowledge of good and evil, and the sword of God's judgment stands between us and His garden.

Ezekiel is another example of the symbolic use of cherubim. Ezekiel described a vision in which he saw what looked like four living creatures:

> In appearance their form was that of a man, but each of them had four faces and four wings. Their legs were straight; their feet were like those of a calf and gleamed like burnished

bronze. Under their wings on their four sides they had the hands of a man. All four of them had faces and wings, and their wings touched one another. Each one went straight ahead; they did not turn as they moved. (Ezekiel 1: 5-9)

As I looked at the living creatures, I saw a wheel on the ground besides each creature with its four faces. (Ezekiel 1: 15)

What significance did cherubim have to Ezekiel? The book of Ezekiel appears to have been written at the time of the Babylonian captivity, and Ezekiel was the prophet for the Jews who were held captive in Babylonia. They had lost the focal points of their religion—the Temple and the Ark of the Covenant, a portable temple that symbolized the presence of God. The Ark of the Covenant has been described in Exodus 25:18 as a simple gold box with "two cherubim out of hammered gold at the ends of the cover."

If one went into the Temple at Jerusalem, he could never see God sitting on His throne because God is not seeable. If God sits above the Ark of the Covenant, and you cannot see God, the only thing you can see are the cherubs. So the cherubs appear to represent the throne of God. In addition, the wheels "on the ground beside each creature" were able to move anywhere, creating a portable Ark of the Covenant. They seem to show that God was not restricted to Jerusalem nor confined to the temple and could go anywhere, so the people had not left Him behind. Though the exiles had experienced great change, God was still in control.

In summary, while the words of a myth are not to be taken literally, the story they tell can be true. Lewis concluded that God has taken myth and other literary vehicles natural to all cultures, raised them above themselves, and served His greater purpose:

The total result is not "the Word of God" in the sense that every passage, in itself, gives impeccable science or history. It carries the Word of God; and we (under grace, with attention to tradition and to interpreters wiser than ourselves, and with the use of such intelligence and learning as we may have) receive that word from it not by using it as an encyclopedia or an encyclical but by steeping ourselves in its tone or temper and so learning its over-all message.[7]

Metaphor

Metaphor is another form of non-literal language used in the Bible. A metaphor is a figure of speech in which a word or phrase for one object, action, or abstract idea is used in a different context than normal, in place of another word or phrase to suggest a similarity between the two. For example, when William Shakespeare said in *As You Like It,* "All the world's a stage," he used a metaphor to convey his idea of the world in which he lived.

The words of the psalmist in Psalm 119:105, "Your word is a lamp to my feet and a light for my path" present another example. Read literally, this verse has to be false. A word cannot be a lamp or light a path. But in the metaphorical sense the verse is true. The word, like a lamp, enlightens, guides, and keeps one from stumbling. Use of the word "lamp" replaces an abstract idea with something that is observable, consequently making the communication more familiar and concrete.

Although the writer may create a metaphor, there is no certainty it will be correctly understood by the reader. What is unknown is explained in terms of what is known, or something is explained in terms that are incongruous or unexpected. The conflict between the two provides the dynamic. A metaphor is likely to be missed if it is too subtle. And the more unexpected or outrageous the comparison, the more vivid the metaphor. To understand the true meaning, readers need to apply their own experience and use their own imagination—a necessary process that nevertheless can open a metaphor to an interpretation unintended by its creator.

Parable

A parable is an extended metaphor in the form of a short narrative that compares one thing to another. Parables often use common or familiar people or circumstances to illustrate unfamiliar truths. Jesus often used parables in his teaching. Some people argue that the events in them are literal historical accounts. Events like these did happen, though it is very unlikely that the stories are literal. Jesus told them because they communicated what he wanted to communicate, even if the events in the parables cannot be attributed to any actual historical characters or situations.

The parable of the prodigal son in Luke 15:11-31 came about when Jesus was seen eating with sinners, which preachers were not supposed to do at the time. Doing so indicated acceptance and recognition. The Pharisees saw this, assumed Jesus was not a very pious teacher, and began muttering in complaint. Instead of giving them a sermon about how wrong sinners are, or how we ought to accept them like everybody else, He told the story of the prodigal son.

The prodigal son parable is the story of a Middle Eastern father who didn't act like any Middle Eastern father any of the listeners had ever seen or heard about. So Jesus was saying, in effect, "You know what Middle Eastern fathers are generally like, but let me tell you about one who is very different, and that's the father of the prodigal son. He is like God. He acts like God. He is an extremist in his love, forgiveness, and acceptance of His son, which is hard for normal human fathers to be." The point of the story is that some normal human fathers can really love their children, but none of them can love their children the way this Middle Eastern father loved his.

The "facts" outlined in this parable may have happened to some historical people, but it's not likely because the son acted not at all like a Middle Eastern son was expected to act, and the father acted totally different from the way a Middle Eastern father was expected to act. He welcomed his son back with open arms as though nothing had happened. That made the parable outrageous and notable. Jesus didn't tell the story just to acquaint us with a good man who lived over in Jericho. He told us about God and showed that God acts toward His children in a way that no normal Middle Eastern father would act. That's the nature of God, Jesus was saying, even though He didn't use the word "God" in the parable.Such stories can be comprehended on many different levels. A child can hear the story of the prodigal son and get one meaning. A teenager can get another meaning. A father whose teenager has been giving him a bad time gets another meaning. The teenager who is causing his father problems gets still another meaning. And all of us can better understand the meaning of love, forgiveness, grace, and our relationship both with our earthly father and our heavenly father. There are just so many levels in this story that one will never fathom the entire mystery.

To understand a parable we need to question all our preconceived ideas and be prepared to consider the impractical, the anomalous, the startling, the paradox. We also need to consider the parable in the context within which it originated. After 2,000 years, the text can convey to modern readers the exact opposite of what was intended. Consider the parable of the good Samaritan in Luke 10. A man has been beaten and left half dead. A priest and a Levite pass him by, but a Samaritan helps him. Now we all "know" today that the priest and Levite were the "bad guys" and the Samaritan the "good guy." But a first-century Jew would have thought just the opposite. The Samaritan was a hated foreigner, yet he was the one commended by Jesus. A different take than one might read today.

Allegory

Allegories have much in common with parables, as each is a narrative intended to teach a truth about human nature. However, it can be said that while the intention of a parable is to clarify, the intention of an allegory is to mystify, as allegories rely heavily on the use of symbols that require interpretation. Understanding allegorical language requires the reader to interpret the symbolism appropriately and ensure that the symbols used correspond correctly to the real world. Because of the strong possibility of interpreting the symbolism of an allegory in an arbitrary or inappropriate manner, turning the language to whatever the reader wants, interpreters have often been reluctant to interpret the details of many parables as allegories.

The parable of the prodigal son presents an example of non-literal, non-historical language where a somewhat allegorical interpretation may be appropriate. For example, one can conclude that the father is a symbol for God, the son represents all rebellious sinners, and the older brother symbolizes the self-righteous hypocrites of the world. Another example that can be interpreted allegorically is the story of the wedding feast in Matthew 22:1-14. This is thought by many to be an allegory in which the King represents God; the son, Jesus; the servants, the apostles; those accepting the invitation, converts; and those excluded, the people who were found unworthy.

A word of warning is in order, however. Sometimes people think that allegorical language is the only alternative to a literal interpretation. They claim allegory to get around the meaning of a passage rather than to accept it for what it is. Although allegory is a symbolic language form, it's not the only way to interpret difficult language. Interpreting language as allegorical when it is not can lead to misunderstanding scripture.

Fable

Fables are another type of non-literal language form found in the Bible—contrary to the arguments of some in the Christian community. Common in the secular world, a fable is a narrative about supernatural happenings, often with animals speaking and acting like people, which is usually intended to teach a lesson. In the fable of the ant and the grasshopper, for example, a grasshopper sees an ant struggling mightily with an ear of corn he is taking to the nest. The grasshopper says, "Why not come and chat with me instead of working so hard?"

The ant responds, "I'm helping to lay up food for the winter, and suggest you to do the same."

The grasshopper does nothing and goes on its way. When winter comes, the grasshopper has no food and finds itself dying of hunger while watching the ants distributing corn and grain from the stores they collected in the summer. Now the grasshopper knows it is best to prepare for the days of necessity. We may not be so sure we believe this conversation actually occurred, but we do believe that the idea attributed to the ant was a good one.

One of the most prominent biblical fables is in Judges 9:7-15. Jotham tells of trees that went out to anoint a king for themselves. They asked the olive tree to serve, and it refused. Then they asked the fig tree, and it refused. Then the vine, and it refused. Then they asked the thorn bush, and it replied, "If you really want to anoint me king over you, come and take refuge in my shade…"

Though this fable appears in the Bible, it is not meant to be taken literally. One view is that the olive tree, the fig tree, and the vine rejected the offer of kingship because they were content to grow where God had planted them and to produce the kind of fruit God desired. The thorn bush represented Abimelech, ruler over Israel, who craved power and prestige. A thorn bush cannot give shade, and a productive person would be too busy doing good to want to bother with power politics. A worthless person, on the other hand, would be glad to accept the honor, but he would destroy the people he ruled. Abimelech, like a thorn bush, could offer Israel no real protection or security. Thus, like the fable of the ant and the grasshopper, Jotham's fable is meant to be taken for the truth it illustrates.

READING THE BIBLE FOR WHAT IT IS

The Bible is not a manual with a 1-2-3 prescription for Christian life. It is a whole library of books with distinct languages, several different genres, and many literary forms. Theologians throughout the centuries generally have been able to go with the flow and understand the Bible as both a divine book and a human book that needs to be read as a whole and within the appropriate context. Reading a form of symbolic language literally is not being true to the biblical materials. Reading literally a symbol, myth, fable, or any other kind of imaginative literature destroys its true meaning. The problem is—When does one stop the symbolic or figurative interpretation? How does one decide what should be read literally and what should be read figuratively? How does one read the Bible for what it is? Even if one accepts the dangers of literalism, how does one avoid inappropriate non-literal interpretations that are equally problematic and, in the words of Amos, cause the reader to flee from the lion only to meet a bear? (Amos 5:19) There are no easy answers, but we will offer some suggestions.

Avoid Potential Mental Traps

To think deeply about the meaning of scripture, we need to first think about how we think. Unless we exercise great care, our minds will play games with us and lead us astray. We will reach conclusions based on what our minds take to the reading rather than on what we read. To prevent this, we need to avoid several mental traps.

The first potential trap is set by our worldview. The term "worldview" has been described as "a comprehensive set of beliefs about the nature and significance of all reality—the physical universe, the spiritual realm, the world of creatures, the realm of God or of gods, and everything else thought to exist."[8] We have noted that the Bible contains a worldview—a presupposition or perspective—that fostered the development of modern science. The writers of the Bible also had their own worldviews, derived from the cultures in which they lived. These views affected what they wrote and how they wrote it.

We are the other side of the proverbial coin. Each of us has our own worldview or individual perspective. We are children of our own age and upbringing, influenced by the teaching of our forefathers, our experiences, and the culture around us. Unfortunately, we rarely take time to think about how our perspective and our unconscious assumptions, attitudes, and biases affect the way we understand what we read in scripture. We all struggle with the tendency to interpret and understand scripture through our own personal lenses in the context of our own cultural setting. Sorting out our own presuppositions, recognizing our blind spots, and avoiding other subjective influences is not always easy, but doing so is essential for seeing the fundamental truths in scripture.

A second potential trap, closely related to our worldview, is the tendency to understand scripture according to the traditions to which we are accustomed, without giving any thought to those traditions and where they came from. As discussed in previous chapters, the goal of biblical interpretation should be to conserve to the best of our ability the primary and original meaning of the text, in its own terms and its own historical milieu. Reading scripture in a traditional way, however, may or may not conserve the intended meaning of particular passages. As we previously discussed, tradition for many people holds that sex is the original sin, or that work is punishment for sin, or that cherubs are little babies with wings, or that Satan had a war with God in heaven. But none of these traditions is based on scripture or biblical stories. They are based on traditional beliefs that have grown up around the Bible, and if we interpret scripture according to them we are making a mistake.

We need, therefore, to examine our traditions and understand how they arose and where they came from. Did they come from secular myths, or philosophy, or biblical language? Are our expressions—like "going to Heaven" or "the immortality of the soul"—biblical expression, philosophical expressions, or traditional expressions? And when we encounter myths, fables, or other literary forms, do we take them for what they are and not try to explain them another way? When we read Genesis 1, for example, do we recognize it as a form of literature that is hard to name and classify, but that is not a scientific account of anything?

A third possible trap is the tendency to see in scripture what we wish it said or believe it should say. There is an old saw that people tend to see what they believe rather than believe what they see, and that probably fits in spades on questions of scriptural interpretation. Aren't we more likely to have the Bible describe sin to cover the speck of sawdust in someone else's eye than the plank in our own? Does our desire for scripture to confirm long held beliefs influence us to read it a certain way? Do we find it necessary to reinterpret various Bible passages from time to time in order to keep up with scientific advances?

A final trap is the tendency to look for easy answers—perhaps a significant cause of overly literal reading of scripture. Let's be clear here. We are not talking about looking for an easy way of life or following Christianity because doing so is easier than following science. Truly following the teachings of Christ requires unparalleled commitment, sacrifice, and tenacity. We are talking about a tendency to look for answers only in the easy places—like looking for a lost golf ball only on a clear fairway when you last saw it headed for a briar patch. It is easy to read Genesis 1 in the literal, young earth creationist sense. Doing so requires no real thought, reflection, or examination on our part and is nothing more than rote memory of presumed concrete facts. Acknowledging its form, manner of speaking, intent, and deeper meaning is much more difficult. The reader must deal thoroughly and honestly with the text and follow accepted principles of interpretation in an attempt to understand the meaning of the passage in its original setting. And she is called to think deeply about the theological and personal implications of the deeper message—all considered, a much more difficult, challenging, and sometimes frightening task than a simple literal reading.

Assess the Probabilities

Unfortunately, we cannot sit down with the composers of Genesis and ask them what they meant. Reasonable people arrive at different conclusions and cannot prove that one is right or that one is wrong. We have to consider all the evidence at our disposal and ask which interpretation is more likely to represent the original meaning of the text.

Again, there are no easy answers, but the best interpretation of a text is likely to be one that conforms to most or all of the following:

- Is consistent with the language and literary genre used by people at the time and place wherein the text was written. Stories, poetry, myths, and other symbolic language—rather than scientific language—were commonly used at the time Genesis was composed. What are the chances that Genesis was intended to be scientific?

- Is in line with interpretations of Christians throughout history. While, no doubt, mistakes have been made, theologians over the centuries have devoted extensive effort to interpreting the scripture. Their efforts should not be discounted, and understandings that vary from their consensus should not be taken lightly.

- Is consistent with the historical meaning of the broader text. Interpreting a single story or passage as inconsistent with the broad biblical message is probably incorrect.

- Does not conflict with readily observable evidence from the natural world. We previously noted that it is unlikely that God intended to trick mankind with natural evidence contrary to the meaning of the Bible.

- Reaches a conclusion that is workable in the lives of believing readers.

The thoughts of C. S. Lewis are helpful in understanding the effect of the last point—whether an interpretation is workable in our lives. As to the literal scientific or historical truth of the biblical accounts, Lewis noted that, "I should have thought the value of some things (e.g., the Resurrection) depended on whether they really happened, but the value of others (e.g., the fate of Lot's wife) hardly at all."[9] He concluded, therefore, that where a literal understanding is appropriate, the need for it will be plain.

Not surprisingly, Lewis treated the Old Testament accounts in a different way than those in the New Testament. With respect to the Old Testament, he said:

> I take it that the whole Old Testament consists of the same
> sort of material as any other literature—chronicle (some of

it obviously accurate), poems, moral and political diatribes, romances, and what not; but all taken into the service of God's word. Not all, I suppose in the same way…. On all of these I suppose Divine pressure; of which not by any means all need have been conscious.

The human qualities of the raw materials show through. Naivety [sic], error, contradiction, even (as in the cursing Psalms) wickedness are not removed.[10]

Thus, Lewis seemed to acknowledge that interpreting most of the Old Testament literally—as history or science—does not make our lives more workable. It seems, however, that Lewis saw the New Testament very differently, and much more literally, not because he took a different approach but because the materials are different. In his view, the New Testament is in the main historically reliable, the apostles were reliable witnesses, miracles are credible in God's scheme of revelation, and the stories told in the New Testament narratives fit perfectly into, and in fact sum up, the great revelational scheme that God has been unfolding from the beginning. And understanding most New Testament accounts this way makes our lives more workable.

In summary, figurative interpretation can be taken too far. But that does not mean we should reject it or resist its every use. When we read, we normally understand words in a literal sense first, then in a figurative sense if the literal doesn't fit. But figurative meanings are not second best or inferior. They are often closer to the truth, more powerful and profound. The Bible discusses spiritual truths, so we should expect to find figurative language. For example, it would be difficult to state literally the profound truth, "I am the resurrection and the life" (John 11:25), or "I am the way and the truth and the life." (John 14:6).

We should not be hasty to seek a figurative interpretation, nor should we too quickly reject one. We need to cautiously examine each passage within its context, and exercise some patience with ourselves and with others who come to different conclusions. We will try to do that in the following chapters, which look in more detail at the origin passages of Genesis.

13

THE ORIGIN STORIES—I

"By the word of the Lord were the heavens made,
their starry host by the breath of his mouth.
He gathers the waters of the sea into jars;
he puts the deeps into storehouses."
Psalm 33:6-7

In the preceding chapter we looked at forms of language contained in the Bible as a whole. But the devil is in the details. Talking in general terms is easy, like strolling along a smooth path through a manicured garden, avoiding the bumps and briars and anything else that might present a problem. Dealing with specifics is like entering the jungle, where there is a tangle of confusion and resistance at every turn. We now enter that jungle. In this chapter and the one that follows we will discuss the specific issues that nearly always surface in any discussion of the Bible and science.

The crux of the Bible and science debate involves questions about the correct interpretation of the first eleven chapters of Genesis. While other scripture may relate indirectly or help us interpret these chapters, Genesis 1-11 contains specific accounts that, if interpreted literally, raise essentially all the issues relevant to today's debate—the creation accounts that present questions of special creation vs. evolution; the use of the word "kind" which some believe equates to "species;" the genealogies that some have used to make a case for a young earth; the fall and its implications for the common ancestry of man and beast; the flood and its alleged relation to geology; the Tower of Babel and questions of diverse languages and races. Consequently, considering whether these chapters contain predominately literal or symbolic language, and whether they are science or theology, are the central issues.

Chapters 1-11 of Genesis, which deal with the period from creation to Abraham, have sometimes been called the prologue of the Pentateuch, the first five books of the Hebrew Bible. They also have been referred to as the Primeval History, because they deal with events that go back to the origin of the universe and mankind. While the five books are traditionally said to have been revealed to Moses and written by him, the clear consensus of Bible scholars today is that they were put together by an editor or editors using a variety of sources. Therefore, Genesis is almost certainly a composite work. Scholars also have concluded that Genesis Chapters 1-11 have two sources—a document, or perhaps even an oral tradition, comprising ancient Hebrew traditions from the Southern Kingdom of Judah, probably after the time of Solomon, and another similar collection of the traditions of Israel that probably came from the Northern Kingdom of Ephraim shortly after the first. Thus, Genesis Chapters 1-11 were not composed as a literary work like Paul's letters in the New Testament, but were instead the end product of a long history of formation.

Scholars are convinced beyond any reasonable doubt that these chapters are best understood as a single unit—a single account of the origins with its own internal consistency and its own context. The stories of creation, Adam and Eve, the temptation, Cain and Abel, the genealogies, Noah and the flood, and the Tower of Babel all have obvious relationships to one another, and they fit together to form one coherent narrative of God's relationship to mankind. They tell of creation and God's blessing of human life, ever increasing sin and rebellion, God's punishment of mankind through the flood, and the persistence of sin and rebellion as addressed at the Tower of Babel.

Although one cannot discern the specific meaning of each story with absolute certainty, one can, with a high degree of probability, draw three conclusions that apply to each story and to the origin account as a whole:

- The chapters were composed before the advent of modern science, with its unique language for describing observations about the physical world.
- Concerns of the original audience would have been very different from our own. They would have been concerned with the nature and characteristics of God rather than with the mechanisms of biological development.

- The text itself indicates that the authors intended Genesis 1-11 to be a consciously symbolic work that uses language artistically rather than scientifically. In fact, scholars generally consider the stories to be similar to parables—not unlike the parables of the Prodigal Son and the Good Samaritan—rather than factual history.

The origin stories that relate primarily to creation will be considered in this chapter. Those that deal with humanity and its fall will be addressed in Chapter 14. In both chapters, a case will be made that each story is a symbolic rather than a literal work—a work that is based on theology and not science, that doesn't explain how mankind came to be, but is part of a whole that reveals deep, fundamental truths about the nature of humanity and our place in the universe.

THE CREATION STORY IN GENESIS 1

We start with Genesis 1:1, which states, "In the beginning God created the heavens and the earth. Now the earth was formless and empty, darkness was over the surface of the deep, and the Spirit of God was hovering over the waters."

Genesis 1:2 through 2:2 relates the creation story through a series of decrees:

> Let there be light ... —the first day.
> Let there be an expanse between the waters ... —the second day.
> Let the water under the sky be gathered to one place ... let the land produce vegetation ... —the third day.
> Let there be lights in the expanse of the sky to separate the night from the day ... God made two great lights ... —the fourth day.
> Let the water teem with living creatures, and let birds fly above the earth ... —the fifth day.
> Let the land produce living creatures ... Let us make man in our image ... —the sixth day.
> on the seventh day he rested ....

The Apparent Conflict

The seven-day time frame of Genesis 1 is the biblical reference most commonly measured against modern scientific accounts. It has perplexed many Christians over the years, particularly as astronomical and geological evidence has so strongly indicated a cosmic history exceeding 10 billion years. Many read Genesis 1 and related references as though God were speaking to them directly in the language, communication patterns, and culture of today. In this context, they take the words to mean God's own clear, straightforward, literal discussion of His specific creation of the universe instantaneously and *ex nihilo* (out of nothing) in seven twenty-four-hour days. This view, held principally by creationists, rejects the widely accepted scientific account of the world's creation over billions of years as unbiblical and the ill-informed speculation of a group of atheists—or at least an account not certain enough to require a non-literal understanding of Genesis.

Others are convinced that we can trust God's revelation in both the scripture and the natural world, and that the story reported in Genesis can be reconciled with science. They attempt to retain the literal meaning of the words by holding to certain beliefs about creation that were in existence for decades before scientific creationism developed. These theories, discussed in Chapter 8, include the gap or ruin and restoration theory and the day-age theory.

All seem to hold their positions because they have assumed that Genesis was intended to answer the question of how and on what timetable God created the universe. When this is the question, they must either dismiss the Bible or science, or they must devise gaps or super long days to accommodate the two. Such an approach allows science to influence scriptural interpretation.

The Purpose of the Story

Another group, often roundly condemned by those with contrary views, accepts the scientific consensus while also holding to the belief that the Bible and Genesis 1 are the inspired word of God. John Stek, professor emeritus at Calvin Theological Seminary, has explained this view as follows:

It is our conviction that these last have chosen the better way, that their way is most faithful to Genesis 1:1-2:3 itself. That word was not intended as a chronicled account of the origins of the cosmos. It speaks of beginnings, but in a manner quite different from that of the historian or scientist. It is a theological word written in the face of ancient Near Eastern myths with their theogonies and cosmogonies. It offers a radically new view of God, humanity, and world that funds the whole biblical witness to God's pursuit of His purposes in history.[1]

Let's consider this interpretation. Simply acknowledging that the real purpose of Genesis has to do with God and His relationship with the world allows the days to be literal twenty-four-hour days, used as literary devices in a story intended to bring the reader into the right relationship with God.

As we consider the scripture, remember that biblical authors were speaking to their contemporaries about issues that were important in their day, using language and literary forms that were familiar to them and that fit within their culture. Thus, we need to think first in terms of what message the words were meant to convey to the people of ancient Israel in their struggle against the pagan religions existing at the time. We then should consider how that meaning applies to us today.

Put yourself in the shoes of one of these people of antiquity and read (or preferably hear read) Genesis 1. What do you, in the mind of the nomad, learn that you didn't already know? Do you learn anything about geology? Does the word "dinosaur" come up? Is there any discussion of the biological history of human beings? Does the story tell you anything about species—how many or even that there is such a thing as "species"? Have you ever heard of science in the first place? Do you lose a minute's sleep in the absence of such discussion?

No! The fundamental question at stake when Genesis was written could not have been the scientific issue of how or by what process things achieved their present form, or the historical issue of chronological time periods. The writers were not addressing issues of modern science or attempting to understand the physical universe, cosmic development, or biological evolution. The issue was idolatry, not science. It was affirmation of faith in one transcendent God, not empirical or speculative theories of origin.

All Genesis tells us is that whatever the people of the day saw with their eyes—cattle, goats, camels, fish, or whatever—was absolutely dependent for its existence upon one all-powerful God. The concerns of the people were religious, and they were addressing the question "Who is God, and how does He relate to human beings and the world?" They were proclaiming the true God as He manifested Himself in His creative works, contrasted with the false religious notions that dominated the world at the time. Recall that in Chapter 1 we cited Conrad Hyers' description of the pervasive polytheism and idolatry of the time. The following is his view of how biblical writers dealt with it:

> In the light of this historical context, it becomes clearer what Genesis 1 is undertaking and accomplishing: a radical and sweeping affirmation of monotheism vis-à-vis polytheism, syncretism, and idolatry. Each day of creation takes on two principal categories of divinity in the pantheons of the day and declares that these are not gods at all but creatures, creations of the one true God who is the only one, without a second or third. Each day dismisses an additional cluster of deities, arranged in a cosmological and symmetrical order.
>
> On the first day the gods of light and darkness are dismissed; on the second day, the gods of sky and sea; on the third day, earth gods and gods of vegetation; on the fourth day, sun, moon, and star gods. The fifth and sixth days remove from the animal kingdom any associations with divinity. Finally human existence, too, is emptied of any intrinsic divinity, while at the same time *all* human beings, from the greatest to the least—not just pharaohs, kings, and heroes—are granted a divine likeness.[2]

The authors proclaimed one God who is creator of all, rather than the gods of the celestial world, the earth, the seas, and the world below. A God who is before all and who created the primordial watery mass, rather than one who came from that mass. A God who sees the sun, moon, and stars as greater and lesser lights providing illumination to the earth and governing day and night, rather than deities who affect events on earth. A God who sees procreation as God's blessing of living creatures, rather than a manifestation of the divine. A God who sees all humanity as fashioned in God's image and appointed to a preeminent status, rather than slaves and pawns subservient to powerful kings who represent the gods.

Consistent with the culture of the time, the writers made their points by relating stories, not by writing a set of instructions or definitions. The stories do not present abstract descriptions or definitions of God. They instead reveal God's identity and character through events and actions. Further, Genesis is not a historical narrative that presents a factual chronology of real events, but instead is a mimetic narrative that helps the reader see the universal truths of God's creation and serves as a prologue for what is to follow. It is more like a parable than a journalistic report of events, and it addresses the character of God and man and the relationship between them rather than detailed scientific questions of what happened at the creation or the chronological order in which it happened. We, the readers, are brought into another time and place and asked to use our imagination to share the experience.

A Framework Interpretation

The late Meredith Kline, an ordained minister in the Orthodox Presbyterian Church and a professor of Old Testament, developed a "framework interpretation" of the first chapter of Genesis. His interpretation holds that the seven-day creation account is not a literal or scientific description of creation, but instead is an ancient text that outlines a religious doctrine of creation. In summary, Kline maintains that a two-register concept structures the whole account—heavens above and earth below set a space dimension, and a heavenly time and an earthly time set a time dimension.

Genesis 1 divides its six days of creation into two groups of three (triads). The first triad (days 1–3) narrate the establishment of the creation kingdoms, and the second triad (days 4–6), the production of the creature kings. The two triads can be compared as follows:

CREATION KINGDOMS	CREATURE KINGS
Day 1—verse 3—"Let there be light...."	Day 4—verse 14—"Let there be lights...."
Day 2—verse 6—"Let there be an expanse between the waters to separate water from water...."	Day 5—verse 20—"Let the water teem with living creatures, and let birds fly above the earth across the expanse of the sky...."
Day 3—verse 9—"Let dry ground appear...." verse 11—"Let the land produce vegetation...."	Day 6—verse 24—"Let the land produce living creatures.... verse 29—"I give you every seed bearing plant...and fruit with seed in it...for food...."

The many similarities between corresponding verses in the two triads lead to the conclusion that there are two descriptions of one single event and that the days progress in topical rather than chronological order. The author used parallelism to describe God's work, not to outline a literal time frame. In this context, "When we find that God's upper level activity of issuing creative fiats from his heavenly throne is pictured as transpiring in a week of earthly days, we readily recognize that, in keeping with the pervasive contextual pattern, this is a literary figure, an earthly, lower register time metaphor for an upper register, heavenly reality."[3]

Symbolic Language

Genesis addresses theology in often symbolic language on a completely different level of thought than modern science. Genesis 1:1 through 2:3 is permeated with the metaphor of king and kingdom. Other religions of the time commonly used such a metaphor, as discussed in Chapter 1 regarding *Enuma Elish*, where Marduk became king among the gods. Theologians have noted that several elements of the Genesis narrative also reflect the metaphor through the use of words having the form of a royal decree; the naming of "day," "night," "sky," and other basic cosmic structure as an expression of lordship;

the assignment of spheres of rule to the sun and moon, reflecting a sovereign overlord; the assignment of specific provisions for humanity, which recalls assignment of food at the king's table; and more. In summary, the metaphor depicts the absolute kingship of one God over the earth and cosmos.

The seven-day structure of the creation story is another metaphor. In the ancient Near East the number seven was frequently used as the primary numerical symbol of fullness, completeness, and perfection. For example, in the epic of *Gilgamesh*, seven days were needed to build an ark, a flood continued for seven days, and another seven days were needed for the water to subside. Thus, seven days symbolically suggested the completeness and goodness of God's created work. Thinking of these "days" in the context of our modern calendar, as is the case with young earth creationism, or of geologic time (as is the case with proponents of day-age creationism) fails to consider the theological purpose and story nature of the verses.

Interestingly, this metaphorical view does, in fact, take the days to be ordinary days. But it considers them as part of an extended chronological metaphor, where they are used to make a comparison with a broader subject. To appreciate this metaphor, consider the words of Jesus as he speaks about Herod in Luke 13:32: "He replied, 'Go tell that fox…'" We suspect that Jesus didn't believe Herod was a furry little critter with a big tail, an interpretation that would be similar to a literal, twenty-four-hour view of Genesis. And He probably didn't say "fox" when he meant "elephant," an interpretation that seems analogous with the day-age view. The more likely case is that when Jesus said "fox" he meant "fox," but was using the word to convey the idea that Herod had a crafty, fox-like nature. He used the word literally, but as a broader metaphor. Similarly, the use of the literal term "day" in Genesis is part of a broader metaphor of completeness.

This view also has its own internal logic and consistency with the culture and problems of the time. For example, the biblical writers, along with Aristotle and other thinkers and philosophers, had never seen more than seven planets. So from their perspective, the number of planets they actually saw corresponded to the number of planets they believed God would make because God only makes perfect numbers. They also saw four phases of the moon, each lasting seven days.

Similarly, Genesis 1 involves seven days and specific creation each day because, in addition to a metaphor for completeness, seven was considered a divine number.

Another example of internal consistency in Genesis 1 is the analogy of the clause "In the beginning God created the heavens and the earth…" to the Babylonian story of pro-creation, or generation of the Gods, as discussed in Chapter 1. The Babylonian account is told in seven tablets, the Genesis account is told in seven days, and the subject matter of each of the days generally corresponds. In both cases things emerge out of the watery chaos. Several other similarities exist between the two accounts as well.

A fundamental disparity between the descriptions of creation in the Babylonian story and in the Genesis story is the difference that makes all the difference in the world, and that highlights the metaphorical interpretation of the scripture. It is the presence of the creator. *Enuma Elish* refers to many gods and goddesses emanating from world matter, with the universe originating in the orderly arrangement of pre-existent matter. In Genesis, one God creates the universe out of nothing. The watery chaos in the Babylonian myth is not a creation. It is the source of the generation of everything there is, but there is nothing beyond it. In the Genesis account, however, the watery chaos itself is a creation, and there is something beyond it—the creator. Thus, Genesis is talking about one God and what the Bible calls idolatry, which we would call polytheism.

This emphasis on one transcendent God and our relationship with Him is confirmed time and again in the Old Testament. One example is found in Exodus, where God brings His people out of the land of Egypt, establishes a covenant relationship with them, and gives them the Ten Commandments. In Exodus 20:2-3, God states "I…brought you out of Egypt," and "You shall have no other gods before me."

Another example is Deuteronomy 4:19: "And when you look up to the sky and see the sun, the moon and the stars—all the heavenly array—do not be enticed into bowing down to them and worshiping things the Lord your God has apportioned to all the nations under heaven." Again, the Bible teaches that if people are worshipping anything besides the God who transcends the gods, they are worshipping the wrong god.

The Creation of Mankind

Genesis 1:26-27 reads as follows:

> Then God said, "Let us make man in our image, in our like-
> ness, and let them rule over the fish of the sea and the birds
> of the air, over the livestock, over all the earth, and over all
> the creatures that move along the ground." So God created
> man in His own image, in the image of God he created him;
> male and female he created them.

The words "in our image, in our likeness" have been interpreted
in widely different ways by various Christian traditions. All seem to
agree, however, that they establish the importance of the doctrine of
creation for an understanding of nature and the human experience.
They help answer the question—What does it mean to be authentically
human?

The words of Genesis make it clear that a human being is very
different from all other animals. While man shares many characteristics
with other living things—including, almost surely, common ancestors—
man differs in many essential ways. Most Christians would agree that
we have been gifted with certain divine likenesses that differentiate
humans from beasts—prominently, freedom. It is a finite freedom,
or course, in contrast to the infinite freedom of God, but freedom
nonetheless—the freedom to partner with God in dialogue, in creativity,
in loving, in commitment (covenanting together), and in living historically in communion. There has been disagreement, however, on a
fundamental issue. This disagreement involves the question of whether
human beings have an immortal soul that is distinct from the body and
that lives forever after death.

Catholic Christianity has generally held that the soul is the
immortal essence of a human—the seat of human will, understanding,
and personality—and that although the human body evolved from a
common ancestor, the human soul was immediately created by God
and introduced into the body at a particular point in evolutionary
history. This view generally holds that the soul is the innermost aspect
of man, by which he is most especially in God's image.

Protestant views about the soul have been less uniform. Leaders of the Protestant Reformation Movement, with the notable exception of Martin Luther, accepted the traditional Catholic view regarding an immortal soul. Despite Luther's reluctance, second generation Lutheran and Calvinist scholastics continued the general Catholic view, which became the default view of the evangelical heirs of the Calvinist tradition. However, many Protestants, particularly those influenced by the Biblical Theology Movement of the twentieth century, believe that the idea of an immortal soul is derived from ancient Greek philosophers such as Socrates, Plato, and Aristotle, and is not a teaching of the Bible. They argue that the term "image" in Genesis does not pertain to either human characteristics or the presence of an immortal soul, but instead simply refers to the fact that God has created humanity as His counterpart, that we have a relationship with Him, and that we are a candidate for eternal life or eternal fellowship with God. In this view, immortality or eternal life is linked with resurrection and is a hope or possibility for the ultimate destiny of humanity, not a certainty incorporated in the creation account.

This general view is shared by many modern scholars who believe that the biblical authors focused on various aspects of human life and relationships, rather than the philosophical question of how many parts are essential components of a human being and whether there is an immortal soul.

Viewing the essence of humanity as our relationship with God, rather than the presence of an immortal soul, makes it easier to address the Bible and science conflict. Naturalistic scientists who have great difficulty crediting a faith that includes an immortal, substantive soul can more easily accept a faith based on a relationship with God. And fundamentalist evangelicals can more easily credit evolution, which would seem to be inconsistent with an immortal soul. Thus, focusing on the concept of relationship rather than the idea of an immortal soul avoids an unnecessary glitch in the dialogue between theology and science.

Importantly, regardless of the differences between the beliefs of various Christian traditions, all seem to agree that man is responsible before God and is the only animal with the responsibility and the freedom to be related to God in faith and obedience. All this brings into sharp focus the question of evolution and the creation of mankind in the image of God. Was it necessary for humanity to be created fully developed, immediately, without a history of common ancestry? Or could we be humans of exactly the same sort, made in the image of God, and still have a history of evolutionary development from a common ancestry with lower animals? Stated differently, does the scientific conclusion as to how humanity was created really matter in our relationship with God? To answer "yes" would be to reach a conclusion based solely on our origin rather than our current meaning or context.

In other words, there is no difference between an existing human person whose ancestor was created instantaneously without progenitors just a few thousand years ago and an existing human person whose ancestors go back much further in time and whose lineage is much more deeply rooted in complex animal biology. Let's consider an analogy. Each human individual, no matter how mature and spiritual, originated as a zygote—a single cell that is the result of fertilization—in his or her mother's womb. Though a zygote shows little evidence of being human, it will eventually (God willing) exhibit unmistakable humanness, and perhaps do so in a way unexcelled by any other zygote. This analogy is not a scientific proof. But hopefully it will help overcome any discomfort associated with matter (such as "dust of the ground"), nature (such as our animal natures, natural relatives, and one cell beginnings), and natural juices (such as "slime") that refer to substances associated with the beginning of all life and the beginning of each individual life of every "kind."

Thus, the biblical doctrine of creation is the affirmation that each human being is "specially" created by God: Adam (as human kind); Adam (commonly regarded as the first man); you and me, our children and grandchildren (specially created individuals). It is a theological conclusion made no more difficult by the findings of modern science. These findings mean only that we should humbly consider science as involving ongoing attempts of faith to seek understanding, and recognize (along with Augustine, Aquinas, Luther, Calvin, Pannenberg, Bonhoeffer, Barth, and many other theologians) that although our ignorance still surpasses our understanding, faith stands.

Summary

The Bible contains two accounts of the creation of man. The one in Chapter 2 will be discussed in the following section. As we have discussed, the version in Chapter 1 has nothing to say about how human beings were created. It clearly places humanity, both male and female, in a special place in the realm of creation, but it preserves in awe the secret of how humanity came to be.

The presence of two creation accounts shows that there is not a single, fixed way. The Bible allows science to explore how man originated without a necessary conflict between scientific findings and the biblical story. A conflict exists only if one believes there had to have been one fixed way for the creation of mankind. Attempting to be loyal to the Bible by turning the creation account of Genesis 1 into a kind of science or history is like trying to be loyal to Jesus by arguing that his parables are actually historical events and are only reliable and trustworthy when taken literally as historical reports. The first creation text is not scientific, or pre-scientific, or unscientific. It is non-scientific, neither agreeing nor disagreeing with science, or even taking a position on science. It is sophisticated and rational, with a logic all its own, but that logic is in the service of theological affirmations.

THE CREATION STORY IN GENESIS 2

The creation account of Genesis 1 started "In the beginning" and climaxed with the creation of man. The story in Genesis 2 begins with God's creation of man, builds from there, and focuses more explicitly on man and woman. Genesis 2 and the next several chapters relate the story of Adam and Eve: there was "no man to work the ground" and God "formed the man from the dust of the ground and breathed into his nostrils the breath of life, and the man became a living being." God planted a garden and put man in it, made all kinds of trees grow, and formed beasts of the field and birds of the air. When Adam found no suitable helper, God "made a woman from the rib he had taken out of the man, and he brought her to the man."

Conflicting Interpretations

Not surprisingly, the creation story of Adam and Eve has been interpreted in various ways. At one extreme, creationists believe that God literally, physically created one man, Adam, directly from the dust of the ground and one woman, Eve, from Adam's rib. Each was specially created as a mature individual from the beginning—the only persons in the world at the time. The corollary, of course, is that God did not use evolutionary processes over a long period of time to create human beings or other organisms.

Many, perhaps most, scholars on the other hand consider the biblical account of Adam and Eve an example of a metaphorical story—one that uses a potter breathing life into an object made from clay to illustrate the creation of humanity and communicate a fundamental truth. They conclude that the literal details are not historically accurate at all, and that the events described by the narrative didn't happen as they were described. For example, people of Old Testament times knew that human beings were created from clay—they saw what happened when people died. The important point was that "the Lord God formed the man" and through this creation established a relationship with Him, which conveys the importance and truth of creation, sin, and human rebellion. This view, of course, is not inconsistent with biological evolution as the origin of human beings.

The Literal View

The view that Adam and Eve were the first mature man and woman presents another example of the awkwardness of literalism when reading the Bible. According to scripture, Adam was created both male and female. Genesis Chapter 1 reads, "So God created man in His own image, in the image of God he created him; male and female he created them." In Chapter 2 Eve was created with and in the man: "Then the Lord God made a woman from the rib..." In fact, the very names are indicative of their roles and meaning. "Adam" comes from the Hebrew "adomah," meaning "man," but Eve is from the Hebrew term for "life." Thus, in the first three chapters of Genesis, Adam almost always means human being—not an individual or a male human being. Male and female are differentiated in Chapter 2 only after it is discovered that there are no other beings on the earth that can be suitable companions for humans. Only a human being can be a suitable helper for another human being.

Many people think that, according to the story, God created Adam and saw that it was not good that he was alone, so He created a woman, Eve. But the scriptural story actually is that after He had put Adam in the garden, "The Lord God said, 'It is not good for the man to be alone. I will make a helper suitable for him.' Now the Lord God had formed out of the ground all the beasts of the field and the birds of the air. He brought them to the man to see what he would name them..." (Verses 18 and 19)

Has God lost His train of thought? He says He will make a helper for Adam and then brings every beast of the field and every bird of the air to him to see what he would call them. And whatever Adam called every living creature became its name. "But for Adam no suitable helper was found."

A Symbolic View

This story has a basic humor and universal truth that people miss when they are trying to read it literally. God sees that the man is lonesome and needs a helper. (The word "helper" does not mean an inferior, but somebody who is suitable to the man.) So God passes all the beasts in front of Adam, and Adam names them. One can almost imagine that he gets to the cow and says, "No, that's not it." He gets to the goat and says, "No, that's not it." And he gets to the aardvark. "No, that's not it either." So no helper was found. Read literally, this interpretation depicts a pretty inefficient God. He should know that a cow or other beast would not be a helper suitable for man. Considering the more fundamental truth, however, one recognizes that the story communicates that there is something about man that cannot be found in the rest of the animal kingdom. "So the Lord God caused the man to fall into a deep sleep; and while he was sleeping, he took one of the man's ribs and closed up the place with flesh. Then the Lord God made a woman from the rib he had taken out of the man, and he brought her to the man." (Verses 21 and 22)

This all, of course, relates to the question of whether human beings were specially created in an instant or evolved over time and whether it really matters. How did Adam and Eve get here? Were the first human beings the result of a long evolutionary development involving concepts such as survival of the fittest and natural selection or of special creation, with Adam appearing instantaneously at the Word of God a few thousand years ago?

The overwhelming majority of credible scientific opinion is that man was created over a long period of time and not instantaneously from the dust of the ground as the literal words of Genesis 2 might suggest. But does it really matter? Is the status of humanity diminished by a longer history of development? It seems that the answer is no. A human being is still a human being. How long his species has been around, and whether it developed from a one-celled organism doesn't change what or who he is.

Think of it another way. The Christian doctrine of creation is not only that Adam was created, but that all of us were created. As noted earlier, we all started out as a tiny one-celled organism in our mother's womb—or, these days, sometimes in a petri dish—and it is a fallacy to say that we are not the result of the creation of God because we came from an ugly, little one-celled organism. If origin from a single cell is okay for one individual, it should work for our whole species. If there is no theological objection to an individual being created from a one-celled organism, there should be no theological objection to our species arising the same way.

Like Genesis 1, the second creation account uses elements that were also used in pagan myths to convey its theology. For example, several Mesopotamian myths depicted human beings as being created out of clay, as was the case with Adam. In Babylon, the tree of life, similar to that in the Garden of Eden, was well known as a symbol of long life or immortality. Sumerian poems discussed a garden paradise. The mystical power of the Tigris and Euphrates rivers was praised in Babylonian hymns and is analogous to the rivers in Genesis 2:10-13. And various pagan myths tell of man attaining God-like wisdom after eating food reserved for the gods, like eating from the tree of life. In fact, the materials in Genesis 2-3 are so similar to so many myths from the civilizations of antiquity that the scripture is almost surely mythological in character. All this does not mean that the stories are untruthful or should be dismissed. But it does mean that to be faithful to the stories' meaning and intent, one must understand and acknowledge their literary form and seek the fundamental truths that are beyond a literal, factual reading.

In summary, we can explain the special nature and status of man theologically, or we can explain it naturalistically. But the human being is the same. The Bible simply communicates that the existence of human beings, and who they are, is dependent absolutely upon the providence and the creative acts of God.

COMPARING THE TWO CREATION STORIES

The two biblical creation accounts differ significantly in the time and cultural background in which they were written and the audience to which they were addressed. Conrad Hyers has explained the differences as follows:

> The differences between these two ways of organizing the issue of origins is the result of two contrasting life-settings in the history of Israel; the agricultural-urban and the pastoral-nomadic. Both accounts have used imagery which arises out of, and closely relates to, their respective experiences of the world. Genesis 1 has drawn upon the imagery of the great civilizations inhabiting the river basins and/or adjacent to the sea, while Genesis 2 has drawn upon an imagery more in accord with the experience of wandering shepherds and goat herders living on the semiarid fringes of the fertile plains. There is precedent in the history of Jewish experience for both, and thus both perspectives are given side by side.[4]

The two accounts also report different sequences of events. For example, in Genesis Chapter 1, vegetation is immediately produced by the will of God, while its existence is made dependent on rain and mist in Chapter 2. In Genesis 1, the first man and his wife are created together, while in Genesis 2, the man is formed first and the wife later, from the man's rib. In Chapter 1, man bears the image of God and is made ruler of the whole earth, while in Chapter 2, man has an earth-formed body and is placed in Eden to cultivate and guard it. In the former chapter, the birds and beasts are created before man, while in the latter, they are created after man. In summary, the creation order in Genesis 1 is: vegetation, day three; sun, moon, and stars, day four; birds and fish, day five; land animals and humans, day six. The order in Genesis 2 is quite different, and creation of the sun, moon and stars is not mentioned.

Commentators have used various trains of logic in their attempts to reconcile the two accounts. Some have developed arguments, often with an alleged scientific basis, that Genesis 2 simply provides details for and is subordinated to Genesis 1. Others believe a better view is to take the passages on their own merits, considering their purpose and literary style. We subscribe to the second view. The contexts and language in each narrative argue for a symbolic, theological, non-scientific meaning, and the writer is using story with different details to convey universal truth.

Stories often differ with each telling and the stories in Genesis 1 and 2 do different things with creation. Because one is older than the other, and they were written in different contexts, interpreting them literally and chronologically leads to a contradiction. Acknowledging that Genesis is literature of the symbolic imagination avoids contradiction by accepting that the two are different ways of telling the story for the purpose of communicating different ideas to different readers.

Considering Genesis 2 in the context of later biblical developments provides compelling evidence that, just as Genesis 1 addressed Mesopotamian polytheism, Genesis 2 was intended to address Canaanite polytheism and idolatry. Genesis 2 was composed around the time of Solomon, a period of increasing urbanism and imperialism when, with official sanction, the Israelites worshipped, served, and built altars to many gods. Israel was becoming like other cultures and losing its ability to fulfill its destiny. With this knowledge, tracing backwards through the Exodus, the patriarchs, the flood, Cain and Abel, to Adam and Eve makes it clear that the writer wasn't interested in dating creation, validating a flood, or determining how human beings were created. The writer was addressing fundamental religious and moral issues, and was encouraging the people of the day to forgo idolatry and the worship of many gods, and to remain faithful to Yahweh and the values of the patriarchs. The same idea applies to scripture dealing with other creation issues.

THE QUESTION OF SPECIES

Species are generally considered to be groups of animals that can breed with each other but not with other types of animals. Before

Charles Darwin, scientists agreed there had been some development of living things over time, but they did not consider it feasible that one species had developed out of a previous species or that ape-like creatures could develop into human beings. Few people challenged the idea of special creation. Therefore, naturalists, including Darwin until he took his trip on the *Beagle,* generally believed in the fixity of the species and the stability of biological forms. From their perspective, the species that existed at the time were those that had populated the earth in the distant past.

Their belief can be tied to an interpretation of the word "kind" in Genesis. Chapter 1, verses 20-26, indicates that God created the creatures of the sea "according to their kinds;" every winged bird "according to its kind;" living creatures on the land "according to their kinds;" and wild animals, "each according to its kind." He then said, "Let us make man in our image." The same language continues in Chapter 7, verse 14, which describes animals entering the ark: "They had with them every wild animal according to its kind, all livestock according to their kinds, every creature that moves along the ground according to its kind and every bird according to its kind..."

Special Creation View

Most people today, even strong creationists, accept the concept of microevolution—change over time within species. They see it in operation where, for example, a breed of dogs like dachshunds that didn't exist in exactly that same form in earlier times has been developed in recent history through artificial selection. Many also have generally conceded that the Hebrew word used in scripture does not mean "species," and that the word has been correctly translated as "kind." From their perspective, use of the word "kind" might allow for development of some species.

However, creationists at some point say, "Wait a minute. We can't trace humans and other animals back to a one-celled animal. Many original 'kinds' were developed by fiat creation at some point in the past when animal kinds were created." They cannot accept macroevolution, or the view that a "kind" is the result of a long development, or that all life, including humans, came from a common source, or that the human species developed its complexity over millions and millions of years. Henry Morris, in *Creation Science*, has argued that the account of creation in Genesis "indicates that at least ten major categories of organic life were specially created 'after His kind,'" and "One 'kind' could not transform itself into another 'kind.'"[5]

Hugh Ross, characterized earlier as a "concordist," developed the "Reason to Believe" creation model and articulated a similar position as follows:

> According to Genesis 1, the Creator actively and purpose-fully built life's diversity as part of the preparation for humanity (in six "days," or eras, of creation), but once humans arrived, He ceased making new kinds of life and no longer replaced extinct life-forms (once the seventh day, or era, of rest came). He assigned humanity the task of managing Earth's living creatures as well as its life-sustaining resources.[6]

Beliefs of those who claim to be part of the Intelligent Design Movement vary considerably. They generally accept that species have been changing for millions of years (microevolution) but cannot accept the full force of Darwinian evolution (macroevolution). They gener-ally reject the notion that natural law and chance alone can explain the diversity of life on earth. Instead, they believe something more—a superior intelligence—is required.

Many who don't believe in macroevolution continue to use scrip-tural language to maintain that God created "kinds" and, thereafter, change is only within the originally created kinds of plants and animals. They argue that there has not been enough time for macroevolution, and that God doesn't want evolution to take place from a single cell or life form. So it did not occur. A corollary is that man and other organ-isms, including apes, have separate ancestry. They may look like they came from the same kind, but that's theologically unacceptable.

Those who oppose macroevolution also argue that evolution has never been observed and is not occurring in the world today in a way that one can observe. Where has anyone observed a one-cell organism evolving into an ape-like animal and eventually into a human? Human beings are unique in all creation and had to be created instantaneously by God, not too long in the past.

To further support their case, as discussed in Chapter 8, creationists and many intelligent design proponents contend that the fossil record has too many major gaps to allow for evolution (some have argued that God put the fossils in their existing patterns in order to test man's faith), and in fact most groups of life came into being 550 million years ago during the Cambrian explosion, a relatively short period of time, perhaps as short as 30 million years.

Evolution of Species—Scientific Conclusions

Proponents of macroevolution, of course disagree. As discussed in Chapter 6, the vast majority of credible scientists—both Christian and non Christian—believe that species evolved over time from a common ancestor. The fossil remains in different strata of rock show that organisms today differ in major ways from those that lived millions of years ago. The long held acceptance of a common ancestor is supported by the presence of similar anatomical structures in various species, and it has been further strengthened by contemporary work involving an understanding of DNA and genetic sequencing.

Proponents make two arguments to rebut the view that evolution has never been observed, a view that Darwin himself anticipated when he wrote, "But the chief cause of our natural unwillingness to admit that one species has given birth to clear and distinct species, is that we are always slow in admitting great changes of which we do not see the steps."[7] First, they point out that while evolutionary theory posits that various species developed from a common ancestor, it has never predicted, for example, that monkeys would change into human beings. Consequently, the fact that science hasn't observed monkeys changing into human beings (hasn't observed what it didn't predict) is not a problem. Second, proponents argue that while the very long time spans involved prevent scientists from "observing" evolution in the literal sense demanded by creationists, evolution has in fact been observed. Think of your favorite oak tree from as many years ago as your age allows. Do you see any change as you observe it on a day-by-day basis? Surely not. But as you think about it over a period of years, do you know it has grown? Surely yes. You make direct observations and logical inferences from what you see, connect the dots, and know that the tree has grown. Similarly, scientists believe that one who takes the time to review the evidence and connect the dots can clearly observe evolution of species.

With respect to the fossil gap suggested by creationists, scientists suggest that "the absence of evidence is not evidence of absence," and that the reason for the gaps is simply that conditions necessary for fossilization are so rare. Most organisms do not make it into the fossil record. Doing so requires a very special combination of physical circumstances such as those found in swamps and estuaries where remains can be buried, compacted, and protected for millions of years and then eroded away without being destroyed. This is a unique situation that makes fossils very rare indeed. In addition, as discussed in Chapter 8, Stephen Jay Gould has developed a theory of "punctuated evolution" to address this issue. He argues that living organisms are generally stable for millions of years. Then, suddenly, for some reason, there is a punctuated jump in evolution, which explains the fossil patterns.

Evolution of Species—Scriptural Arguments

Most importantly, there is no scriptural argument against the evolution of species. The religion and science controversy is fraught with cases where one suspects that one side or the other adopts a position for practical or philosophical reasons and then goes looking for scripture to support the position. The question of species is a prime example. One suspects that opponents of macroevolution came to their beliefs because of the influence of philosophy or perceived atheistic and materialistic influences of social Darwinism, and then did exactly that—they went looking for scripture to support their ideas.

Let's go back in history and consider philosophy. Aristotle believed the world was comprised of substances occurring in fixed natural kinds, and each substance or individual grows toward self-realization within its own type. In his view, individual biological organisms are primary substances, their forms are eternal, and their essence unchanging. Predictably, the Aristotelian philosophy of science and the biblical text were combined to, in effect, result in a literal interpretation of the Bible that considered "kind" as species and had them unchangeable. Consequently, forerunners of Darwin—prominent scientists like Charles Lyell and Carl Linnaeus—believed that species were fixed, and if they weren't fixed, they could only move slightly one way or the other. They were very Aristotelian in their biology and were Aristotelian creationists.

Thus, just as Galileo and Copernicus were objecting centuries earlier mainly to Aristotelian astronomy rather than the Bible, Darwin's problem was principally with Aristotle, not the Bible. To overcome the Christian traditionalists of his day, Darwin had to attack the Aristotelian concept of forms rather than the Bible, which doesn't say anything about species or the fixity of species. Even today, a Christian who says "The Bible teaches the fixity of the species," is not a literal Bible interpreter because those expressions are not found in the Bible.

Genesis is a broad, general theological story that does not address the question of species. In fact, according to Bernard Ramm, writing in *The Christian View of Science and Scripture*:

> Few reliable conservative scholars today would state that we can positively identify the Hebrew word *kind* (Hebrew, *min*; LXX, *genos*; Vulgate, *genus* and *species*) with the modern scientific notion of *species*. None would certainly identify *min* with varieties. To attempt to identify *min* with species or varieties is making the record speak with a scientific particularity it does not possess. We judge it improper for the theologian to try to settle specific details about scientific matters by forcing the Bible to speak with a degree of particularity its language does not indicate.[8]

As in so many other biblical stories, the use of "kind" in the creation story conveys a universal theological truth rather than scientific facts. Think of Genesis as originally heard or read in the culture in which it was written. What does it tell a person in that setting about the species? It doesn't tell him anything he doesn't already know. It doesn't tell him what a species is, how many species there are, or even that animals can be divided into species. It tells him that whatever he has seen with his eyes—cattle, goats, sheep, sea monsters, or human beings—were created by and absolutely dependent for their existence upon God. It doesn't say whether new species have evolved over time. That is a scientific question.

THE ORIGIN STORIES—II

"It is a disgraceful and dangerous thing for an infidel to hear a Christian, while
presumably giving the meaning of Holy Scripture, talking non-sense."
Augustine (354 – 430 A.D.)

Chapter 13 addressed the two creation accounts of Genesis and questions relating to the origin of species. But the controversies arising from the early chapters of Genesis don't end there. In this chapter, we will discuss several other issues that commonly arise when the topic of religion and science is discussed—the genealogies, the fall, the flood, and the Tower of Babel.

THE GENEALOGIES

Genesis contains several accounts of descendants of Adam and Eve. Genesis 4:17-22 traces ten generations from Adam to Tubal-Cain. Genesis 5:1-32 also traces ten generations from Adam, but with significant differences, including ending with Noah rather than Tubal-Cain. Genesis 11:10-32 continues the progression from Genesis 5, listing generations from Noah to the call of Abraham. All have been used over the years to support the idea of a young earth.

Literal Interpretation

The scientific revolution brought about by Copernicus and Galileo changed the general view of the universe from geocentric to heliocentric, but it left the traditional beliefs about the earth's age intact. In the seventeenth century, Dr. John Lightfoot, vice-chancellor of the University of Cambridge and one of the most eminent Hebrew scholars of his time, estimated that creation occurred at nine o'clock in the morning on October 23, 4004 B.C. A decade later, Bishop James Ussher, an eminent churchman and confidant of Charles I, made the same estimate—without the nine o'clock time—and received almost all the credit. He, like Lightfoot, painstakingly followed the series of "begats" in the book of Genesis back in time and determined that the universe was created in the year 4004 BC, on October 23. This chronology was accepted by almost all of Ussher's contemporaries and was inserted in the margins of many editions of the "King James Version" of the Bible in the nineteenth century.

Ussher's approach continues to be used by some believers today as "proof" of the fallacy of evolution, molecular biology, astrophysics, and many other scientific endeavors of the twentieth century, as conclusions based on evolutionary theories do not make sense if the earth is really that young. Some who believe in a young earth defend their position by attempting to demonstrate weaknesses in the scientific methods of determining the antiquity of the universe. Others admit the reasonableness of scientific conclusions as to the age of the earth. But they claim this only demonstrates the apparent age, not the actual age, because anything instantly created must look as though it had been there before creation.

Symbolic Interpretation

The biblical timescale began to be seriously questioned in the late 1600s and in the 1700s as the implications of the emerging fossil record and other discoveries of the growing science of geology became better understood. Those who doubted a young earth raised numerous practical objections to the literal biblical version of events that assumes that Adam and Eve were specially created as mature individuals at a specific point in time. They asked tough questions: Who did the sons of Adam and Eve marry? If they married their sisters, how is this reconciled with biblical proscriptions against such marriages? Could the world have reached known population levels in the relatively short period of time between creation and the flood, and between the flood and now?

Problems with a literal interpretation continue to be raised as interpreters aim to read the Bible for what they believe its writers intended to communicate. The genealogies of Genesis 5 and 11 sound to people today like specific, accurate chronologies, from which the age of the earth can be calculated. However, Old Testament scholars generally agree that chronology was not the purpose of the genealogies; instead, they were literary devises used to bridge the gaps between individual stories and to suggest passage of considerable periods of time. The Bible does not directly or indirectly address the age of man, the time of creation, or the age of the earth. The earth may be younger or older than the 4.5 billion years estimated by evidence from astronomy, physics, geology, and archeology, but there is no conflict between the physical data and what the Bible actually says. We need to be very careful about turning the information contained in the genealogies to purposes beyond its intent.

The sequence of people in a biblical genealogy does not reliably represent accurate history. Hebrew writers were more concerned with noting significant individuals than with documenting complete family histories. Consider Genesis 5:32, where the sons of Noah are listed in what appears to be birth order as Shem, Ham and Japheth. However, Genesis 9:24 tells us that Ham, not Japheth, is actually the youngest. Thus, the order given in 5:32 reflects the relative importance of each to the events that transpire in subsequent history. The biblical writer did not adhere to our twentieth century western literary forms that would typically sequence by age. Instead, the writer adjusted the sequence of events to fit the relative importance of the individuals.

Similarly, writers often omitted the "black sheep." One author put it this way: "If Uncle Harry was a horse thief, then usually Uncle Harry wouldn't be included in the genealogy. If Uncle Harry was a brave king, then you could count on his name showing up on every genealogy that could reasonably claim him."

The words begat and son are used to indicate descendents some place down the line, rather than immediate. For example, Genesis 5:9 reads, "When Enosh had lived 90 years, he became the father of Kenan." Kenan may or may not have been the paternal son of Enosh. He could have been a grandson, or a great-grandson or a great-great-great-grandson. The scripture doesn't provide enough insight into the lineage to decide the matter, but the practice allows for the omission of many individuals or generations.

In addition, biblical writers often referred to a whole lineage by its chief member. This kind of usage is taken further in the genealogies of Genesis 10, where one person's name may be used to refer to a whole nation, tribe, or even a geographical region. For example, most biblical scholars believe that the "sons" referred to in Genesis 10:2 and 10:4 are countries, not just individuals. Verses 5, 20, and 31 make very clear the nonspecific aspect of these genealogies of Shem, Ham, and Japheth. We are so accustomed to these names that we forget the significance such a usage has in the biblical genealogies.

While this view of genealogies seems odd today, it apparently was quite common in biblical times. The Hebrews never seemed to have had a problem with the approach because the lists and ages were never intended for the chronological purposes to which we wish to put them. They showed the descendants of the throne and illustrated other universal truths. For example, the literal language of Genesis 5 and 10 indicates ages ranging from Enoch at 365 years to Methusala at 969 years, but the stated times have a contextual purpose that does not relate in any way to overall chronology. Theologians believe that Genesis 5 illustrates the surety of death, regardless of long lives, following the sin of Adam and Eve. The genealogy of Genesis 10, which occurred after the flood, uses shorter life spans to demonstrate man's humbling and loss of a grasp on life.

Thus, we should not try to use these genealogies to determine how long ago God created the heavens and the earth, or to attempt to refute scientific explanations. The Bible only says, "in the beginning," so to assign a date based on scripture is presumptuous. If we knew in fact that there was one Adam, knew when Adam lived, and knew the exact meaning of *yom* (generally the word for day, but actually having at least four different meanings) each time it is used in Genesis 1... If we knew the time between each *yom* of Genesis 1... If we knew how long the earth was formless and void before God initiated the events of the first *yom*...And if we knew the genealogies were accurate chronologies...Then we might hazard a guess as to the time of creation. But these are big ifs. They suggest that we need to read the genealogies as they were intended and let science stand on its own.

THE FALL

Many people believe there is a story in the Bible about some folks eating an apple six thousand years ago, and because they ate the apple, we all die. But the Bible contains no such story. In Genesis 3, a snake tells Eve that God has lied to her and Adam concerning the Tree of Knowledge of Good and Evil. It convinces her to eat the fruit of the tree so they will become like God, and Adam later partakes as well. Their eyes are then opened and they realize they are naked. God curses the snake, Adam, Eve, and even the earth itself, and banishes them from the Garden of Eden. This story is seen in many parts of the Christian tradition as the beginning of the human problem, or as "original sin."

Few, if any, theologians believe this story should be interpreted literally. Conservative Protestant James Orr (1844–1913), one of the most important Christian apologists of the nineteenth and twentieth centuries, wrote two articles on Genesis and science in *The Fundamentals* and has said with respect to the fall:

> I do not enter into the question of how we are to interpret the third chapter of Genesis—whether as history or allegory or myth, or most probably of all, as old tradition clothed in oriental allegorical dress—but the truth embodied in that narrative, viz. the fall of man from an original state of purity, I take to be vital to the Christian view.[1]

Thus, Orr thought that the story of the fall was "probably" told in an "allegorical" manner. In Orr's view, "… we do not know what Adam and Eve actually did in their rebellion against God. We only know Eve was deceived by Satan and sinned. Then she tempted Adam, who sinned and was ultimately responsible. Thus humanity fell from original righteousness and immortality."[2]

Genesis says that Adam was forbidden to eat from "the tree of the knowledge of good and evil," but was allowed to eat of the "tree of life." We know that apples grow on apple trees and acorns grow on oak trees. But what grows on a "life" tree? Or a "knowledge of good and evil" tree? And how did the serpent speak to Eve? Clearly, the author of Genesis had a more poetic imagination than most of us and, therefore, could deal with subjects in a more profound way than we usually do. The writer didn't tell a literal story about somebody eating an apple and causing us to die. He wrote symbolically about life and death and the knowledge of good and evil. Thus, we can only understand what eating from the tree of life or the tree of knowledge of good and evil means if we accept that Genesis 3 is not a literal, historical account of a man and his wife snitching an apple.

Pagan myths from Mesopotamia and Babylon, including the legend of *Gilgamesh*, explore similar themes of humans losing their chance for immortality, but they are different in a significant way. These myths generally assumed that the gods purposely kept humans from immortality so there would be no threats against the gods. The story of Adam and Eve, on the other hand, teaches that we are to blame for our own transgressions and that our downfall is a consequence of human choice. It presents a very profound account of the meaning of life—an account we must probe deeply to understand. Its imagery expresses the idea that human nature has fallen from its original sinless state into a state that God did not intend. We see that the choice Adam and Eve made was in reality the choice human beings make between the tree of life and the tree of the knowledge of good and evil. Adam and Eve were free adults and were taught about guilt and shame, which are rooted in human pride and disobedience. It's the story of you and me—of all of us. Adam and Eve's disobedience created a massive gulf, which can only be bridged by the salvation offered by Jesus Christ.

This story gives us a way to think about our problems and the fallen world in relation to God. We all probably know that we have eaten of the tree of the knowledge of good and evil and that we have deep problems because we are human beings and are living in a fallen world. However, we may not know that the reason we have deep problems is because we have broken our relationship with God. So the story's purpose is not to tell human beings that they have problems and have fallen. Its purpose is to tell us why.

Some question whether the doctrine of sin has any meaning and whether human beings can be considered fallen angels if man evolved from a common ancestry with apes. But the Bible doesn't consider us as either fallen angels or descendants of apes. Instead, the story of Adam and Eve symbolically illustrates that we are human beings with free will, responsible for the consequences of our own actions. Creation was good, and sin came after creation in the form of voluntary acts. While temptation may lead to sin, it does not cause sin so long as the sinner has free will—which we all do. Thus, sin was not a necessary part of creation. It was voluntary, and it doesn't have to last forever. The fundamental truth and relevance of this story is not affected by when and how we became human beings. We have the same freedom and responsibility, commit the same acts, and behave the same way regardless of whether we were created instantaneously six thousand years ago or have been around for millions of years.

THE FLOOD

The flood of Noah discussed in Genesis 6-9 is one of the most familiar of all biblical stories. Moral decay and corruption had gradually filled the earth in the generations, according to the genealogies, since the time of Adam and Eve. God found the world so corrupt He was sorry to have created it and was determined to "wipe from the face of the earth every living creature I have made." He warned Noah, the only righteous man, of the impending disaster and promised to save him and his family. Noah was instructed to build a wooden ark according to certain specifications and to take into it male and female specimens of all the world's living creatures, from which the stocks might be replenished after the devastation of the flood. Noah and his family entered the ark, and "all the springs of the great deep burst forth, and the floodgates of the heavens were opened." Rain fell for forty days and nights and covered the entire earth, including the mountains. Then, according to Genesis 7:18-20, "The waters rose and increased greatly on the earth, and the ark floated on the surface of the water. They rose greatly on the earth, and all the high mountains under the entire heavens were covered. The waters rose and covered the mountains to a depth of more than twenty feet."

The water flooded the earth for 150 days and "Every living thing on the face of the earth was wiped out." After the water dried, God blessed Noah and his family, and He put a rainbow in the sky as a visible guarantee of His promise in the covenant.

A variety of views exist as to the real meaning of this story.

Global Flood View

In the absence of understandings from modern geology (relating to issues such as the marine origin of fossils, the earth's strata, glacial theory, and plate tectonics), most early Christian and Jewish writers believed the flood events of Genesis actually happened as recounted. Bishop Ussher, introduced earlier in this chapter, even calculated that the flood occurred 1,656 years after the Creation: Noah and his family entered the ark on Sunday, December 7, 2349 BC, and exited on December 18 of the following year. Many early writers tried to fill in the gaps that remained in the scriptural account by speculating about issues such as the detailed plan of the ark, the nature of the food eaten during the flood, the chaos that occurred when the doors to the ark were closed, and daily life on the ark. They often used allegory, sometimes rather extreme, to relate flood details with the Bible, and they tried to understand what the events meant for the present and the future.

By the seventeenth century, doubts began to arise—about previously unknown species, or the presence of noxious creatures in America that should have vanished in the flood, or where all the water came from and where it went after the flood, or how to explain fossils in various earth strata. The notion of a local flood began to gain traction as many Christians modified their beliefs to harmonize them with emerging scientific understanding.

Attempts to find remnants of the ark have continued for centuries. Since the end of World War II, nearly a dozen Christian organizations have mounted serious expeditions to Mt. Ararat in search of the remains of Noah's ark. None have been successful.

Many, however, have continued to maintain a literalist view. They believe that if flood geology—the view that the flood and its aftermath are the origin of most of the Earth's geologic features, including sedentary strata, fossils, fossil fuels, canyons, salt domes, etc.—could be established on a sound scientific basis, the Darwinian system of biological evolution as we know it could not be reconciled and would collapse. Ideas of social Darwinism would then be deprived of the intellectual foundation they claim from Darwin.

The creationists' view, often called catastrophism, follows a tradition launched by the numerous works of George McCready Price in the early 1900s and continued by John C. Whitcomb Jr. and Henry M. Morris in their 1961 book, *The Genesis Flood: The Biblical Record and its Scientific Implications*. They argue that the Genesis account is an absolutely authoritative account of a divinely ordained event and is to be taken literally in all respects. The flood of Noah was a global event that destroyed all the earth's land-dwelling animal life, and all of today's animal life descended from those on the ark. The flood was the cause of all the earth's major geological features as sudden up-thrusting occurred when the fountains of the deep broke open, causing mountains to form. And the water scooped out valleys and canyons (including the Grand Canyon), laid down gravel and rocks, destroyed all life on earth, and created the fossil record in the geological strata. Noah's sons were the progenitors of the entire human race. Creationists see the flood as a great miracle in the sense that it was caused by God, and also in the sense that forces were unleashed that are not now available for scientists to study.

Reminiscent of early biblical apologists, creationists have responded to doubters by filling in the gaps in the biblical record in a number of ways. For example, when skeptics wondered how animals in remote areas found the ark, or how so few humans could have fed the animals and cleaned the manure, Whitcomb and Morris responded:

> Even as God instructed Noah, by specific revelation, concerning the coming Flood and his means of escape from it, so He instructed certain of the animals, through impartation of a migratory directional instinct which would afterward be inherited in greater or less degree by their descendants, to flee from their native habitats to the place of safety. Then, having entered the Ark, they also received from God the power to become more or less dormant, in various ways, in order to be able to survive for three years in which they were to be confined within the Ark while the great storms and convulsions raged outside.[3]

Local Flood View

Many people, including most intelligent design proponents, have concluded that the scientific evidence contrary to a worldwide flood is clear and compelling. Some, perhaps more accurately in the concordist camp, suggest instead that a very large regional catastrophe did occur, which effectively destroyed the world and its people and simultaneously changed the geography and geology of a section of the world. However, because it was a local rather than a universal flood, we are not dependent upon it for all the answers to geology, and it could not have been the source of the fossil record.

Those who advocate a scriptural basis for a local flood point out that the words usually translated as "earth"—*adamah* and *erets*—do not necessarily mean what we call the earth, and that those words also can mean country, earth, ground, land, and nation. While our Bible discusses the destruction of the human race, they add, we should not rule out the likelihood that mankind lived only in a small portion of the earth and could have been destroyed by a local flood. Thus, they argue that the flood destroyed the entire human race (except Noah's family) and all the birds and mammals associated with mankind, so it could be a universal event without being global—an interpretation that violates neither the text nor the available scientific data. The web site for the Reason to Believe organization, states:

> Given that Genesis 6-9 tells the story of God's act of judgment against wholesale reprobation and spiritual ruin, scriptural integrity hinges primarily on whether the Flood killed all humanity except for the family of the one man who feared God. In other words, the key theological point is whether or not the Flood was universal in its effect, regardless of its physical extent. The original Hebrew text supports a universal flood impact and allows for a regional locus when viewed in context.[4]

Similarly, many local flood proponents contend that other passages are subject to interpretation. For example, they believe the correct interpretation of the provision in Genesis 8:9, which records that the dove sent out by Noah could find no place to set her feet, depends on establishing the dove's frame of reference. The fact that the dove couldn't find land doesn't mean that there wasn't any. And the reference "under the entire heavens" in Genesis 7:19 must be interpreted from Noah's perspective in Mesopotamia, not from a modern global perspective. Both allow for a regional flood that fits scientific facts such as those about the quantity of water available in the earth's crust and atmosphere. Therefore, the biblical ark did exist. The remains will never be found simply because the timbers of the ark would have been too valuable for the ancients to leave lying around. The important point is that a local flood accomplished the biblical purpose—to wipe out most human beings—because that very small area is where civilization and most human beings were located at the time.

Nonbeliever View

The view of nonbelievers is simple and straightforward. They generally argue that the story of Noah was intended to be taken literally, although it is a legend with no truth at all. There is no scientific evidence confirming the flood. In fact, a great deal of evidence refutes such an event. The flood described in Genesis would have been physically impossible. The nonbelievers contend, for example, that Noah and his sons could not possibly have built such an ark in the time allotted, that collecting two of each animal would have been impossible (and in any event their weight and the weight of their food would have collapsed the ark), and that the subsequent animal population could not possibly have developed from only two of each kind. Also, nonbelievers generally maintain that if the flood were a true account, it would demonstrate an appallingly negative and vindictive God.

Symbolic View

We suggest a fourth view—the conclusion of most Bible scholars, archeologists, historians, and even intelligent design proponents—that starts with the conclusion that there has been no global flood. While the prevalence of flood accounts suggests the strong likelihood of a major flood event in the distant past, the problems in connection with a universal flood are just too great to overcome; i.e., the amount of water required, the mixing of fresh and salt water, getting rid of the water, all the problems connected with the animals, and on and on. After literally hundreds of attempts archeologists have never been able to find credible evidence of a worldwide flood event or of a ship resting on the top of any mountain anywhere in the Near East. Even if a major local flood did occur during the time of Noah, one should not attribute the earth's geology to it. Variables such as land drift, land shifting, earthquakes, water cycles, and heat from inside the earth seem to better explain the age and structure of the earth.

However, archeological evidence confirms that in ancient times, floods often devastated large areas of Mesopotamia, known today as Iraq. As a result of heavy rains and melting snow, the Tigris and Euphrates rivers often expanded beyond their banks and submerged hundreds of miles of land in the spring. This phenomenon gave rise to powerful traditions. Aristotle and Plato referred to great deluges in their writings, and flood stories similar to the one of Noah were common in Sumerian, Mesopotamian, Greek, and Babylonian cultures. In the Babylonian epic *Gilgamesh* (previously discussed), a deity warned of a great flood; an ark with seven levels was built and loaded with personal possessions, animals, and birds; mountains disappeared under the devastating water; the ark came to rest on a mountain top; a dove, swallow, and raven were sent out; and mankind survived.

The biblical flood story has an interesting historical context. Importantly, many scholars believe that several ancient sources lie behind the version that appears in our Bible and that different themes have been woven together to comprise the biblical story. Ancient Near Eastern literature commonly used storms and floods sent by divine decree to symbolize invasion and conquest. Evidence strongly supports the view that the biblical story was written between 550 and 450 BC, around the time of the Babylonian Exile—when most inhabitants of Jerusalem were exiled to Babylon, the walls of Jerusalem were destroyed, Solomon's temple was burned to the ground, and the Davidic monarchy was eliminated. Thus, many aspects of the biblical story are consistent with the literary practices of the time that often related floods to conquests.

The story of Noah's flood was handed down by oral tradition and has obvious similarities with flood accounts in Mesopotamian and other epics. However, the biblical story is different from the pagan ones in many details, including the size of the ark or the time the water stayed on the land. More importantly, while the pagan stories reflect unpredictable gods prone to divine anger and wrathful actions when humans annoyed or disturbed them, the biblical account affirms a God who is consistent, faithful, just, and loving. He punishes only for clear moral evil and is quick to forgive.

Alan Richardson, in his book *Genesis I-XI*, brings a great perspective to the story of the flood:

The story, like the creation stories, conveys truth in the form of parable. The wonder is that the divine revelation can take the primitive and childish speculations and legends of the pagan world and can make of them the vehicle of ultimate truth—truth in a form which the "pre-scientific" contemporaries of [the composers] could grasp, and which can speak in every age to all who are willing to lay aside their sophistication and become as little children. Only those who are "wise in their own conceits" will think that they have nothing to learn from the divinely inspired children's story of Noah's ark.[5]

The bottom line is that the argument seems to be about nothing of substance. Regardless of whether or not the account is based on a spectacular local flood, the Genesis story was never intended as a form of science that would describe how the earth's geologic features were formed or indicate the age of the earth, and it was not intended as a history of events. It is much more likely that the flood story was included in the Bible to illustrate and explain theological ideas. Like the creation stories, it provides a resounding rebuke to polytheism and a confirmation of one true God, as He says, "I will wipe mankind, whom I have created, from the face of the earth..." It tells the story of human depravity and man hitting the bottom, and of God's attempt to redeem man and provide us a new start. The ark is a beautiful picture of salvation by grace through faith. There was no other way to be saved from destruction in that day except by coming into God's ark of refuge. And the story of the salvation of the man, his family, and every living creature is the picture of a creation restored, where life will go on to be lived in covenant with God in a cleansed world order. That is the story we need to learn and appreciate, and it is not science.

THE TOWER OF BABEL

The story of the Tower of Babel follows the story of the flood of Noah. God had almost given up on the whole human race because of the wickedness of mankind, but He found in Noah hope for a new beginning. After the flood, God promised Noah that He would never again destroy the world because of man's evil, and He sent the survivors forth to multiply.

Unfortunately, the flood did not stem man's evil ways. The sons of Noah and their wives repopulated the world with their offspring, all of whom spoke with "one language and a common speech." This linguistic unity made Noah's descendants ambitious and powerful, and they wanted to make a name for themselves. They began building a town with a tower—the Tower of Babel—which would reach to the heavens. The tower glorified man rather than God, and showed that man loved himself more than any god. God noticed the activity and observed, "If as one people speaking the same language they have begun to do this, then nothing they plan to do will be impossible for them. Come, let us go down and confuse their language so they will not understand each other." (Genesis 11: 6-7) Thus, God removed the source of their power by creating many languages. Since the people were unable to communicate, they were forced to stop building their town, abandon the tower, and scatter across the face of the earth.

The Conflict

This biblical story concerning our diversity of languages is closely analogous to the earlier story of creation. Just as a literal reading of the language of the creation account suggests special creation, a literal reading of the story of the Tower of Babel suggests that various languages were a special creation of God. And just as science holds that species, including human beings, evolved over many years, linguistic theory holds that different languages evolved over a long period of time. Like the creation story, the Tower of Babel is an incredible story that needs to be understood in light of its context and purpose.

The Context

People in Old Testament times lived in cities and constructed elaborate temple complexes to provide a place to worship their most important god and to testify to the royal power. They commonly constructed a ziggurat—a very large, stepped pyramid that served as the base for the temple. Since they considered the sky to be the floor of heaven, not so far above the earth, it seemed possible that one could pile enough bricks, one on top of another, to reach the heavens.

Not surprisingly, stories developed about these imposing structures. "Enmerkar and the Lord of Aratta," a Sumerian myth similar to that of the Tower of Babel, had Enmerkar of Uruk building a massive ziggurat in Eridu. Enmerkar implored the god Enki to restore (or to disrupt in some translations) the linguistic unity of the people in the region.

The name "Babel" referred to Babylon, a city that reflected everything wrong with humanity. Babylon was both envied and loathed. It was beautiful, graced with streets and palaces, and was a center of intellectual development in the ancient world. But to the Hebrews, a nomadic society concerned with day-to-day survival, Babylon represented oppression, cruelty and violence. So Babel (Babylon) is portrayed as a society whose members, filled with an outsized pride, sought to dominate and exploit others. Everyone spoke the same language, and through human cooperation, the Babylonians attempted to glorify themselves by climbing to heaven on a tower. This was not a God-centered society, but a group of people dedicated to elevating man to a position as God. The ziggurat or tower was the evidence.

The Theology

Bible scholars are convinced that the story is theology, not science. First and foremost, it is a parable—similar to the parable of the Good Samaritan or the parable of the Prodigal Son—that uses familiar people or circumstances to illustrate unfamiliar truths. The parable covers several recurring biblical themes. It condemns the overweening pride of the people of towering cities who defy God's purpose and law. It emphasizes that man's exaltation of himself as opposed to God is the prime cause of divisions and rivalries. It teaches that human beings cannot speak to one another in a common tongue because people have no common interest or mutual regard. The parable of the Tower of Babel is not a literal history that accounts for differences of race and language as the result of a single divine intervention at a particular moment. Instead, it is a story using familiar circumstances of the time to tell of the encounter of sinful humanity with the God of righteousness. It would have spoken powerfully to the Babylonian exiles of antiquity.

It is a story told from the viewpoint of an ancient society—a parable about mankind—God's story about where man's heart is and

God's concern about it. It is the story of God's dealings with the citizens of Babel, who thought they were technologically able to challenge God's leadership and who were willing to press forward in the name of progress without reference to or respect for God. It told the citizens of Babel, and tells us, that the road without God is doomed to disaster.

15

CONCLUSIONS

"Do not be conformed to this world, but be transformed by the renewing of your minds, so that you may discern what is the will of God—what is good and acceptable and perfect."
Romans 12:2

So many questions. So many different responses based on hard evidence, working theories, revelation, or faith, and often involving ignorance, uncertainty, arrogance, ambivalence, or fear. How does one reach his or her own personal decision on such complex and important issues? Is there a single right answer? If so, what is it?

We will not have all the answers, but we aim to be "somewhat more partially right." We acknowledge the broad range of biblical interpretations and believe the Bible allows room for a range of beliefs on matters of science. Against this background, we cannot be dogmatic and assume that you should agree with us. We hope you will honestly consider our views.

Our beliefs, as suggested earlier, include accepting the theory of biological evolution, along with other contemporary, scientific propositions. Accepting such conclusions requires some judgments in areas where we are not experts. However, all of us make decisions every day when we don't have direct knowledge or expertise in the matter being considered. Most of us buy cars without any real, direct knowledge of which make or model is best. We fly on a plane without understanding why it stays in the air. We have a doctor carve us up without a detailed understanding of why an operation is necessary or how she will go about it. Courts and juries make life and death decisions on the basis of the testimony of others.

We apply what we know and what we can see for ourselves, but we also assess the knowledge and expertise of others, placing the most weight on those who have the greatest credibility. Your authors have taken such an approach in reaching the conclusions outlined below. You may use the same process and reach different conclusions. However, we hope you will read the Bible for what it is and judge science on its own merits. We offer the following in this spirit.

THE MYSTERY

We suspect that some questions will be around, unanswered for as long as human beings exist to ponder them. Our universe is stranger, more complicated, and more mysterious than we can imagine. And we are not omniscient. So we need to be honest with ourselves and acknowledge, perhaps thankfully, that no one has all the answers and we suspect no one ever will. There are so many mysteries.

Two Levels of Mystery

Think of two levels of mystery. One level involves questions to answer or problems to solve: "Why the planets move as they do?" "What causes cancer?" "Who killed JR?" Many have been answered, and others, no doubt, are answerable as human beings continue to ask and to explore. Such questions often have led to a God of the gaps when people try to use God to explain what they don't understand, or until they understand it, as if He were a stand-in for a scientific explanation. Once they find the answer or solve the problem, God goes Poof!—up in a cloud of smoke or an exhibition of arrogance because there is no perceived need for Him any longer.

This response to the unknown would have been shocking to many pioneers of science. From their perspective, the real mystery is much deeper and more fundamental, not just a gap that God fills until man finds the missing link. The real mystery involves God as the source of all that is—a much greater issue involving more fundamental questions: "What is the source of the universe?" "Why is there something and not nothing?" "Whither lies human destiny?" "Do human beings have a purpose?" Despite all of humanity's efforts in philosophy and science, such questions remain—apparently unanswerable, often unfathomable. Theology will not resolve them either. Certainly, neither

Jewish nor Christian theology claims to resolve the mystery of God. All they can do is provide a greater awareness of the mystery.

Augustine used the doctrine of the Trinity as an example of the deep mystery of Christianity. He did not believe this doctrine really explained the relationship between God and Jesus Christ; instead it was just a human attempt to comprehend the relationship. For Augustine, theology was faith seeking understanding—a journey that human beings will never complete and that will not solve the fundamental mysteries. Our journey is simply an exploration of more mysteries.

Luther believed God is both hidden (1 John 4:12, "No one has ever seen God.") and revealed (John 14:9, "Anyone who has seen me has seen the father."), which is perhaps what makes a mystery—enough known to pique our curiosity and enough unknown to be mysterious. That which is hidden about God is broader and more important than what is revealed, because all that human beings can know about God is what He has chosen to reveal. And He hasn't revealed much about Himself. The Bible is a book of stories about God, in which He reveals something of Himself and what He is like. Yet most everything is still hidden. Any person who thinks she has God boxed up, and therefore knows exactly who He, or perhaps She, is or how He works, is badly mistaken. Augustine, Luther, and other thoughtful theologians for centuries have understood that the God of the Bible is not an understandable God. We all need to understand that, too.

The Deeper Mystery

Even talking about God challenges the limits of our language. But symbolism in naming, describing, and elaborating on the mystery perhaps can help us comprehend some of it. Hyers has suggested that four biblical words—maker, word, wisdom, and person—have been used to name God, and that these words provide "clues to the ultimate source and basis of things—a source and basis which is also sensed as being superior, rather than inferior, to its highest known forms in human existence."[1] These words provide a symbolic richness and power that can be appreciated even by small children, but really understood by not even the most brilliant adult. Consider the word "person." We try to describe God by referring to a person because we are persons. But the biblical teaching is the other way around. We are persons because God is a person. And the mystery continues.

Science is inadequate in the face of such mystery. Some say science assumes that nature is all there is, or as Carl Sagan noted in his televisions series, *Cosmos*, "the Cosmos is all that is or ever was or ever will be." Sagan writes God off and doesn't address what he believes does not exist. Others simply refuse to make judgments about God because scientific inquiry cannot address or test the supernatural. So even if we human beings learn everything there is to know about nature, we still would not comprehend the ultimate mystery. It is beyond us.

How one addresses this great unknown varies with one's point of view. On a particular issue, say a question about God's interaction with the world, an agnostic might be uncertain because the empirical evidence of God's existence and interaction simply doesn't reach the level of proof or non-proof. A Christian, on the other hand, "knows" that God interacts with the world because this is a tenet of his faith.

The writer of Hebrews seems to have anticipated the problem and provided the answer in Hebrews 11:1-3: "Now faith is being sure of what we hope for and certain of what we do not see. This is what the ancients were commended for. By faith we understand that the universe was formed at God's command so that what is seen was not made out of what was visible." And Jesus said to Thomas in John 20:29, "Blessed are those who have not seen and yet have believed." While such belief without seeing is anathema to the scientific method, it seems to describe the essence of the mystery that exists within religion.

Theology is man's attempt to understand what faith is and how it works. It is our attempt to understand who we are and how we are saved, and it requires faith because we don't know all the answers. Your authors certainly don't claim to have all the answers in the Bible and science debate, but we have elected to deal with the mystery as discussed in the following sections.

SCIENCE VERSUS SCIENTISM

In earlier chapters, we noted that the science we are considering includes, at a minimum, conclusions from the application of the modern scientific method to astronomy, geology, and biology. Most of those conclusions—like a round rather than a flat earth and a helio-centric rather than a geocentric universe—have been resolved for many years. Even the more recent big bang theory is not the focus of much controversy. While some disagreement remains between certain elements of astronomy and geology, and some religious persons, the divisive issue today is evolution. Accordingly, our discussion of science focuses primarily on evolution.

Science

We respect the views of anyone who honestly and thoughtfully considers all the scientific evidence and believes that evolution has not occurred. But we respectfully take another view. Your authors believe there is substantial hard, observable evidence of evolution. We can observe the unique characteristics of a pet dog or cat and appreciate the microevolution, or change over time, which has resulted from selective breeding. We can go to a good museum and observe fossil records or drive cross-country and observe geological outcroppings consistent with an old earth and evolutionary change. We can observe our own bodies' vestigial organs—appendix, body hair, or tailbone—that have no current use. More importantly, while we cannot specifi-cally see evolution and no piece of evidence is proof in and of itself, we can merge all the bits of data from myriad fields to form a rich picture of how the world and its inhabitants came to be over a very long period of time.

Of even more importance, the vast majority of credible scientists, Christian and non-Christian, support the theory of evolution and do so in the macroevolution sense. It's important to note that this theory and its related conclusions—such as the very old earth and the gradual appearance of new life forms over billions of years—are not peripheral issues on the margin of science and our lives. Instead, they are at the core of much of today's science and technology. Nearly all credible scientists, including physicists, geologists, biologists, astronomers, and others, hold to them with absolute certainty. These conclusions are so fundamental that, if they were wrong, the disciplines themselves would fall.

Allied against these forces are a small number (six to a dozen, depending on one's definition) of creationist/intelligent design organi-zations that object to macroevolution, some on purely religious rather than scientific grounds, some apparently driven by religious beliefs to find the scientific answer they want, and others driven by their honest views of the scientific evidence. According to *Newsweek* in 1987, only 700 U.S. earth and life scientists out of a total of 480,000 with respectable academic credentials, or less than one quarter of one percent, give credence to creation science. A 1997 Gallop poll more recently found only five percent of scientists—broadly defined to include those on the very margin of this issue, such as computer scientists—object to evolution.[2] As we saw in Chapter 9, even many proponents of intelligent design accept nearly everything that evolution comprises.

Thus, while this issue cannot be decided by vote, the view of credible scientists is so overwhelmingly in support of biological evolution that, when combined with what we otherwise know and can observe, we feel compelled to accept it. And since evolution is the most controversial issue in the religion and science debate, we are, in effect, accepting science and all that it appropriately entails.

Scientism

Modern science tries to document the factual character of the natural world and develop theories that coordinate and explain these facts, using an empirical point of view (What is the universe made of?) and a theoretical point of view (Why does it work as it does?). Science and its spin-off, technology, have changed our world literally before our eyes and made it what it is today. However, science and evolution have birthed a number of "isms" that we see as their illegitimate stepchildren.

"Scientism" is a concept that "...adds to science two corollaries: first, that the scientific method is, if not the *only* reliable method of getting at truth, then at least the *most* reliable method; and second, that the things science deals with—material entities—are the most fundamental things that exist."[3] Stated differently, scientism assumes there is no God; therefore some alternative explanation of the origin has to exist. It presumes that the scientific account of the world is all there is and that anything that cannot be discovered through the scientific method cannot be true.

The term itself is highly controversial. Some view it as an appropriate way of capturing the two corollaries, which are seen as arbitrary and unsupported assumptions or opinions of an overreaching scientific community. Others view scientism as a pejorative used by creationists and others to discredit vocal critics of religion when someone puts forward a scientific theory they don't like. But in fact many, perhaps most, scientists recognize that science has its boundaries and that such an exclusive attitude is not legitimate. Setting aside the linguistic argument, we disagree with the basic idea. Our reason for doing so is simple. We believe that science isn't all there is because there is a God and creator. We will discuss this point in more detail in the following section.

Now, let's review the specific "isms" involving evolution and Darwin that are especially relevant to our discussion. The term "evolution" commonly envisions biological evolution—the scientific proposition that species of organisms arise from other species through a process of natural selection over time. Thus, Darwin's theory of evolution is specifically limited to biology and has to do with how living organisms change over time.

Although Darwin's theory was a biological concept that had nothing to do with cultural practices, ethics, social policy, or how the universe originated, it was immediately seen by many as a threat to the foundations of civil society. It subsequently has been applied to many areas of life, sometimes with devastating results. The terms "evolutionism," "Darwinism," and "social Darwinism," often used interchangeably, refer to this broader application. They have come to be a part of the evolution myth, even though they go well beyond Darwin's theory of biological evolution.

Evolutionism is more than a scientific theory of evolution. Even before the time of Darwin some people were beginning to believe that evolution was the key to understanding the whole of reality and was, in fact, a kind of substitute for the traditional theistic or Christian view of God. It was seen to provide a philosophical, and perhaps even a scientific, explanation of the origin and continuance of things that did not need a specific biblical conception of God. Thus, the stage was set for a scientific theory of evolution, particularly in the cultures of Great Britain and Germany. After Darwin's biological theory was presented, evolutionists expanded it to include several "isms." Evolutionism is a term most often used to suggest a belief, rather than a scientific theory, that there are forces within nature or within matter itself that will eventually produce progress and change as natural and unplanned outgrowths of those that went before. These changes ultimately will result in a natural evolutionary outcome within cultures and civilization. Thus, evolutionism has connotations of atheism.

Similarly, Darwinism encompasses the idea that the universe, the earth, and all living organisms have evolved in a naturalistic process without any divine direction or intervention. Social Darwinism—a part of evolutionism and Darwinism but not a part of Darwin's theory of evolution—expands the idea of struggle and survival of the fittest into the social sphere, and it has been used to justify practices such as those involved with Fascism, racism, eugenics, or Hitler's master race. For example, the Nazis used an extrapolation from the scientific theory of evolution to a more general theory of social Darwinism as one way to rationalize World War II.

A related concept involves evolutionary ethics, an approach to morality based on the role of evolution in shaping human behavior. During the mid 1900s, Julian Huxley, Thomas Huxley's grandson, was an influential proponent of the application of scientific knowledge to social and political problems, formulating a theory of "evolutionary humanism" that dealt with eugenics and population control among other ideas. The theory was a combination of Victorian liberalism, Victorian ideas of progress, and the scientific theory of evolution. It was an illegitimate, illogical, and theologically unsatisfactory convergence.

Although Darwinism still influences modern political thought, most of us would not want to live in a society governed by Darwinian evolution as a societal morality. Darwin, his wife, Emma, and his defender, Thomas Huxley, as well as latter day opponents like William Jennings Bryan and Henry Morris all disagreed with the evolutionists, whom they believed were taking a purely scientific concept and making it into a social, philosophical, and ethical theory. They believed that one cannot establish an ethic based on evolution that will keep human beings superior to any animal. Thus, one can't blame social Darwinism on Darwin, but one can blame it on the evolutionists who thought they were appropriating Darwin.

That which is ethically best—what we call goodness or virtue—involves conduct that would not necessarily lead to success in the cosmic struggle for existence. In place of ruthless self-assertion, human morality demands self-restraint. In place of thrusting aside or treading down all competitors, virtue requires that the individual shall not merely respect but shall help his fellow man or woman. Goodness and virtue repudiate the gladiatorial theory of existence and are directed not so much to the survival of the fittest as to the fitting of as many as possible to survive. The development of more scientific knowledge hasn't solved the problem of how to relate the morals of society to scientific data. It has only exacerbated it. But it hasn't changed the fact that we can believe in Darwin's theory of biological evolution without endorsing the "isms" that have illegitimately grown from it.

CREATION VERSUS CREATIONISM

We believe that the origin stories of Genesis 1-11 reveal who the creator is, but that they do not address when or how God created. This is the reason we believe in creation, not in creationism.

Creation

The theological doctrine of creation holds that God is the source of all and that creation is an absolute origination out of nothing through a purposive act of His free will—*creatio ex nihilo.* No material, process of nature or even of chaos was there at the origin. God is the source of everything, and we ultimately owe our being, our existence, and our future to Him. The doctrine of creation addresses who did what. However, it does not speculate as to how and over what time frame God created the earth, man, or other living organisms, except for an implication that creation is not just an original activity. Instead, it is an ongoing and constantly new reality. As Ian Barbour noted in *Religion and Science*, the fundamental theological affirmations of Genesis— "(1) the world is essentially good, orderly, coherent, and intelligible; (2) the world is dependent on God; and (3) God is sovereign, free, transcendent, and characterized by purpose and will"[4]—all relate to God and the world at every point in time, not just at a time in the past. And they do not designate a time frame or a process for creation, one way or another. Instead, the creation stories' emphasis on God as the source of all excludes nature gods, polytheism, pantheism, dualism, idolatry, and other such practices of antiquity, and it helps us understand who we are within a context of larger significance.

Your authors believe in creation. Scripture reveals that God is the creator and originator of all things. Genesis 1:1 states, "In the beginning God created the heavens and the earth." Hebrews 11:3 states, "By faith we understand that the universe was formed at God's command, so that what is seen was not made out of what was visible."

Scripture also teaches that God preserves, sustains, and governs His creation. Acts 17:24 and 28 state, "The God who made the world and everything in it is the Lord of heaven and earth and does not live in temples built by hands. ... For in him, we live and move and have our being." Hebrews 1:3 states, "The Son is the radiance of God's glory and the exact representation of His being, sustaining all things by His powerful word."

Read also Psalm 147, a passage that contains poetic references to God determining the number of stars, covering the sky with clouds, supplying the earth with rain, spreading snow like wool, or hurling down hail like pebbles. These references do nothing to advance our scientific knowledge, but they surely do make a strong case that God acts not only as original creator but also as preserver, sustainer, and governor.

Creationism

Creationism, sometimes called "scientific creationism," is a different matter. This belief views the Bible as a scientific account of creation and Genesis as the literal, historical, scientific account of how the world was created. While creationism covers a broad spectrum of views, as discussed in Chapter 8, it generally endorses a literal interpretation of the Genesis creation accounts as well as the scientific validity of "special creation"—the view that the universe and all living organisms were instantaneously created in their mature form by divine fiat at a specific point in time, a few thousand years ago according to many. Modern scientific creationism has its roots not in the work of the fathers of fundamentalism or conservative religious teaching, but in the efforts of their successors to introduce their religious beliefs into the public school curriculum under the guise of modern science.

Your authors do not believe in scientific creationism. Our reason is simple. The fundamental, root premise underlying creationism is that the Bible is a book of science and is to be interpreted literally in all respects, except, it often seems, when science is just too compelling.

This is a premise that we reject. Consider two basic ways of interpreting the Bible. The first is to hold that the Bible in its original form is to be literally interpreted as a scientifically accurate history. The second is to read the Bible in the historical and linguistic context in which it was written, to accept its mysteries, and to appreciate its fundamental truths about the relationship between God and man.

We choose the latter approach and readily admit that we are comforted by the observation that this is the approach that does not conflict with all that we observe and learn about science. We don't believe God intended to deceive or trick us with the book of nature, which is what creationism seems to require. More importantly, we believe that a literal/historical/scientific reading of the creation accounts of Genesis negates their fundamental truth and power. A biblical view of creation is unlike anything man, including scientists, can comprehend. Nothing in our experience brings something into being. We may understand a change or a rearranging of what is already there, but we cannot fathom bringing something into existence. Only God can do that, as He is the source of space, time, and being, not just an actor within that context. Langdon Gilkey has noted:

> This means that the ways in which we talk about this event must be different from the way in which we seek to describe natural or human processes. The relation between the Creator and His creation cannot be the same as the relation of one finite event to another; hence we cannot understand the former relation in exactly the terms of the latter relation. Any attempt, therefore, directly and precisely to describe creation in the terms of our experience will inevitably fail in its object. Such a description, set in the terms of finite events, will reduce the unique divine activity of the creation of finitude itself to the level of natural and human actions within finitude. Creation then becomes an event within process rather than the origination of process, and God becomes a finite being in the world, rather than its almighty Creator. The claim to be able literally to describe God's creative act does not so much reflect piety as it reveals the loss of the religious sense of the transcendent holiness and mystery of God.[5]

Thus, with all due respect to sincere proponents of creationism, such a literal interpretation of Genesis, which aims to tell how creation occurred by spelling out finite deeds, times, and facts, seems to cast God as a construction worker—a finite being within the universe—rather than the source of being. This approach plays into the hands of modern secularists, who delight in accepting a literal intent for Genesis and then challenging its scientific accuracy. We also believe it confuses many youth and "seekers," sets them up for faith crises, and fosters disrepute of the evangelical faith. Therefore, we prefer an approach that recognizes the ultimate dimensions and depths of existence of God's creation. And we believe this approach is consistent with a correct understanding of the biblical text.

INTELLIGENT DESIGN VERSUS THE INTELLIGENT DESIGN MOVEMENT

We are comfortable with "intelligent design" but have concerns about the "Intelligent Design Movement." Just as with discussions of creation and creationism, assessing one's belief about intelligent design needs to start with some clear definitions—a difficult task in this controversial area where intelligent design (ID) has been used to encompass a broad range of views of how life originated and developed on the planet. For the discussion that follows, let's define intelligent design as the theological idea that the complex characteristics of living things are best explained as having an intelligent plan and origin, a concept that allows for recognizing a God and creator who works through evolution—more commonly referred to as theistic evolution. The "Intelligent Design Movement," as suggested in Chapter 9, is a scientific program based on the idea that the complex characteristics of living things are best explained as having an intelligent plan and origin. In summary, we define intelligent design as a broad theological and philosophical belief, and "Intelligent Design Movement" as an attempt at a scientific theory—that is widely criticized and largely rejected by the scientific community.

Intelligent Design Movement

Your authors have serious questions about the Intelligent Design Movement. Our concern starts with its apparent origin. You will recall that it began to take its present shape and course in the 1990s, following and apparently in response to the 1987 *Edwards v. Aguillard* United States Supreme Court case that prevented the teaching of creationism in public schools because proponents failed to prove that their views had scientific merit. Efforts to have intelligent design taught as science in public schools have continued. The latest significant public effort was the *Kitzmiller v. Dover* court case in 2005, which was defeated. This sequence of events has led some critics to refer to ID as "neocreationism" or "stealth creationism." Thus, the Intelligent Design Movement is sometimes suspected of being an attempt by more scientifically sophisticated creationists to insert "scientific creationism" into the American educational system. It is argued that they aim to use a "Trojan horse" to break into science classrooms, where they would not be allowed if they were flying their true flag of Bible doctrine.

We reject this harsh characterization. It may be consistent with the intent of certain lay people—parents, school board members, and others—who aim to use intelligent design as a means to accomplish what they have been unable to accomplish under the creationist banner. However, this characterization appears to misrepresent the intentions of many scientists associated with the Intelligent Design Movement, who indicate they do not expect their theory to get into classrooms until they can successfully convince the broader scientific community that it is valid.

Notwithstanding the various views, we must admit in all candor that history has caused us to cast a wary eye on this movement. As in the case of evolution, the question of whether or not ID qualifies as a scientific theory is not decided by vote. The fact is that most scientists who have spoken to the issue doubt that ID rises to the level of valid scientific theory, although their criticism admittedly sounds often like an emotional reaction against old style creationism.

The United States judicial system, considering testimony from these scientists, has consistently reached the same conclusion in a significant number of cases, notwithstanding the best efforts of the Intelligent Design Movement to present evidence to the contrary.

Reasons for these conclusions have varied. Some feel that the inability to test or falsify ID's concepts, and its proponents' failure to predict other findings or suggest approaches for further experimental verification, prevent it from being considered a science. Some see ID as based largely on negative attacks against evolution—attacks that have failed dramatically. Others argue that irreducible complexity, a key part of the ID case, is flawed and that many proposed examples have turned out after further scientific investigation not to be irreducibly complex after all. All considered, we simply are not convinced that intelligent design is science.

Finally, and perhaps most importantly, intelligent design seems to be a recent example of the "God of the gaps" fallacy. It accepts science that it concludes is irrefutable—a round earth; a heliocentric universe; in most cases, an old earth; in some cases, major aspects of evolution—regardless of literal biblical language. But where science doesn't know, or where there is significant controversy, it looks to God and/or the Bible for an answer. When science fills the gap, answers change. We believe such a view diminishes the character of God, casting Him as a repairman who has to intervene from time to time to fix what is broken about His creation.

Intelligent Design

We do, however, believe in intelligent design as contemplated by the basic concepts of theistic evolution. Why do we hold this belief? We do not have an answer that will satisfy the rigors of science or that will be viewed as credible by those who do not believe God exists. And we do not claim to be able to answer in a couple of paragraphs what others have left unanswered after volumes and volumes. But we do believe, and we must respond.

Just as we don't have all the answers, neither does science, not even about our natural universe or evolutionary development. Science can never deal adequately with issues such as values, purpose, the meaning of life, the final cause as to why things really happen, or the hereafter. With respect to the natural world, we shouldn't allow theology to try to fill the gaps temporarily until science comes through. And we shouldn't look to science to do what it cannot do. This leaves many unanswered, perhaps unanswerable, questions.

The Bible calls out God as the creator, but it doesn't say how He went about His task. We believe that God has created a world that contains the capabilities for self-organization and change, such that an unbroken line of evolutionary development has in fact taken place. In this regard, we are comforted by intelligent design, meaning that God had a creative plan that included natural consequences and divine governance over a continuing and ever-changing process. The material behavior that we observe, including evolution, is a consequence of God's plan and a continuing expression of His plan for the development of the universe. Natural laws describe this behavior as well as a patterned succession of related phenomena—a succession that demonstrates that God did not act impulsively or on a whim. The glory of the creation commands reverence regardless of when or how it took place, and the awe it engenders is not diminished by an evolutionary view of how organisms developed from original life. We have to accept the mystery of the details. We must have faith.

SUMMARY

The preceding sections suggest that the crux of our views on the apparent conflict between the Bible and science involves a number of "isms" and concepts derived from both fronts. Include them, and the debate seems like a fight between two thousand-pound gorillas. Avoid them, and you have a fairly narrow conflict that seems resolvable. Let's briefly summarize the various elements of the debate and see how they affect the problem by considering two cases.

Case 1
The elements of Case 1 are as follows:

BIBLE	SCIENCE
Creationism	Biological Evolution
Intelligent Design	Scientism
Movement	Evolutionism
	Darwinism
	Social Darwinism
	Evolutionary Ethics

If one views the conflict as between the Bible as defined in Case 1—creationism and/or the Intelligent Design Movement—and science as meaning biological evolution and its illegitimate stepchildren from scientism through evolutionary ethics, resolution seems impossible. The gorillas are just too big. Creationism and the Intelligent Design Movement—scientific claims often infused with ideas from secular philosophers and based on super literal scriptural interpretation of Genesis and other passages—simply cannot accommodate even biological evolution. The two are fighting in the same ring, the Bible against science, and there isn't room for both. And all the "isms" and evolutionary ethics make the problem even more insurmountable, as the social ills that accompany them have a psychological effect that adds fuel to the intensity of the fight.

Case 2

The elements of Case 2 are as follows:

BIBLE   SCIENCE
Creation   Biological Evolution
   (intelligent design
   or theistic evolution)

If one accepts Case 2, with the Bible envisioning creation (by whatever method God chose) and science meaning biological evolution, one gets an entirely different answer. No conflict exists between biological evolution and the belief that God is the source of all there is, with a creative plan that includes natural consequences and divine governance over a continuing and ever changing process. The Bible makes no claim as to how or when organisms develop or change, and God can do it any way He wishes. Conversely, the theory of biological evolution, based on empirical evidence, makes no claim as to why first life originated or who was or is the moving force. It explains **how** things happen, not **why** they happen. The "isms" simply are not science. They are beyond science—predicted social implications of evolution that may or may not occur and in any event are not necessarily a result of evolution. They are not dogs in this fight.

In summary, nothing in creation (or theological beliefs contemplated by intelligent design or theistic evolution) conflicts with biological evolution. While various biblical passages no doubt condemn aspects of evolutionary ethics and the evolutionary "isms," that's a different, non-scientific matter. Without condemning biological evolution, we can condemn murder, war crimes, torture, mistreatment of one group of human beings, social gains through the exploitation of human beings, or other myths of evolution.

While we have been considering the question of "the Bible vs. science," perhaps the real question is whether we believe in creation or creationism, or whether we accept intelligent design or the Intelligent Design Movement. For many, this still is not an easy question to resolve, but it is a very different one. Like the debates in the time of Galileo and Copernicus, it is a debate among Christians, not between Christians and others. It does not minimize the role of God in the creative process. It can be resolved with faith and careful attention to the two books of God. We encourage you to try.

NOTES

CHAPTER 1—RELIGIOUS ANTIQUITY

1. *The Oxford History of the Biblical World*, edited by Michael D. Coogan (New York: Oxford University Press, 1998), p. 4.
2. Hyers, Conrad, *The Meaning of Creation: Genesis and Modern Science* (Atlanta: John Knox Press, 1984), p. 44.

CHAPTER 2—NEW TESTAMENT CHRISTIANITY

1. *Ancient Christian Writers*, trans. J. H. Taylor (Newman Press, 1982), volume 41.

CHAPTER 3—MODERN SCIENCE

1. Barbour, Ian G., *Issues in Science and Religion* (Englewood Cliffs, New Jersey: Prentice-Hall, Inc., 1966), p. 57.
2. SUNY Fredonia, *Department of Geosciences* (www.fredonia.edu/ department/geosciences), 2009
3. Fordham University, *Internet History Sourcebooks Project* (www.fordham. edu/halsall/mod/galileo-tuscany.html), 2009
4. *Issues in Science and Religion,* pp. 35-36.
5. *Principia,* trans. Andrew Motte, edited by Florian Cajori (Berkeley: University of California Press, 1934), pp. 544-546, as quoted in *God and Nature* (Los Angeles: University of California Press, 1986), p. 229.
6. *Wikipedia: The Free Encyclopedia,* (www.en.wikipedia.org/wiki/ Isaac_Newton), 2009
7. *Issues in Science and Religion,* p. 48.

CHAPTER 4—CHARLES DARWIN

1. Aydon, Cyril, *Charles Darwin: The Naturalist Who Started A Scientific Revolution* (New York: Carroll & Graf Publishers, 2002), p. 80.
2. Darwin, Charles, *The Origin of Species* (London: Penguin Books, Ltd, 2003), p. 88.
3. Shermer, Michael, *Why Darwin Matters* (New York: Times Books, 2006), p. 24.
4. Moore, James R., *The Post-Darwinian Controversies* (New York: Cambridge University Press, 1979), p. 125.

CHAPTER 5—DARWIN'S AFTERMATH

1. *Why Darwin Matters*, p. 118.
2. Larson, Edward J., *Summer for the Gods: The Scopes Trial and America's Continuing Debate over Science and Religion* (Cambridge, Massachusetts: Harvard University Press, 1998), p. 34.
3. *Issues in Science and Religion*, pp. 89-98.

CHAPTER 6—SCIENCE

1. The American Scientific Affiliation (www.asa3.org/), 2009
2. Collins, Francis S., *The Language of God: A Scientist Presents Evidence for Belief* (New York: Free Press, 2006), pp. 127, 141.
3. Leaky, Richard, *The Origin of Humankind* (New York: Basic Books, 1994), p. 79.
4. *The Language of God: A Scientist Presents Evidence for Belief*, pp. 136-137.
5. The National Academies (www.nationalacademies.org), 2009
6. National Center for Science Education (www.ncseweb.org/resources/articles/1144), 2009
7. Polling Report.com (www.polingreport.com/science.htm), 2009

CHAPTER 7—NON-BELIEVERS

1. Morris, Henry M., *Scientific Creationism* (Green Forest, Arizona: Master Books, 1974), p. 19.
2. Strobel, Lee, *The Case for a Creator: A Journalist Investigates Scientific Evidence That Points Toward God* (Grand Rapids, Michigan: Zondervan, 2004), p. 82.

3. Dawkins, Richard, *The God Delusion* (New York: Houghton Mifflin Company, 2006), p. 49.
4. *The Case for a Creator*, p. 83.
5. *The Language of God: A Scientist Presents Evidence for Belief*, p. 218.
6. *The Encyclopedia of Religion and Ethics*, edited by James Hastings. T.H. Huxley, quote. (Charles Scribner's Sons,1908).
7. *The God Delusion*, p. 31.
8. *Charles Darwin: The Naturalist Who Started a Scientific Revolution*, p. 259.
9. *The God Delusion,* p. 31.
10. *Science and Religion,* edited by Paul Kurtz. (Amherst, New York: Prometheus Books, 2003), p. 67.
11. *The God Delusion,* p. 158.
12. Geisler, Norman L., *Christian Apologetics* (Grand Rapids, Michigan: Baker Book House, 1976), p. 234.

CHAPTER 8—CREATIONISM

1. Morris, Henry M., *Scientific Creationism* (Green Forrest, AR: Master Books, 2003), p. 12.
2. *God & Nature: Historical Essays on the Encounter between Christianity and Science,* edited by David C. Lindberg and Ronald L. Numbers (Los Angeles: University of California Press, 1986), p. 407.
3. Creation Research Society (www.creationresearch.org/belief_wndw.htm), 2009
4. Creation Moments (www.creationmoments.net/about/doctrinal.php), 2009
5. *Susan Epperson et al., v. Arkansas,* U.S. Supreme Court, 1968 (www.law.umkc.edu/faculty/projects/ftrials/conlaw/Epperso.htm), 2009
6. Ibid.
7. Institute for Creation Research (www.icr.org/home/faq/), 2009
8. *Scientific Creationism*, p. 203.
9. Institute for Creation Research (www.icr.org/home/faq/), 2009
10. Polling Report.com (www.polingreport.com/science.htm), 2009
11. *Scientific Creationism*, p. 251.
12. Ibid., p. 26.
13. Institute for Creation Research (www.icr.org/), 2009

14. *Scientific Creationism*, p. 92.
15. Creation Research Society (creationresearch .org/), 2009
16. *Scientific Creationism,* pp. 171 and 216.
17. Houston Chronicle, February 8, 2007.
18. Ross, Hugh, *Creation as Science: A Testable Model Approach to End the Creation/Evolution Wars* (Colorado Springs, Colorado: NavPress, 2006), p. 76.

CHAPTER 9—INTELLIGENT DESIGN

1. *Mere Creation: Science, Faith & Intelligent Design,* edited by William A. Dembski (Downers Grove, Illinois: InterVarsity Press, 1998), pp. 16-17.
2. *McLean v. Arkansas Board of Education*, 529 F. Supp. 1255, (E. D. Ark., 1982).
3. Ibid.
4. *Edwards v. Aguillard*, 482 U.S. 578 (1987).
5. *Mere Creation: Science, Faith & Intelligent Design,* p. 17.
6. *Tammy Kitzmiller, et al. v. Dover Area School District, et al.*, 400 F. Supp 2d 707, (M. D. Penn., 2005).
7. Hume, Edward, *Monkey Girl: Evolution, Education, Religion, and the Battle for America's Soul* (New York: HarperCollins Publishers, 2007), p. 93.
8. Kitzmiller, 400 F. Supp 2d 707.
9. The Talk OriginArchives (www.talkorigins.org/faqs/dover/day1am.html), 2009
10. *Creation as Science: A Testable Model Approach to End the Creation/Evolution Wars*, p. 32.
11. Behe, Michael J., *The Edge of Evolution: The Search for the Limits of Darwinism* (New York: The Free Press, 2007), p. 233.
12. *Creation as Science: A Testable Model Approach to End the Creation/Evolution Wars*, p. 53.
13. Ibid., p. 152.
14. *Mere Creation: Science, Faith & Intelligent Design,* p. 364.
15. Behe, *Darwin's Black Box: The Biochemical Challenge to Evolution* (New York: The Free Press, 2006), p. 193.

16. Ibid, p. 5.

17. *The Edge of Evolution: The Search for the Limits of Darwinism*, p. 3.

18. Ibid, p. 72.

19. Wells, Jonathan, *The Politically Incorrect Guide to Darwinism and Intelligent Design* (Washington, DC: Regnery Publishing, Inc., 2006), p. 84.

20. *Mere Creation: Science, Faith & Intelligent Design*, Chapter 4.

21. *The Politically Incorrect Guide to Darwinism and Intelligent Design*, p. 84.

22. Moreland, J. P. and Reynolds, John Mark, *Three Views of Creation and Evolution* (Grand Rapids, Michigan: ZondervanPublishingHouse, 1999), p. 205.

23. *Creation as Science: A Testable Model Approach to End the Creation/Evolution Wars,* p. 179.

24. Darwin, Charles, *The Origin of Species* (New York: Signet Classic, 1958), p. 175.

25. *Darwin's Black Box: The Biochemical Challenge to Evolution,* p. 39.

26. National Catholic Bioethics Center (www2.ncseweb.org/kvd/trans/2005_0930_day5_pm.pdf), 2009

CHAPTER 10—TWO BOOKS

1. Bacon , Francis, *Essays, Advancement of Learning, New Atlantis, and Other Pieces*, edited by R. F. Jones (New York: Odyssey, 1937), p.179, from Charles E. Hummel, *The Galileo Connection* (Downers Grove, Illinois: InterVarsity Press, 1986), p. 165.

2. Gould, Stephen Jay, *Rocks of Ages: Science and Religion in the Fullness of Life* (New York: Ballantine Books, 1999), pp. 5-6.

3. Ibid., p. 63.

4. Ibid., p. 21.

5. *The Language of God: A Scientist Presents Evidence For Belief,* p. 5.

6. *The God Delusion,* p. 58.

7. *Perspectives on an Evolving Creation*, edited by Keith B. Miller (Grand Rapids, Michigan: Eerdmans Publishing Co., 2003), p. xii.

8. *Three Views of Creation and Evolution,* p. 175.

9. Ibid., p. 185.

10. *The Language of God: A Scientist Presents Evidence For Belief,* p. 200.

11. *Perspectives on an Evolving Creation*, p. 335.
12. Russell, Robert John, *Cosmology from Alpha to Omega: Towards the Creative Mutual Interaction between Theology and Science* (Minneapolis, Minnesota: Fortress Press, 2008).
13. *Perspectives on an Evolving Creation*, p. 368.
14. Coalition for Excellence in Science and Math Education
15. (www.cesame-nm.org/index.php/name), 2009
16. Lewis, C. S., *The Problem of Pain* (New York, HarperSanFrancisco, 1940), p. 72.
17. The United Methodist Church (www.archives.umc.org/interior.asp?mid=10422), 2009
18. Ministry and Mission of the Presbyterian Church (USA) (www.pcusa.org/theologyandworship/science/evolution.htm), 2009
19. *Mere Creation: Science, Faith & Intelligent Design*, p. 20.

CHAPTER 11—BIBLICAL CONTEXT

1. McGrath, Alister E., *Christian Theology: An Introduction* (Oxford: Blackwell Publishing, 2001), p. 202.
2. *Scientific Creationism*, p. 15.
3. Ibid., p. 203.
4. Marsden, George M., *Fundamentalism and American Culture* (New York: Oxford University Press, 2006), p. 113.
5. Creation Research Society (creationresearch.org/hisaims.htm), 2009
6. *Creation as Science: A Testable Model Approach to End the Creation/Evolution Wars*, p. 53.

CHAPTER 12—SCRIPTURE

1. National Catholic Bioethics Center (www2.ncseweb.org/kvd/trans/2005_0930_day5_pm.pdf, p. 23), 2009
2. Ramm,Bernard, *The Christian View of Science and Scripture* (Grand Rapids, Michigan: Wm. B. Eerdmans Publishing Co., 1954), p. 52.
3. Tate, W. Randolph, *Biblical Interpretation: An Integrated Approach* (Peabody, Massachusetts: Hendrickson Publishers, 1997), p. 83.
4. Cotterell, Peter and Turner, Max, *Linguistics and Biblical Interpretation* (Downers Grove, Illinois: InterVarsity Press, 1989), p. 298.

5. *Biblical Interpretation: An Integrated Approach,* p. 109.
6. Lewis, C. S., *Reflections on the Psalms* (New York: Harcourt, Brace, and World—A Harvest Book, 1958), p. 110.
7. Ibid., p. 111.
8. *Three Views on Creation and Evolution,* p. 165.
9. Kilby, Clyde S., *The Christian World of C. S. Lewis* (Grand Rapids: Wm. B. Eerdmans Publishing Company, 1964), p. 153.
10. *Reflections on the Psalms,* p. 111.

CHAPTER 13—THE ORIGIN STORIES-I

1. Van Till, Howard J., et al, *Portraits of Creation: Biblical and Scientific Perspectives on the World's Formation* (Grand Rapids, Michigan: Wm. B. Eerdmans Publishing Company, 1990), p. 262.
2. *The Meaning of Creation: Genesis and Modern Science,* p. 44.
3. Kline, Meredith G., *Space and Time in the Genesis Cosmogony* (www.asa3.org/asa/pscf3-96kline.html), from *Perspectives on Science and Christian Faith: The Journal of the American Scientific Affiliation* (1996)
4. *The Meaning of Creation, Genesis and Modern Science,* p. 41.
5. *Scientific Creationism,* p. 216.
6. *Creation as Science: A Testable Model Approach to End the Creation/Evolution Wars,* p. 143.
7. Darwin, Charles, *The Origin of Species,* (London: Penguin Books, Ltd, 2003), p. 453.
8. *The Christian View of Science and Scripture,* p. 37.

CHAPTER 14—THE ORIGIN STORIES-II

1. American Scientific Affiliation (www.asa3.org/asa/PSCF/1999/PSCF6-99McGrath.html), 2009
2. Ibid.
3. Whitcomb, John C. Jr. and Morris, Henry M., *The Genesis Flood: The Biblical Record and its Scientific Implications* (Phillipsburg, New Jersey: P&R Publishing, 1960), p. 74.
4. Reasons to Believe (www.reasons.org/), 2009
5. Richardson, Alan, *Genesis I-IX: Introduction and Commentary* (London, SCM Press LTD, 1953), p. 97.

CHAPTER 15—CONCLUSIONS

1. *The Meaning of Creation: Genesis and Modern Science,* p. 111.
2. Religious Tolerance.org (www.religioustolerance.org/ev_publi. htm), 2009
3. Smith, Huston, *Why Religion Matters* (New York: HarperSanFrancisco, 2001), p. 59.
4. Barbour, Ian G., *Religion and Science: Historical and Contemporary Issues* (New York: HarperSanFrancisco, 1997), p. 202.
5. Gilkey, Langdon, *Maker of Heaven and Earth* (Garden City, NY: Doubleday & Company, Inc., 1959), p. 54.

INDEX

Made in the USA
Columbia, SC
20 July 2018